'A wonderful and vital account of a city ruled by, and for, extreme wealth' Anna Minton, author of *Big Capital*

'A rage-inducing tour . . . Knowles' book helps readers to see [London's super-rich] as less secretive, more troubling and a great deal sadder . . . The anonymised plutocrats and their hangers-on who fill the book reflect limitless arrogance, waste and injustice. The excesses of planet plutocrat are particularly shocking because they happen alongside the world in which the rest of us live . . . *Serious Money* has a serious mission. These vast fortunes, Knowles argues, do not just make people miserable. They are rotting the ties that hold our society together'
Edward Lucas, *The Times*

'Fascinating, punchy, thought-provoking. *Serious Money* exposes the corrosive impact of London's super rich on our economy, society and politics, and comprehensively busts the myth that their wealth trickles down to the rest of us' Frances O'Grady

'Startling, spirited . . . Knowles is alert to arresting details . . . a wry primer to the extravagances of the super-rich'
Alex Diggins, *The Critic*

'Years of footwork through the streets of central London have gone into producing this magnificent but disturbing book on the lives and influence of the super-rich. Knowles writes with enviable lightness and pace about how money, property, birth, breeding, contacts, secrecy, parasites and servants have created a class that owns and milks London, a world away from the city's ordinary citizens. A powerful ethnography of plutocratic power'
Professor Ash Amin, author of *Seeing Like a City*

'An innovative and disturbingly entertaining travelogue covering one of the most important issues of our time . . . could not have been published at a more critical time'
Matt Reynolds, *LSE Review of Books*

ABOUT THE AUTHOR

Caroline Knowles is a Global Professorial Fellow at Queen Mary University of London. Currently the Director of the British Academy's Cities and Infrastructure programme, she has carried out research in London, Hong Kong, Beijing, Fuzhou, Addis Ababa, Kuwait City and Seoul. Knowles is the author of *Flip-Flop: A Journey Through Globalisation's Backroads*, and co-author of *Hong Kong: Migrant Lives, Landscapes, and Journeys*. Information about her latest book can be found at https://seriousmoneybook.com.

CAROLINE KNOWLES

Serious Money

Walking Plutocratic London

PENGUIN BOOKS

PENGUIN BOOKS

UK | USA | Canada | Ireland | Australia
India | New Zealand | South Africa

Penguin Books is part of the Penguin Random House group of companies
whose addresses can be found at global.penguinrandomhouse.com

First published by Allen Lane 2022
Published in Penguin Books 2023
001

Printed and bound in Great Britain by Clays Ltd, Elcograf S.p.A.

The authorized representative in the EEA is Penguin Random House Ireland,
Morrison Chambers, 32 Nassau Street, Dublin D02 YH68

A CIP catalogue record for this book is available from the British Library

ISBN: 978-0-141-99437-6

www.greenpenguin.co.uk

MIX
Paper from
responsible sources
FSC® C018179

Penguin Random House is committed to a
sustainable future for our business, our readers
and our planet. This book is made from Forest
Stewardship Council® certified paper.

To Bill and his many 'revelations'

Contents

Cast of Characters

(in order of appearance)

The Boy: young Shoreditch entrepreneur and owner of Looking Glass.

Quant: algorithm writer for a bank.

Banker: high-up in an international bank in the City, dealing with many of the world's billionaires.

Searcher: researcher at one of the world's biggest hedge funds.

Genius: billionaire hedge fund owner.

Cake: former banker and private equities dealer specializing in fintech.

Doorman: stands outside The Dorchester hotel.

Cop: head of security at a famous five-star London hotel.

Night Manager: works the night shift at a top London hotel.

VIP Service: Colombian woman who specializes in elite-guest relations at top London hotels.

Big Spender: anyone who stays in the most expensive accommodation in top hotels.

Legacy: director of communications in a private investment group.

Sturgeon: Russian investor whose hobby is producing sustainable caviar.

Arty: former Mayfair gallery curator turned expert on art collections for the wealthy.

Investigator: young lawyer, who reports from the impenetrable 5 Hertford Street club.

Blazer: former private equity dealer from an elite colonial background, resident of Mayfair.

Buffer: urbane urbanist who fronts for His Grace The Duke of Westminster.

Runner: runs a Mayfair family office and his own property development company.

Walker: works on the domestic and family services side in a family office.

Wig: the hippest judge and QC, expert in the international dimensions of family law.

Palace: Notting Hill mum and volunteer, who hails from the landed aristocracy.

Desk: wife of a Notting Hill private equities dealer.

Physics: Notting Hill mum with two young daughters and a home renovation project.

Elgin: resident of Elgin Crescent in Notting Hill and mother of a son at Eton.

Rebel: nineties merchant-class squillionaire, who dropped out in Chelsea.

Lady: elderly minor aristocrat living in an attic in Kensington.

Officer: former civil servant and neighbourhood activist in Kensington.

Historian: Opera's husband, retired conservation architect and local Kensington historian.

Opera: Historian's wife and friend of Opera Holland Park.

Soviet: nostalgic Russian multi-millionaire and art collector.

Journo: Russian journalist and chronicler of London's invisible Russian entrepreneurs.

Butler: has worked in some of the wealthiest households in London.

Bags and Barbour: two players on the young Chelsea scene.

Student: went to a private university and travelled in private planes with wealthy classmates.

Colour: flamboyant designer to the super-rich.

Atmosphere: designer who creates atmospheric interiors.

Light: maker of light sculptures and other light creations.

Traveller: organizes unusual luxury journeys and unique travel experiences.

Party: socialite who inherited his wealth and has nothing much to do all day.

Assistant: opinion-maker who worked for Party.

Author: novelist and historian, who is long-term resident of and guide to Richmond.

Sailor: former banker turned maritime security expert.

Babysitter: young woman who is guide to domestic life in Virginia Water.

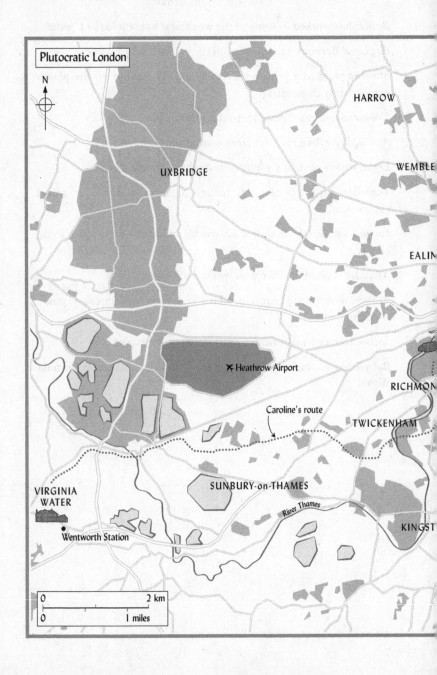

Plutocratic London

N

HARROW

WEMBLE

UXBRIDGE

EALIN

✕ Heathrow Airport

RICHMON

Caroline's route

TWICKENHAM

VIRGINIA
WATER

SUNBURY-on-THAMES

River Thames

● Wentworth Station

KINGST

0 ——— 2 km
0 ——— 1 miles

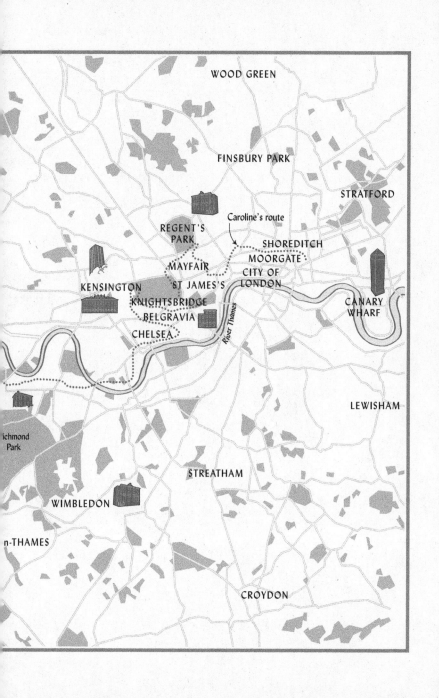

Prelude

You don't expect to meet a zebra in London. Standing on a low wooden plinth, turned sideways to reveal the full length of its handsome body to the street, it lives in a brightly lit shop window, dazzling in the eerie orange of the night street. Brass tortoises nestle between its legs, reflecting the light above, and a life-sized stone statue of a black pug sits in the foreground. The ceiling is hung with elaborate brass light fittings secured with chains; a large Chinese vase and an intricately carved wooden chair are carefully positioned behind. The zebra stares blankly into a framed poster that depicts a group of surreal, distorted Picassoesque revellers, with the word *cocaine* written above their heads and a devil hovering over them.

I am on South Audley Street in Mayfair, the most expensive district on the Monopoly board of my childhood. Along the street, more bright shop windows reveal themselves, displaying tiny elaborate designer handbags, impossibly impractical high heels and small, glittery dresses, made to adorn women whose own function too must be purely decorative. Further on still, three male mannequins in shooting-party tweed, plus-four britches and jackets, with gun cases and a stuffed black dog at their feet, stare vacantly back at me; behind them the heads of stuffed animals are mounted on the wall next to glass cases of dead birds, the prizes of predatory activity. This combination of urban and rural caricatures a certain kind of wealthy Englishness, constructed for the benefit of wealthy international visitors and wannabes. Old money has always modelled wealth for new money.

These uncanny tableaux suggest the careful consideration given to museum exhibits, fastidiously curated to display objects of significance and evoke people who matter. They show a few of the many faces of wealth in London. The dummies in tweed project traditional upper-class Englishness, the fantasy of an eager audience at both home and abroad. The zebra hails from another kind of habitat entirely, a reminder that wealth in London today is concentrated in the hands of an international, globalized plutocracy. These and the other kinds of plutocrat that appear in this book, people whose power and influence derive from their money, have amassed inconceivable levels of wealth. And these extreme concentrations of wealth, not seen in a century, are radically reshaping London and the lives of its residents.

The city has been shaped by money in different ways since Roman times. But we know, because those who provide financial services offer ready calculations, that both the number of rich people and the size of their assets are growing at an alarming rate. Globally there are 20 million US dollar millionaires.[1] This includes high-net-worth individuals (HNWIs): people with more, sometimes much more, than a million dollars – or pounds in the United Kingdom – in investable assets, excluding their main residence. Furthermore, ultra-high-net-worth individuals (UHNWIs) are those with over £20 million in investable assets. Their number has been rising steadily: in 2020, despite (or perhaps, because of) the global pandemic, both the number of UHNWIs and their wealth grew by almost 10 per cent on the previous year.[2] At the same time, Oxfam reported that the highest concentrations of wealth, not just in London but globally, are concentrated in fewer hands than ever. Today, the combined wealth of the world's richest eight billionaires – who would easily fit into two London taxis – have accumulated as much wealth as the poorest 3.6 billion people on the planet.[3] The 'World Wealth Report 2021',[4] meanwhile, reveals that the United Kingdom has just over half a million resident HNWIs and UHNWIs: most of them live in London, making it the city ranking sixth in the world for where local and international billionaires choose to live.[5] In 2021, the *Sunday Times* Rich List, which only a few years ago reported that the United Kingdom had 93 resident sterling billionaires – more than New York, San Francisco, Hong Kong or Moscow – revealed that this number had risen to 171.[6] The United Kingdom, and London in particular, is one of the most appealing destinations for plutocrats looking for a home.

In 2020, 49 per cent of property sales in central London were to overseas buyers, according to Hamptons estate agents. Some have even dubbed this moment in plutocratic fortunes as a 'second gilded age',[7] recalling the era of Rockefeller, Carnegie and Ford, the US robber barons and captains of industry who made obscene amounts of money.

That this is so, is no accident. Successive UK governments have deliberately constructed a political and economic ecosystem that supports extreme concentrations of wealth in private hands. Eliding individual and collective wealth, insisting that rich people make for a rich country – or, as they like to put it, 'a rising tide lifts all boats' – UK governments have encouraged international investment and stashing money in British banks. Only recently have money laundering laws been introduced, reflecting a worry about where that money might have come from. There are no restrictions on the sale of property to overseas buyers. Governments have been forced to acknowledge creative accounting and money hidden in offshore tax havens, prompted by the revelations of the Panama, Paradise and Pandora Papers. Meanwhile, luxury industries supporting wealthy lifestyles have flourished in London, while the city's cultural and educational offerings, attractive neighbourhoods and housing, and well-respected schools and universities, are all part of the draw. Consequently, HNWIs and UHNWIs are clustered in tightly circumscribed areas, a vortex of wealth extending across central London, where I encounter them as I walk the streets in which they live and work.

To me plutocrats are both familiar and strange. Like most people, my knowledge of the fabulously wealthy comes from the fictional world of film and television: *Brideshead Revisited*, *Upstairs Downstairs*, *Dynasty*, the *Kardashians*, *Made in Chelsea* and my favourite, *Billions*, a series in which the full regulatory apparatus of the US state, armed with instruments of law and taxation, struggles to curtail the excesses of the uber-wealthy. I am simultaneously envious, seduced and appalled by these displays that are so far removed from my everyday experience.

As a child raised in the 1960s in a tiny Devonshire village, where my grandmother ran the post office, my understanding of what it meant to have money was shaped by the village's wealthy residents, whom I met through helping out in the shop. Village social life centred on the Church of England – visibly the Conservative Party at prayer – and it was characterized by former participants in colonial wars and occupations, colonels and majors 'returned' to a rural idyll they had not previously lived in. Their homes, cavernous detached nineteenth-century houses with wrap-around English gardens, into which I was occasionally invited to hand out canapés, or to babysit, were furnished with the trophies of lives spent in East Africa, India and the Far East: tiger-skin rugs, ivory ornaments, wood carvings, elephant feet turned umbrella stands, and the wall-mounted quarry of far more distant lands than South Audley Street. Echoes of elsewhere. I listened to their conversations without understanding: 'Do you remember the Parsons?' 'Were they Kenya? No wait, they were Hong Kong.' The village counted among its residents a smattering of aristocrats, including the sisters of the Earl of Devon, who ran the Sunday school I was forced to attend, and lived on an avenue we referred to privately as 'Quality Street'. Our envy and deference – my grandfather always referred to the aristocrats reverently as 'elites', and always used former army titles – was tinged with ridicule, a small way to rebel against the rigid social order of the village, even as we observed and served it. Wealth in the countryside in the 1960s meant something very different from what it does in London today. It was small, accessible to me as part of its serving class, and based on hereditary connection with land and titles, as well as on colonial military conquest.

From this hinterland of a rural proletarian childhood, observing the wealthy became a habit. It lurked in the background while I was at university. Later, like other academic sociologists, I threw myself into researching the injustices of city life: poverty, racism, migration and the inequities of globalization. In my study of migration, I followed Brits who left to live in other places, like Hong Kong, some of them wealthy, some of them 'returned' to villages like the one I came from. When a group of researchers at my own university was commissioned to study London's super-rich,[8] I convinced them to let me join the team. Through our research I came to understand the profoundly damaging impact of the super-rich on city life. When the study finished, I realized that I hadn't finished with the super-rich, and carried on alone, determined to get closer still to what *makes* the rich and their neighbourhoods. Following the money, in the shape of the lives, bodies and habitats of the wealthy, throughout the streets of London, became a preoccupation, and this is how *Serious Money*, my exploration of the city's wealthiest residents and areas, began.

The super-rich are the city's most troubling and secretive presence. Their lives are socially, politically and environmentally unsustainable, making them one of the most pressing problems of our time. Some counter that they generate prosperity for all, alongside their own, since by investing their money they create jobs. Others see them as a parasite rentier class who live in luxury and fail to pay enough tax – a claim substantiated in the 2016 Panama Papers, leaked by the law firm Mossack Fonseca. Portraits of the wealthy in the popular media depict them as celebrities and truculent billionaires; when their excesses in the face of growing urban poverty are considered, these casual portraits only serve to obscure who they really are. Plutocrats have become a caricature of themselves: a new urban myth. How little we really know about them and the opaque worlds they inhabit beyond the tabloid and *Tatler* myths. Who are they? How do they think about themselves, about other people, about London? Where does their money come from? How do they spend it? How do they live with their money, and how does money live with them?

I explore these questions on foot. Walking is how I make sense of the world. A slow way of taking stock of places and people, walking makes time for thinking and close observation. And it has a good pedigree in urban exploration. My guides are Virginia Woolf's descriptions of the everyday pleasures of walking London's wintry streets; Walter Benjamin's wanderings in the Paris arcades; Iain Sinclair's London ramblings; Teju Cole's ruminations on New York City; and Raja Shehadeh's walks in the Palestinian Territories. All these writers show that walking exposes politics, like a sediment in the landscape.[9]

Money forms the fabric of the city, shaping streets and buildings, especially as government has allowed property to become a primary store of unprecedented wealth. The Shard, towering over the River Thames at London Bridge, is really a stack of money accumulated from oil – a glass and concrete arrangement of the Qatar sovereign wealth fund. Buckingham Palace is a repository of entitlement and a store for accumulated treasure cast in stone. The makeshift cardboard beds of the homeless reveal where state money ought to be. And London's ubiquitous Victorian terraced houses are one form of money (loans) repaid over time through another (wages). Here, despite being abstract and digital, money becomes a living and vital matter: a character in this story, because it is the realization of wealth. Though this a London story, it is also a global tale of our time, since it chronicles the acquisitions of the global super-rich and the city their money shapes. Melbourne, New York, Mumbai, São Paulo, Moscow, Shanghai: all have their own versions of this story.

In London, money rises in the East and sets in the West, and *Serious Money* follows this arc. It starts with visits to the places where money is generated, around Shoreditch and the City, through financial institutions, property speculation, business and especially tech: together with inheritance, this is how serious money is acquired. It then calls in on the hidden money engines of private equity and hedge funds in Mayfair, Belgravia and St James's: areas that simultaneously create vast wealth and offer opportunities for wild consumption. Continuing westwards through a vortex of wealth, I take an intimate look at domestic life in Kensington, and then Chelsea, take in the northern spur of Regent's Park, and then move on to Richmond. Along the way I visit palaces, polo fields, private clubs, art galleries and auction houses, luxury shops and the capital's most expensive residential streets. I examine the wealthy's housing; their vacations and their clubbing and dining habits; how they graze on London's vibrant arts scene; how a matrix of advisers guides their spending; how women fare in these habitats; and, especially, how mothers produce the next generation of plutocrats, by teaching their children how to be rich. Following the money finally takes me all the way to the city's western border, and the sinister and silent streets of Virginia Water in suburban Surrey.

If money is ingrained in streets and cityscapes, it is animated by people. People *are* the city, its human fabric. Without people, cities would neither exist nor function, and it is people's individual stories and actions (really just stories told by other means) that make cities run. *Serious Money* is an attempt to access these stories from the inside, offering views into the buildings and lives that are deliberately kept out of bounds. Money is animated when entangled in people's lives and aspirations. It comes to life when people use it to build or buy stuff, when they splurge it on good times, when it bales them out of hard times, when it lurks in cupboards, mattresses and under floorboards, in houses or in neighbourhoods, when it is piled in dark corners, when it is exchanged for zebras, fancy shoes and shooting gear, when it is taken away. People are money in motion; people act out the authority that money confers. In this book, money has bodies, habits, routines, priorities, orientations, ways of being at home, strategies for shaping neighbourhoods and streets; it has friends, families, children, hopes, fears, insecurities and crippling anxieties.

A cast of wealthy characters and, sometimes, those who serve them, people who live and work in plutocratic London, populate these pages; they tell me about their lives and labours, as I move through the city. In the style of *The Canterbury Tales*, I have given them all typological names. This protects their anonymity, which research-ethics protocols (and the rich themselves) demand.

The hidden lives of the super-rich have an undeniable allure. But public fascination and voyeurism obscure their real significance. Media and political attention focus on the habits of the poor, with impecunious migrants and refugees providing a focus for popular discontent. While this argument rages, the influence of wealth and the damage it inflicts go unnoticed, intentionally unacknowledged politically, as private equity and hedge funds take over shops and businesses, and close them down, destroying jobs and reshaping high streets. Plutocrats are a tiny proportion of London's population, yet their wealth is extraordinary – the median pre-tax annual wage in London is a very modest £34,073[10] – and the influence wealth secures is disproportionate. Yet, as wealthy residents increase,[11] so do the ranks of the dispossessed. The number of homeless people in London without a fixed residence, some of them rough sleepers, increased sharply from 2010, when, following massive public investment to forestall financial collapse threatened by the banking crisis of 2008, a politics of austerity hit the public finances and the budgets of local councils.

A direct line can be drawn between London's housing and social welfare crisis and the super-rich, including international developers and investors who have bought up the city's real estate, and wealthy residents who – permitted to do so by indulgent governments – avoid making a fair contribution to the public finances. Post financial collapse and post austerity, London has witnessed greater social inequalities than ever. The Royal Borough of Kensington and Chelsea, home to many of the city's wealthiest residents, admits to 265 rough sleepers. Yet it fails to report its total homeless population, which, according to the geographer Danny Dorling,[12] numbers more than 5,000, while the Office for National Statistics (ONS) recently calculated the total for London as a whole at 8,555. More telling perhaps, are the 38 per cent of Kensington and Chelsea's children living in poverty – according to the Borough's own estimates. Poverty and unimaginable wealth coexist, often in the same London streets, connecting the fortunes of the super-wealthy with increasing immiseration and dispossession of the poor.

These stark inequalities risk serious social and political unrest. London is an experiment in the social consequences of the coexistence of want and wealth. This makes understanding and exposing the lives and habitats of the city's super-rich, and the mechanisms creating their fortunes, an urgent priority. It reverses the usual order of things. The poor are historically the focus of social research, social policy and social reform. Charles Booth's ambitious late-nineteenth-century research, which mapped poverty onto the streets of London with neat colour-coding, is a shining example of humanitarian concern, which, however well intentioned, suggests that poverty and the poor are problematic. The implication is that the rich are above investigation, and the unforgiving framework through which the poor are viewed – from family breakdown and substance abuse to cheating the government through 'benefits fraud' – could never be applied to them. *Serious Money* overturns this assumption, as I collect stories about the rich, bringing *their* London into view, lifting the curtain on their prized anonymity and security.

Cities are always a work in progress, becoming what they are or might be, but sometimes they change dramatically and suddenly. Two such developments with consequences still unfolding scaffold *Serious Money*. The first is the banking crisis of 2008. This generated massive cuts in public finances and reductions in welfare benefits, while also helping a small number of Londoners to become richer than ever. The second is the Covid-19 pandemic of 2020, another seismic event which entrenched and extended existing inequalities. In its early days, the pandemic emptied the city of traffic, people and commerce, as London's momentum drained away. Some of the homeless were swept from the streets into budget hotels, the rest had the streets to themselves. Many people worked from home, or struggled with skeleton public transport to fill critical roles, or left the city altogether. Commercial life ground to a halt as shops, restaurants and bars were shuttered. Tourists left and stayed away. And ghost buses winged through deserted streets with no one aboard. At the same time, Covid-19 offered a vision of what London could look like without the super-rich: rent became (marginally) cheaper, community networks strengthened and local traders flourished as the glass towers of finance emptied out – all reminders that London does not have to be this way, that it could be made differently. *Serious Money* explores twelve years that have been crucial in shaping London, capturing a moment when it has the potential to become another kind of city.

London's Financial Districts

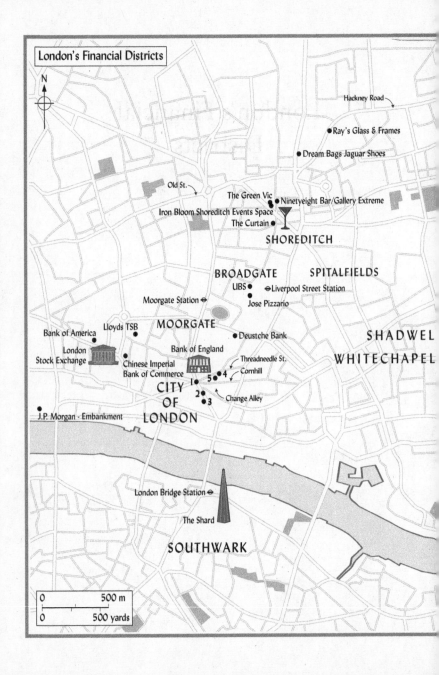

London's Financial Districts

N

Hackney Road

●Ray's Glass & Frames

●Dream Bags Jaguar Shoes

Old St.

The Green Vic ●
Iron Bloom Shoreditch Events Space
The Curtain ●

●Ninetyeight Bar/Gallery Extreme

SHOREDITCH

BROADGATE   SPITALFIELDS

UBS ●   ●Liverpool Street Station
Moorgate Station ⊖
                    ● Jose Pizzario

MOORGATE
Bank of America Lloyds TSB ●   ● Deustche Bank   SHADWEL

London   Bank of England   Threadneedle St.   WHITECHAPEL
Stock Exchange   ●Chinese Imperial   Cornhill
               Bank of Commerce   1 ● ● 5 ● 4
                    CITY   2 ● ● 3   Change Alley
● J.P. Morgan - Embankment   OF
               LONDON

London Bridge Station ⊖

The Shard

SOUTHWARK

0   500 m
0   500 yards

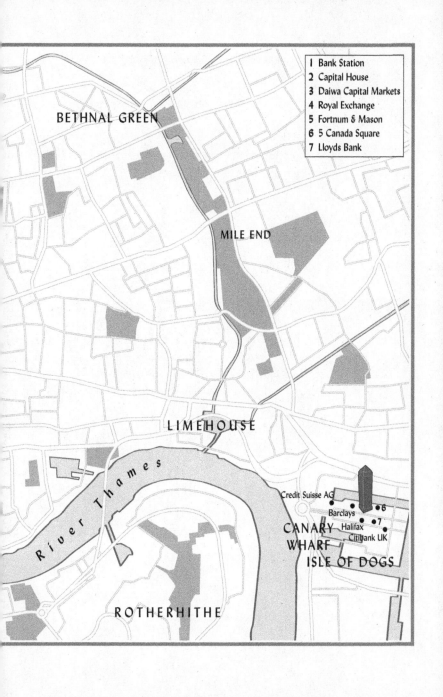

1 Bank Station
2 Capital House
3 Daiwa Capital Markets
4 Royal Exchange
5 Fortnum & Mason
6 5 Canada Square
7 Lloyds Bank

BETHNAL GREEN

MILE END

LIMEHOUSE

River Thames

Credit Suisse AG

Barclays

CANARY
WHARF

Halifax

Citibank UK

ISLE OF DOGS

ROTHERHITHE

I

The Quant in the Ditch

The Ditch is what the Boy calls his area of East London. This is where he curates stripped-back cool, all in distressed leather and polished concrete, in a cocktail bar on Hackney Road. The bar in question, Looking Glass, belongs to a landscape strung with other bars, clubs and restaurants. The Ditch – Shoreditch – is also these days an extension of London's financial district just down the road in the City. Its proximity to finance, London's money-generating machine, means it is a good place to catch rising young financial-industry workers, 'bankers', to most of us, in indiscreet, off-duty moments. As every senior banker I approached refused to meet me, I am looking for finance workers, the not-yet-super-rich, whose work enriches others, to explain how money is made through financial instruments. The Boy[1] – now in his early thirties – studied anthropology at university, just long enough to hone his ability to read the street and help it spend its money, which he has done successfully now for a decade. When I explained my difficulties, he offered to connect me with one of his regulars: Quant. Quant is a significant cog in the money-expanding game, the varied, complex enterprise that underpins the generation of extreme wealth in London.

Hackney Road was, until recently, full of wholesale outlets, selling luggage, handbags and colourful high-heeled shoes. The wholesalers themselves replaced small factories, making rope, rubber, varnish and paint, when East London was at its industrial peak, at the turn of the nineteenth and twentieth centuries. But as the night-time economy pushed its way east of Old Street, connecting it to the financial district to the south around Liverpool Street Station, so new industries spread along Hackney Road like a rash. Reclaimed mid-century furniture shops; barber shops reinvented to trim and sculpt hipster beards; body-art tattoo parlours; restaurants, pizza-joints and bars: these are the new commercial-rent-hiked face of Hackney Road. The Jaguar-Shoes Collective, a venue, performance and exhibition space, trades on the authenticity of the venue's former function as a bag and shoe wholesaler, created in the 1980s and recently decommissioned. The remnants of this recent past, still visible in the landscape, are all repurposed.

As I arrive, a yellow digger is ripping up the pavement outside Looking Glass to fix leaking pipes. Inside, the decor is Shoreditch-chic: bare brick walls, concrete floors. A vast mirror separates the bar at the front from the bar at the back, hidden speakeasy style, the mirror marking its Alice-Through-the-Looking-Glass promise. A colourful plastic deer head, mounted on the wall, gestures ironically towards the country house aesthetic that the curio cabinets of South Audley Street pursue in earnest. Ramshackle trunks turned into tables, fading velvet and leather sofas and mismatched chairs are carefully arranged. The lighting is seductively low. The soundtrack is upbeat, but struggles against the drilling outside. It is a warm Thursday summer evening, still early, and the busiest part of the night, between 11 p.m. and 2 a.m., is yet to unfold.

The atmosphere in Looking Glass is chilled and welcoming. I watch José the barman ply his trade in offbeat cocktails; an inventive mixologist commands a premium round here. He wipes the edge of a glass with lemon peel before filling it with the precision of an alchemist – £12.50. The Boy, in black jeans and T-shirt, flat cap pushed back on his head to catch his unruly hair, with a miniature Kalashnikov on a thick chain in rose gold around his neck, stops to talk between running around sorting things out. He restarts the sound system as it falters, then fiddles with the card machine; no one uses cash. He tells me that the rise in local stabbings is worrying police and curators of the night-time economy alike. My drink arrives in a small, deep, earthenware bowl, a tiny bay leaf attached to the outside of it by an even tinier plastic clothes peg. I perch on a bar stool and wait.

Next to me a young woman in a short grey dress is sampling cocktails in preparation for her birthday party. She has hired the room on the other side of the mirror and must decide which cocktails to serve.

She tries several before speaking to José, who is balancing a coffee bean on top of a drink. She wants something that looks pretty, maybe something layered in different colours. José tries to talk her out of it: Looking Glass does not approve of such mass-market gimmicks. The cocktails' names – *ash and coal*, *fickle millennial*, *identity blossom* and *changing perception* – betray the Boy's liberal arts education. Anticipating her friends' tastes, she checks if José can make a drink she likes but without raw egg whites. The lemon-based cocktail is nice, but just too sour. Could it be adjusted? As she samples each cocktail, she photographs and uploads it onto Instagram.

A British-born Nigerian with an economics degree, she tells me she works in one of the big City banks in customer relations, serving clients who invest in their financial products. We talk about a town on London's periphery, where her well-paid job enabled her to buy a flat, and I worry about her getting back there after road-testing the cocktail menu. We talk about Lagos. She likes to take her London friends there to stay on swanky Victoria Island, which she knows is 'another world', blessed with constant water supplies and electricity generators, set apart from the rest of a city which struggles to supply these staples for the masses. For her, Lagos is party town, to the despair of her parents who struggled to relocate the family to London.

Quant arrives looking apprehensive. 'Nothing good can come of this,' he says as he sits down. He is trying to imagine the banker-bashing moves of which I might be capable, and to which he is accustomed in the media. He looks geeky and solemn – he doesn't smile once – in dark, round-rimmed glasses, a sleeveless pullover over his shirt, and smart casual trousers; he has changed out of his banker uniform. We have found a table in one of the bar's many dark corners, and ease into the conversation by talking about his background. His father was an anaesthetist, and Quant grew up in a solidly middle-class town beyond the western edge of London, graduating first from Oxford and then from Cambridge. With degrees in mathematics and computer science, he joined the financial workforce. A lot of the best-paid jobs seemed to be in banking at that time – not that he is solely motivated by money, he assures me. He reasoned that a job that depends day-to-day on financial markets, and the ever-changing events to which they respond, would be interesting, challenging.

Quant, who spends his days estimating the price of things with no obvious value, believes that wages are a measure of human worth, and his are high.

His first job was with a City hedge fund that specialized in 'structured credit products'. This meant that they repackaged debt: mortgage, corporate, credit card and other kinds of debt, for wealthy people and institutions to invest in. Quant was tasked with analytics and structuring, to better understand the risks involved in these financial transactions. A big US bank bought one of their structuring tools, so Quant moved to New York, working on secondment in the US bank, while also setting up a New York office for his London company. Because debts are sold in mixed bundles carrying different risks of default, the risks are hard to calculate, hence the need for analytics, the work that earns him the pseudonym Quant. Low-risk debts have a high value and low returns on investment; high-risk debts have a lower value and earn higher returns. But the structured debt market sells bundles of debts combining different levels of risk, making them especially complicated to value, and posing challenging puzzles for a maths and computer enthusiast.

It was 2007, and Quant was about to be caught up in a financial storm of monumental significance. On his way from Las Vegas airport to Caesars Palace and the American Securitization Conference – featured in Michael Lewis's book and subsequent film *The Big Short* – as they passed boarded-up, dilapidated houses, the taxi driver entertained Quant with stories of local mortgage borrowers facing foreclosure. He described homeowners stripping their houses of all saleable materials, including wires and pipes, and, sometimes, doing a bit of revenge-vandalism before surrendering the keys to the bank. Later Quant realized that the taxi driver was describing the sub-prime mortgage crisis that began in the United States with catastrophic consequences for the bond market, the banks and, eventually, the rest of us. In 2008, when Lehman Brothers bank collapsed, what might have been a local banking crisis spread from Wall Street to Main Street and along the superhighways of international finance to cities like London.

The sub-prime mortgage crisis occurred because mortgages are rated as low-risk investments by agencies like Standard and Poor's

(S&P), as they are based on the solid ground of American homes. Who doesn't pay their mortgage? But by 2007, the housing market was no longer the sure bet it once was. At the American Securitization Conference, Quant listened to debates about the risks of investing in mortgage-backed securities. He says: 'I had no idea. I just heard all these differing views.' His firm already knew that there were 'a lot of risks here that are not well understood', and so, 'For our own funds, we didn't trust rating agency analysis. We'd always stressed the [composition of the] investments much more than the rating agencies did.' It was, he said, 'becoming clear that the way that they had rated mortgages was based on a history of benign house-price growth, and didn't capture the potential for house-price decline or the potential for very poor origination standards, selling mortgages to people who didn't have a job, who had no income.' Real estate agents are incentivized by commission and bonuses to make fast sales, without considering whether people can actually afford their mortgage repayments. The agents use attractive 'teaser' rates of interest – which quickly give way to higher interest rates – to tempt into home ownership those people who might normally consider it unaffordable. Which it rapidly becomes. Asset and hedge fund managers are assured by the rating agencies that these are low-risk investments, and, anyway, the high-risk investments are hidden from view, because the different levels of risk – mortgage, corporate and credit card debt – are all repackaged together in 'tranches' and shifted on to investors. Pass the debt parcel. Investors are assured by rating agencies that property is a safe investment that will rise in value in perpetuity. Quant knows that 'things can go very badly wrong as well as right.' It was to be an important lesson for him and for governments around the world.

As the financial crisis hit and people across the world lost their jobs and houses, a minority of financiers who successfully anticipated the crisis became very rich indeed. Michael Lewis argues that financial markets are rigged in favour of financial institutions – that they are not, in fact, really *markets* at all. A few investors who were already rich grew even richer.

Quant's insider knowledge enabled him to survive the financial collapse of 2008, in which many lost their jobs. By 2007, he said, 'the writing was starting to come on the wall that there were going to be severe problems', and so he decided to leave New York and return to the London office. Ultimately, he did better than survive. His skills serve a more highly regulated financial future. The financial crisis revealed the need for better risk assessment models of the kind Quant was working on, and, as a new era of financial regulation dawned, independent risk valuations from outside the banks that could better assess the value and risks of hard-to-value financial products became a part of the measures introduced to forestall future financial collapse. Quant's firm now sells its risk assessment and valuation of investments models to all kinds of financial operations. The financial crisis of 2008 routed his career in new and prosperous directions, while some of his colleagues lost their jobs. Here is another lesson in how to make serious money: at the expense of others.

At Looking Glass, the bar is beginning to fill up. The room behind the mirror has been hired for a speed-dating event. Eager twenty-somethings are milling around the bar making stilted conversation while surreptitiously eyeing each other's assets. They are wearing badges made with sticky tape, names like Tom and Victoria scrawled in felt-tipped pen; it looks a bit homemade, a bit like a nursery school event, but with more adult intentions. When the hopeful participants have all arrived, the organizers usher them into the space behind the mirror so that the main business of the night – auditioning potential intimate partners – can begin.

Meanwhile Quant sips his pint and explains the complexities of value in structured finance markets. 'If you split the investment universe up, you have equities, which is investing in stocks and shares in companies. Then you have the fixed income space, which are things like bonds and loans. Structured finance falls in the fixed income space, so it's called fixed income in a sense that if you buy a bond, the contract of that bond will state exactly what it is you're due to be paid, so you'll pay the fixed portion of interest. And then your principle at the end imitates [the value of] your bond.'

Establishing the value of the bond is the tricky part. Quant says: 'If you want to know the price of a loaf of bread, you can go to the supermarket and you can see a price tag on it. But with the things that we invest in, it's a bit like asking, "What's the price of your house?" There isn't a price tag on that, but you know the area it's in, you know when it last traded, and you know that the next-door neighbour sold for this, and they've got one fewer bedrooms, and this guy has one more, so you can interpret in the markets that we invest in.' He adds that '25 to 30 per cent of the market has a direct bid on it' – meaning Goldman Sachs, for example, are willing to pay a certain amount for it, 'which is a good indication of a price that's close to that value'.

The Boy brings us more beer. Quant notes, 'That still leaves 70 to 75 per cent of the market.' So, he explains, they analyse comparable quoted securities with a direct price, and translate it across. He can't tell you the price of your house, but he can make a fairly accurate estimate once he knows its size and its neighbourhood. But, he continues, 'That's quite a data intensive exercise, you need to scan through thousands of securities to figure out their different characteristics. So, we will sell prices, evaluations, just data; our products are all data, and some software as well.' Risk, he concludes, 'is more about having established where we are today, what's the likely trajectory in the future, and what's the risk if things go terribly wrong'. It's all about algorithms: the ordered sequences, instructions and variables that establish the value of a bond.

Quant's analytics makes money for people who are already wealthy, and for big institutional investors like pension funds and sovereign wealth funds. It is a rich person's (or institution's) game for knowledgeable investors. In the process his analytics also makes money for banks, hedge funds and other institutions working in structured credit. Chief investment officers (CIOs) sit at the head of an institution's investments. Below the CIO are portfolio managers, and below them are senior and junior analysts specializing in particular sectors. Recommended investments, Quant says, are submitted to the investment committee, as long as they 'will make lots of money, and it's not very risky'. The 'not very risky' part is where analytics comes in. This is the money-expanding game, the varied, complex enterprise that underpins the generation of extensive wealth in London.

Money makes more money, and those who understand the alchemy of money's expansion skim the profits. Fund managers overseeing investments 'will be paid usually a fixed-rate fee on the assets that they manage. So, if they manage $1 billion of assets, they'll be paid, say, 2 per cent just as a flat fee. Then they are paid an incentive fee.' This means that if the value of that portfolio goes above a certain threshold, they will be paid the 2 per cent base fee, plus 20 per cent of the increase in value: '2 and 20' is the industry standard. This is how money expands, 'because 2 per cent of a return on a multi-billion-pound portfolio can be a huge amount of money for a very small number of people, and in most of finance these big sums of money come from small percentages of vast sums of money'. Mariana Mazzucato, an economist and expert in the alchemy of finance, says this practice extracts rather than creates money, by circulating it among a wealthy few, and skimming it for fees.[2] She calls this 'rent seeking', taking unearned income from unproductive activities. Mazzucato sees financiers as 'takers' rather than 'makers', and argues that their supposed value in generating wealth for society and for cities, through job creation and taxes, is overestimated.

The money machine driving plutocratic London makes a small number of people very rich indeed and leaves those who advise them, like Quant, quite comfortable too. Although he earns considerably less than a chief investment officer or a portfolio manager, Quant lives in a Shoreditch warehouse conversion, conveniently close to his workplace in the financial district. He likes the buzz of bars like Looking Glass and the gentrification, which, he tells me, is advancing apace. Apartments in this area change hands at £1.5 million. We have been talking for several hours, and Quant has arranged to meet with his friends, so we finish our drinks and he heads off into the night. The bar is quieter now, and the Boy agrees to show me the Shoreditch night.

We amble along Hackney Road until it reaches the A10 and the railway arches with their sprouting buddleia. This is where the financial district marches up from the south into the London Borough of Hackney, and the tentacles of finance grope humbler parts of the city, turning them into a corridor of expanding money with high-spec apartments and shops. We pass The Stage, a half-finished concrete shell of an apartment block, on the corner of Bethnal Green Road, wrapped in brown hoardings. Artists impressions below depict a vision of ideal urban living – mostly young and white – opposite the pop-up shops of the BOXPARK shipping containers. Whatever they once contained, they now sell expensive clothes and inessential goods.

Following the railway arches, once the domain of informal car repair shops piled high with used tyres, we move along Great Eastern Street towards the centre of the night-time economy of the Ditch.

On Great Eastern Street, we stop at the Boy's other venue, Iron Bloom, an event space he rents out as a pop-up, often to corporate types who want to project a certain edge. Like a stage, dressed for different productions, complete with on-call set designers, it takes on different forms and activities. The Boy says its current iteration is the Green Vic, 'an ethical pub', a play on the Queen Vic, of *EastEnders* fame. The Boy tells me, 'All of the beer and the spirits and the wine are ethically sourced; they employ people from disadvantaged backgrounds; the food is vegan; it's got minimal environmental impact.' All over this area, wealthy corporations seek credentials by flirting with alternative value systems.

As we move on to Scrutton Street, the Boy points to a red brick building where he used to go to impromptu warehouse parties, now the Curtain Hotel and Members' Club: 'Beyond gentrification!' Young finance workers stand outside pubs with pints (men) and large glasses of white wine (women). He describes Shoreditch in its earlier days as having plenty of bars and underground cultural venues, which attracted artists because of cheap rents. Others followed in the artists' wake, which hiked the price of property, and the artists moved out, to be replaced by a new, wealthier demographic serving finance: by people like Quant. The Boy says: 'They want to live in these vibrant areas, but they don't want noise. Hence the authorities are trying to strike a balance between keeping residents happy and keeping businesses going. Everyone slags off the authorities, but really, they've got a job to do.' The night economy grates against getting a good night's sleep.

We drop into a basement bar called Ninetyeight, which is barely visible from the street. Long and thin, it is lit by pink and purple lights and decorated with a jumble of objects suggesting a children's play area: knitted teddy bears on the backs of chairs, jars of sweets on the bar, feathered lamps, toy monkeys and sheep, a rocking horse. 'Madame 98' appears and hugs the Boy. What makes Ninetyeight unusual, the Boy explains, is that 'Madame' owns the entire seven-floor building. She bought it over thirty years ago when Shoreditch was a more sinister place, its pubs allegedly full of East End gangsters. When

Shoreditch's former landlords took the money offered by the big buyers who were moving into the area, sensing there was money to be made on leases, Madame, a no-nonsense East Londoner by now in her seventies, refused to sell. Consequently, she is a wealthy woman, raking in rents. Finance and property speculation are key routes to London riches. This area, she says, with a mixture of scorn and awe, is 'completely owned by hedge funds'.

Do hedge funds own Shoreditch? We walk to the eastern end of Hackney Road that leads to Bethnal Green. This end of the street is clearly in transition. Its cafés and small shops are boarded up. There are big gaps where Victorian buildings have been knocked down. The old gay pub, the Joiners Arms, has disappeared despite attempts to save it as a community resource. Entire sections of the street are cleared as developers bide their time and make offers that owners and leaseholders cannot refuse. Ray's Glass and Frames shop stands defiantly in the way of the new street. It is what the Chinese, accustomed to large-scale urban renewal, call a 'nail house': a place that sticks up out of the landscape, disrupting the new city.

Rising out of the pools of orange lamplight are two new apartment blocks in brown brick called Shoreditch Exchange: 184 flats, with gym, cinema, 'club lounge' and twenty-four-hour concierge. Prices begin at just under £800,000, unaffordable to most Londoners. The developer is Regal London, a privately owned company that buys up small plots of city land in London, Hong Kong, China and Dubai. It is, according to its website, 'underpinned by significant assets'. In fact, Regal London is financed by a private equity firm called KKR, which has its London offices in Mayfair's Carlton Gardens. It takes advantage of the gap in city building left by the retreat of the big house builders like Barratt, who are only interested in large developments, not small plots of land like these. With $129 billion in assets under management, KKR is the world's biggest private equity fund. It boasts what is called an internal rate of return (IRR) – a metric used to calculate the profitability of investments, often criticized for over-estimating profitability – of over 25 per cent on money invested. We have found Madame 98's hedge fund, actually a private equity fund – an equally high-return investment instrument – caught in the act of recasting London, building by building, street by street.

As we wander back along Hackney Road towards Looking Glass, I wonder whether the Boy can survive a game rigged in favour of private equity, sure to demand ever-increasing commercial rents. Looking Glass is filling to bursting point as the pubs begin to close and the benefits of its late-night licence come into play. Some of the speed daters have stayed and joined the throng as the night moves on. Quant has returned with a gang of his friends, all lawyers and accountants in corporate finance, ordering rounds of beer and cocktails. I'm struck by how the Ditch, a seemingly trendy alternative space, is full of big-finance money. Shoreditch houses and entertains finance workers; it bolsters and extends London's money machine through commercial investments; and yet it looks like a cool place to party after work. How well money and the rich hide in plain sight.

2

Bankers in Glass Towers

No fewer than nine streets converge on Bank junction, at the heart of the money machine's long-standing engine room of finance colloquially called 'the City' or 'the Square Mile'. One of them is Threadneedle Street, where the Bank of England sprawls in windowless Corinthian-columned grandeur. It is an imposing presence at the junction, steadily printing money and formulating policies to sustain the United Kingdom's finances. The Bank of England creates digital money, through a process known as quantitative easing, and injects it into the economy by buying assets and government bonds (debt). Because quantitative easing inflates asset prices, it also increases the wealth of already wealthy people. Key mechanisms of central banking favour the rich. Bank junction is also a focal point for London's traffic: taxis were recently banned in efforts to ease the traffic congestion. I am standing on the pavement at 7 a.m., in a light rain, and it is already cranking into gear. I am going to visit Banker in his glass, steel and concrete tower. But first I want to wander the streets and soak up the atmosphere.

The human cogs of the money machine arrive from all directions. From Shoreditch and points north, they arrive along the A10, the road that runs all the way to King's Lynn in Norfolk. From the south, from the suburbs and the towns and cities that extend to the coast, they pass through London's oldest railway station, London Bridge. At peak morning commuting time, a crowd like a protest march without the placards moving from the direction of the station crosses the actual London Bridge and streams into London's ancient financial district. (In the evening, the same crowd crosses the Thames in the opposite direction, heading homewards.) Liverpool Street Station receives the melee that arrives from the east. And from all directions, thousands of workers emerge above ground and into the working day at Bank Underground Station. The vibration of bodies in motion, on the business of finance, animate these narrow streets.

The Bank of England's imposing columns stake a bold physical claim for London's global financial significance. Through slave ships, Lloyd's coffee house and shipping insurance, the City managed the financial architecture of Britain's imperial and mercantile wealth from the seventeenth century onwards. The global reach of finance, connecting London to all corners of the world, is imprinted in its ancient streets, which are, as historian David Kynaston suggests, paved with the right stuff, with money.[1] The racial politics embedded in the voyages of 'discovery' – financed by London's banks – that opened up the New World, and led to slavery and the entire imperial apparatus of human and material-resource extractions, are not immediately discernible. But an earlier machine for expanding money, with an invisible dark past, stalks these streets.

Finance's ancient operations are everywhere named in these labyrinthine passages and alleys – from Change Alley to Cornhill's Royal Exchange, now the refuge of smokers, and women leaning against the wall to eat hasty lunches who fill the not-so-well-paid service roles that hold the money machine together. In her study of the city's financial workers, sociologist Linda McDowell described an elitist masculine environment, with an atmosphere of exaggerated masculinity that makes it difficult for women – who predominate in administrative, rather than more prestigious, better-paid, positions – to take leading roles.[2] The masculinity of finance starts to become visible.

Walking from Bank junction to Moorgate, I pass strings of cafés with familiar names crammed into ancient buildings: Pod, Starbucks, Eat, Pret, Coco. And in stylish Michelin restaurants like Hispania waiters in white jackets serve men in dark suits. The requirements of contemporary finance have reconfigured the business of these ancient streets. Backroom financial service centres fill the gaps between eateries. In companies like Capital House, offices stuffed with lawyers and accountants steer finance through regulation while minimizing the tax liabilities of wealthy clients and corporations with imaginative accounting. I walk on past Daiwa Capital Markets, a Japanese investment and brokerage firm, and the Chinese Imperial Bank of Commerce. These channels circulate finance between London and a tangle of other places. The United Kingdom's 250 foreign banks, originating in more than twenty-six countries, cluster in these streets. The door to London's financial markets was blown open by the Big Bang of 27 October 1986, in which the London Stock Exchange became a private limited company and welcomed foreign financial institutions to London. This coincided with electronic trading facilitating a second explosion, this time of trading volumes, enabled by new digital technologies. Waves of internationalization, in money, style and food, wash through these streets and refashion them.

Formal in dress and demeanour, finance workers move through the streets in a purposeful, routine, self-assured and, sometimes, intimate manner; secrets and endearments are whispered in doorways. The men striding past me wear sharp dark suits and pastel shirts: ties are no longer necessary. Women's dress codes mimic the men's, with the addition of high-heeled shoes. The streets are openly luxurious and subtly securitized. I pass the entrance of the Royal Exchange, where an African security guard stands watching. Repurposed from its 1571 origins and its 1844 refurbishment, the Royal Exchange now hosts expensive restaurants, one run by Fortnum & Mason where I stop for lunch, and shops selling lavish watches, jewellery and other glittering baubles – means of dispersing surplus income. Seemingly insignificant things like these hold this place together and make it work.

I eat my salad and tune in to the conversation of a mother and her daughter, both lawyers, at the next table, consuming elegantly small portions of seafood. With the rich reluctant to speak to me, I often have to resort to eavesdropping. Their quiet conversation reveals the concerns that create the atmosphere of this place. They discuss workplace relationships, abilities, performance-related bonuses and the injustices of their distribution; then move on to classical dressage, the riding academy, competitive horsemanship, international equestrian events in Switzerland and Paris, and their mutual appreciation of 'beautiful horses'. Finally, they recover their identical Burberry macs and head off into the rain. Two men on the other side of me are discussing the challenges of good leadership, their aspirations, the difficulties of office politics, and people who could be 'useful to you'. 'How is family life?' 'Not so good: I am trying to spend more time with my family.'

Walking from Moorgate to Liverpool Street and the south-eastern edge of the financial district, I pass Spaces, a room full of desks rented to the city's itinerant workforce. There are further huddles of smokers, and homeless people shrouded in damp sleeping bags, who tell me it's safer to sleep during the day and stay watchful at night. A street sweeper passes, employed by the French company Veolia, pushing a cart along the road. These are just some of the everyday activities creating the vibrations of the streets where the money machine churns.

The traditional financial district ends abruptly towards Liverpool Street Station, where a modern city is breaking out of the ground at Broadgate, the entire area dug up for Crossrail. This vast cross-city transport infrastructure project promises to reduce unbearable congestion on the Underground. A pedestrianized square owned by British Land is almost finished, yet still shielded by construction hoardings that announce the new commercial lease possibilities of the square, while hiding its army of construction workers, many of them from less prosperous parts of North East England. It is a city landscape in constant upheaval in a thousand different ways. Near the square are new buildings clad in dull metal, UBS and Deutsche Bank among them, which mark the seam between the ancient and the new city of money. A twenty-first-century financial district built in glass and steel sweeps down Bishopsgate back to London Bridge and three miles eastwards along the Thames to London's new financial annex, its confident banking and insurance towers reaching into the sky, described by architect Rowan Moore as a 'canyon of swagger'.[3]

This is Canary Wharf, a private-sector city regeneration project developed by the Canadian company Olympia and York. It struggled at first, and was liquidated with debts of $20 billion in 1992, when few of the global financial corporations searching for office space in the Square Mile were persuaded to move to its gleaming glass towers. The Docklands Development Corporation and the Canary Wharf Group took over in 1995, with Olympia and York's owners, international property developers Paul and Albert Reichmann, remaining active in the new company. The development then attracted wealthy investors, including Prince Waleed bin Talal of Saudi Arabia, and large public investments in transport, which connected Canary Wharf to the London Underground in 1999 and to the City Airport, opened in 1987. Credit Suisse, Bank of America, NatWest, Citibank, the Hongkong and Shanghai Banking Corporation (HSBC) – with its Tower designed by Norman Forster – and J. P. Morgan, among others, set up shop, establishing a new model of city building later rolled out worldwide, notably across China and in the remaking of Beirut.[4] In this model, private developers take responsibility for everything from buildings and public spaces, to street food and security. Green squares and so called 'circuses' – private spaces that look like public spaces, closely patrolled by private security companies – provide the new template for private-sector urbanism.

London's new financial district was built on land occupied by social housing and disused docks. The Thatcher government's movements in the 1980s to privatize public housing and make it a 'residual option', combined fatally with strategic neglect resulting from local authorities' strained budgets. Social housing estates were allowed to crumble into dereliction, supporting the case for demolition, and providing the land for the eastward extension of London's financial hub, spurred on by the kind of public investment in infrastructure denied to social housing tenants. Canary Wharf was constructed on the dispossession of London's poor, dismantling the soft social infrastructures built between neighbours and communities over years. Its streets and buildings express a particular political orientation, in glass, steel and concrete.

But, for now, I am still on Broadgate heading to meet Banker. Planning restrictions that once constrained this historic area were loosened with the help of early millennial star-architects, whose work was judged by the then Labour government planning appeals system as offering significant contributions to the architecture of the city. This reasoning allowed developers to exceed the height of St Paul's Cathedral and open up London's skies to international finance. Renzo Piano designed The Shard, Norman Foster 30 St Mary Axe ('the Gherkin', formerly the site of the Baltic Exchange) and James Stirling the postmodern building No. 1 Poultry. In a building like these – I cannot say where Banker actually works – security personnel stand by glass revolving doors leading into a marble hallway. The scale projects importance, and protects Banker from the activity of the street. A smiling woman on reception lets me through the glass barriers; another escorts me further into the bank and into an anonymous meeting room, among other meeting rooms, each a perfect clone of the last: tables, chairs and bottled water create scenes for conversations about growing money. I stop to admire the Damien Hirst paintings.

In his early forties, Banker wears a well-tailored grey suit and shiny black shoes. He tells me about 'rules' preventing him speaking to journalists and researchers. Most financial sector workers think it best to fly 'under the radar', he says: 'There is no upside to being conspicuous.' Separation and concealment make this place; I am pleased and surprised that he has agreed to meet me, to tell me more about how the very rich make their money through the dark arts of finance. I do my best to assuage his concerns about anonymity – and call him Banker. Now in a senior management position, Banker keeps the money machine ticking over and paying out for the bank's clients.

Banker joined the financial workforce just before the millennium. Through the stories of older colleagues, he learned about the trading floor where stocks were physically and noisily exchanged, and saw traces of the 1980s' Big Bang, when American banks arrived in London mob-handed. No longer did East End scrap-metal and market traders, who could formerly progress through back office routes onto the trading floor in the era of call-out trading, man the machine. Banker arrived at the end of 'high touch trading', when clients' orders were executed manually. He describes this as 'a bit like being a coal miner in the late eighties and nineties'. 'By the time I was doing it,' he says, 'it was all on computers and the banks' recruitment policies were transformed.'

In this brave new digital world, banks needed the brightest and best-educated to explore the financial engine's more oblique and lucrative possibilities, and exploit opportunities that far exceeded in complexity the buying and selling of shares. A new era of financial instruments, including a burgeoning asset management industry run by intermediaries, was dawning. Banker was recruited on 'the milk round': an annual visit by banks to elite universities that funnelled talent into finance. From Oxford, Banker became a trader at Lehman's. He was flown first class to New York where the bank gave him an apartment and he rode around the city in taxis. He was back working at Lehman's in London when it collapsed, on 15 September 2008; Ben Bernanke at the US Federal Reserve described this as the worst financial crisis in global history. Banker was living at the epicentre of the financial crisis.

He tells me: 'I remember going to bed on the Sunday night and it was the headline. We were aware that there were crisis talks in New York. I was monitoring it on NBC or Bloomberg News or something.' Then he saw a breaking news strapline across the screen: *Lehman files for chapter eleven* [bankruptcy]. Banker had no idea what to do. He went into work the next morning, as usual, and there was someone standing in the foyer handing out photocopied pieces of paper saying that Lehman Brothers International had been removed from the central corporate structure of Lehman Brothers Holdings and taken into receivership in the United Kingdom. He and his colleagues were asked to keep going in to work for the next month. They weren't allowed to trade, but Lehman's were trying to sell parts of the business as going concerns. If its workforce had disappeared, it would have been harder for them to negotiate those sales. A week before their usual pay day, Banker remembers, 'Senior management said, "Unfortunately, we haven't even got any funds to pay you on the 21st."' This was worse than his worst-case scenarios. He says, 'Typically you think in banking, even if, let's say, I lose a lot of money as a trader, the worst that could happen is that you get made redundant.' This isn't usually disastrous: 'You get three months' notice, and you get all your accumulated stock, typically, your deferred compensation.' Instead he was unable to pay that month's bills. It was, he says, 'quite stressful'.

Lehman's collapse provided some of the most widely circulated images of the banking crisis, as employees were caught by television cameras carrying their boxed personal effects from Canary Wharf's office towers. Recalling the moment when the glass towers of banking splintered, Banker reveals his insecurities and anxieties about his future. The anticipated safety net, liquidated stock options and redundancy pay, had been temporarily withdrawn. But Banker's wife had a well-paid job and could easily cover their living expenses, and he soon found another job as a trader with comparable seniority and pay. His setback was temporary and his story reveals one of money's manoeuvres. It protects itself by staging what looks like business as usual, while selling parts of its operation to cut losses. Its international arm is cut adrift to limit the damage. Money is cunning and resilient, and, in these qualities, it shows its character.

Banker is now part of another bank, a global stock market trading and wealth management enterprise operating in fifty countries, managing the wealth of over half of the world's billionaires. In this context, again, London sits at the centre of global finance. He tells me his work involves bespoke services: in assessing the needs of wealthy clients and advising on the expansion of their wealth through a spectrum of financial instruments, including investment and stock market trading, as well as estate planning and protection from taxation. This bank provides 'pretty much every type of financial service that you can offer' to large sections of the global plutocracy, providing the building blocks of the plutocratic city.

Are these activities not also public benefits? The financial sector added £58.2 million to London's economy in 2016, accounting for 14 per cent of the city's total economic output, 1.1 million jobs and 25 per cent of UK service exports.[5] Yet, the economist Brett Christophers suggests otherwise.[6] He says finance money was always considered unproductive, until the 1970s when new methods of accounting were adopted. These emphasized employment and tax figures which suggested that finance made important contributions to the public life of the city in providing work and tax revenues. The voices of bankers insisting on the contribution of finance in creating collective prosperity were amplified by the media and supported by a politics that is embedded in financial industries. Christophers, like Mazzucato, argues instead that the finance machine simply churns, expands and skims money, redistributing it from outsiders to insider wealthy investors and into ever fewer hands. No less a figure than UK Financial Services Authority Chairman Adair Turner described banks as engaged in 'economically and socially useless activity'.[7] The 'social benefits of finance' story is a political manoeuvre. The jobs created all serve the money machine. But one thing is clear: from the seventeenth-century voyages of the East India Company, which gave way to the speculative gains of Empire, to today's complex financial architecture of derivatives, bonds and the rest, the City of London is finance money in bricks, stones, bodies and bones.

· While Banker's colleagues offer wealth management services to the world's billionaires, he advises and trades on behalf of institutional investors, asset managers, private equity and hedge funds. He says, 'As a trader I'd typically start at 6 a.m. or 6.30 a.m. You are preparing for the market to open, which happens at eight o'clock, and that involves understanding any news that happened in the stocks that you cover.' He checks what the US and Asian markets have done after the European markets closed the previous day. Then he begins the 'real business' of trying to generate new business, to get orders to execute on behalf of institutional clients. 'Then the market opens at eight and you spend the day executing those orders, buying and selling, trying to cross stock between different clients, monitoring the news and the order flow, to see how the instruments that you are trading are going to perform.' He describes his workplace as a 'high octane, high pressure environment'.

Banker reads the markets, their broader financial and political landscape, and seizes investment opportunities that expand money, ideally ahead of other traders: competitive advantage is crucial in accumulating money. Banks like his trade commodities, buying and selling shares in publicly listed companies and financial instruments like futures (bets on the future value of commodities). He says: 'We service hedge funds and advise them on what to buy and what to sell. Then we ultimately take those orders and buy and sell those things on their behalf.' They also act as a 'prime broker' for hedge funds, meaning that they take care of their money and other assets, and settle their trades for them. 'We'll provide them with leverage, so that if, say, they've got $1 billion dollars to invest, if they give us that $1 billion we might allow them to take positions worth $2 billion.' He compares it to spread betting, since, with a spread bet, 'You don't have to put down the full amount, you put down the margin. Essentially they give us the margin and we allow them to take our balance sheet to invest.' Economist Susan Strange calls this 'casino capitalism'.[8] We all have chips in this game, whether we like it or not, through savings, pension funds and loans, instruments that leave ordinary people vulnerable to the fluctuations of markets, which enrich the already rich.

Banker tells me that most trades work through automatic programs – algorithms – instead of high-touch manual trading. Algorithms track shifting markets and opportunities across equally shifting landscapes automatically, through the kinds of programs devised by people like Quant. These programs and models are sold to the bank's institutional clients and the bank uses them to trade for wealthy customers. 'Bank employees,' he says, 'must build, maintain and adjust algorithms to accommodate shifting circumstances, including the unpredictable performance of markets, so these are not fully automated processes.'

Hedge funds are the pooled funds of experienced (wealthy) investors who aim to shield investment portfolios from market risks as investments go up or down. Banker explains, 'Hedge funds manage money on behalf of wealthy individuals, but also other institutional asset managers, who will allocate money to hedge funds to manage on their behalf.' High risks yield high returns. While traditional trading operations went *long*, buying assets in the expectation that they would rise in value, hedge funds go *short*, and profit from falling asset values. Being able to bet in both directions protects as well as grows money, but hedge funds have recently shown lacklustre performances in growth. As financial markets are dynamic, investment funds go up and down over time. And more questionable practices include misleading investor reports intended to undermine a stock and diminish its value. As more investors rush into the space, so returns fall, and the search for asset value moves ever onwards elsewhere. Churn, shift and skim are the rhythms of money as it works its way through the City's financial institutions.

He tells me that private equity is a similar concept. Private equity funds are also investing money on behalf of other people, more typically institutional money, but, to some extent, also the money of private individuals. 'It's longer term, so instead of investing in listed securities and trading them on the market, what they'll do is, they'll take a private stake in a company that isn't listed.' These alternative assets such as private equity and hedge funds, which are not publicly traded, give the wealthy direct access to channels of investment for expanding money, which are closed to other investors.

Banker says private equity searches for small successful businesses that can be scaled up through private investments, and earn high returns for investors. The sandwich chain Pret a Manger began this way – started by small entrepreneurs and scaled up by private equity. Parts of the high street, as well as the streets I walked to Banker's office, from Shoreditch to Moorgate, are private equity in action. Private equity invests in failing businesses too, by taking a controlling interest and then driving reforms or closure, whichever makes them the best returns. He gives the example of Monarch Airlines, bought by private equity: 'Unfortunately that went down. They ended up making money though, because, despite the fact that the company then had to wind down, there was still great value in the landing slots.[9] When they got sold off, [private equity] ended up making a profit, even though the company went bankrupt.' Private equity also bought Comet and British Steel. 'In both those cases, those companies were about to go bankrupt.' The predatory practices of private equity shape high streets across the United Kingdom. It seizes opportunities to expand money and lives on the road kill of failed money, when it engages in asset stripping, rather than saving a business that is about to go under.

We don't talk numbers, but Banker's handsome salary is supplemented by bonuses and stock options that reflect his contribution to the bank's profits skimmed from his deals. From the 1990s, there was a boom in profits that was reflected in giant hikes in the salaries and bonuses of top financial workers, putting some of them in the ranks of the super-rich. 'I would say that most people who work in finance, are, to some extent, motivated by earning money, or they probably wouldn't do it,' Banker muses. 'There are easier ways to earn a living, just in terms of the hours and in terms of the pressure. I think, that said, it is enjoyable.' He feels fortunate that 'banking does pay relatively well, given that I actually also find the work quite interesting. But I think most people are motivated, to some extent, by money and the status; there's probably some element of what it affords someone, the nice lifestyle, the house, the holidays.' Banker is a HNWI. He lives in style on the northern, Primrose Hill side of Regent's Park, one of London's wealthiest neighbourhoods.

The 'money and the status' are motivational because money has come to be seen as a measure of individual worth, as finance-men have absorbed the logics of finance into their emotional life. Finance is a testosterone-fuelled competitive sport driven by fear and greed.[10] Banker puts it more delicately: 'People who end up working in these roles are bright people who have gone to the best universities, who have done well, typically, academically.' A broader social question concerns whether amassing still more money for the already rich is the best use of the United Kingdom's most educated talent. Banker does just that; he is a cog in the human-algorithmic money machine that drives the plutocratic city in certain directions.

Banker tells me that the money machine is more dispersed than I had thought. Although the financial district is important, he mentions Mayfair as an alternative centre for hedge funds and private equity. Where the City and Canary Wharf have large, purpose-built offices designed for international banks, hedge fund and private equity operations are smaller and can easily fit into the town houses of Mayfair. I resolve to head to Mayfair next, to explore these super-lucrative worlds of hedge funds and private equity.

I leave Banker's glass tower the same way I came in. He walks me to the lift and we chat about football. After we say goodbye, I wander back towards Liverpool Street Station. A row of taxis is waiting to take people all over the city. A man and woman in their forties are concluding a discussion in Italian over cigarettes. Two women who were sheltering from the rain under a shawl when I went into the building have gone. The rain has stopped. I head for the sunken circle at Broadgate, ringed with bars and restaurants. On the way, I think about Banker's experience of the financial crash. I think about Lehman's recovery tactics and I think about Banker's sense of insecurity, which turned out to be temporary.

The rest of us were less fortunate. Following what the UK National Audit Office describe as a sustained period of instability in financial markets and an economic downturn of global proportions, British taxpayers stepped in with financial support for the banks totalling £1,162 billion between 2007 and 2010, in order to protect the financial system from collapse. This hit to public finances justified a politics of austerity, which brought massive cuts across public services from

2010. In the London Borough of Tower Hamlets, which abuts the city's financial district, four out of ten households live below the poverty line, one of the highest rates in England and Wales.[11]

After-work drinks are already under way as I arrive in Broadgate Circle. It's like being in the bottom of a crowded bowl, with steps ranged around the sides to higher ground. Customers of José Pizarro and Mrs Fogg's are sitting at tables outside or standing in small groups. The men have removed their jackets, and talk loudly – to each other, or into their phones – while juggling pints of beer. Women with blond ponytails and suntanned, toned legs, designer handbags and understated jewellery stand with pink wine and orange Aperol spritzes. Shoreditch cool has a commercial rival. Broadgate Circle, which was once fortified against areas to the east, opened up as Shoreditch became a super-cool after-work destination and commissioned public artworks, like Richard Serra's 55-foot steel sculpture, *Fulcrum*, to suggest it, too, embraced artists. Uniformed security men on minimum wages patrol the bowl from its rim, which provides a lookout onto the unfolding activities of the evening. I squeeze onto a table at José Pizarro and tune in. It is crowded and the men talk over each other, making it difficult for me to hear. One is complaining, 'All the action's down your way. He sits at your desk.' The other talks about another of their colleagues, saying, 'He's soft as shit, that's what frustrates Andy. He doesn't have the bullets in his gun.' They note, 'There's not been any new girls in a while', and laugh. The second man continues, talking about a colleague with a 'number one account' whom he is trying to cut down to size. Their friendly 'banter' comes with an undercurrent of menace, competition and just a hint of predatory intentions towards the women they work with.

Behind Broadgate Circle cranes tower overhead. Construction workers are still building the city. Taller buildings are stacked behind the circle and the cranes, creating a landscape of layered heights. I step inside José Pizarro to pay my bill and watch a chef in the open kitchen carry the most beautiful pink octopus to the counter to slice into tapas.

Mayfair, St James's and Belgravia

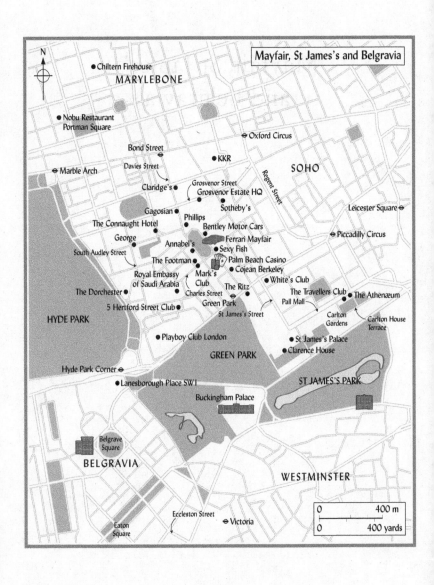

Mayfair, St James's and Belgravia

N

● Chiltern Firehouse

MARYLEBONE

● Nobu Restaurant
Portman Square

⊖ Oxford Circus

Bond Street

● KKR

SOHO

Davies Street

⊖ Marble Arch

Regent Street

Claridge's ●

Grosvenor Street
Grosvenor Estate HQ

Leicester Square ⊖

Gagosian ●

Sotheby's ●

Phillips

The Connaught Hotel

Bentley Motor Cars ●

⊖ Piccadilly Circus

George ●

Ferrari Mayfair ●

Annabel's ●

● Sexy Fish

South Audley Street

The Footman ●

Palm Beach Casino

● Cojean Berkeley

Royal Embassy
of Saudi Arabia

Mark's
Club

● White's Club

The Ritz

The Travellers Club ●

● The Athenæum

The Dorchester ●

Charles Street

Pall Mall

5 Hertford Street Club ●

Green Park

Carlton
Gardens

Carlton House
Terrace

St James's Street

HYDE PARK

● Playboy Club London

● St James's Palace

GREEN PARK

● Clarence House

Hyde Park Corner ⊖

● Lanesborough Place SW1

ST JAMES'S PARK

Buckingham Palace

Belgrave
Square

BELGRAVIA

WESTMINSTER

Eaton
Square

Eccleston Street

⊖ Victoria

| 0 | 400 m |
| 0 | 400 yards |

3

Mayfair Magic

Palaces, private members' clubs, luxury hotels, art galleries and auction houses, embassy outposts of oil-rich nations, darkened casinos, emporia stuffed with exotic objects, private equity enterprises, wealth management operations and hedge funds: all the fun of the fair. The affairs, whims and foibles – the lives of the uber-wealthy – shape these streets. There are many 'May fairs', tiny traces of this area's eighteenth-century past of theatrics, puppet shows, comedians and eccentric vendors – a world of 'low pleasures' as it was described at the time, recast in the present.[1] Mayfair. Following the money to the West of the city, Mayfair is altogether glitzier, more complacent, more brazenly rich than anywhere else in London. Concentrations of wealth, sometimes concealed and sometimes openly displayed, stare down at me from all sides. I get off the Tube at Green Park, a good place to start exploring.

At the northern end of Green Park a tangle of tourists waits for the Hop On Hop Off bus that tours the city's attractions. Two women in full burkas, pushing strollers while managing multiple carrier bags of designer shopping, are navigating the crowds congealing around the bus stop. Three homeless camps outside the Tube, surrounded by ragged luggage and underlaid with cardboard, observe distances tacitly agreed between the occupants. At one, where a dishevelled man is drinking coffee, a handwritten sign simply says *I'm hungry*; the sign at a second suggests a £1 donation towards a shelter for the night.

I walk down the long row of arches that run the full length of the front of The Ritz, forming a covered passageway between one of London's most famous luxury hotels and the road, now also providing shelter for further homeless campers and *Big Issue* sellers. Guarding the entrance to another world, the doorman at The Ritz, in a grey-trimmed double-breasted black coat and top hat, shrinks into the recessed doorway as if to remove himself from the goings on in the street.

Banker's tip-off and my subsequent research have taught me that hedge funds and private equity move large volumes of money through Mayfair's streets, and I want to know what this looks and feels like. Hedge fund central, it turns out, is on the other side of Piccadilly from The Ritz, on Berkeley Street and Berkeley Square at its northern end. The street, the square and the streets around house a significant pro-portion of London's 400 hedge funds, with $395 billion, second only to New York City's $1,024 billion, in the value of assets under man-agement,[2] which is how these things are estimated. Private equity offices are more dispersed, and, though estimates differ widely, there may be as many as 347 private equity firms, with £30 billion under management,[3] clustered in this area. This may not be the case for ever: like the city itself, London's financial architecture is ever-changing. Since the United Kingdom left the European Union, some private equity operations have moved to Holland, France and Spain, all look-ing to stake their claims as London's rival. Even without Brexit, there has been what *Financial Times* journalists call 'over fishing of the London market',[4] driving some operations to Manchester and Leeds. But, for now, the money is here in Mayfair, both concealed and out in plain sight.

I meet Searcher at Cojean, a casual lunch place on Berkeley Street. He works on this street as a researcher for a large American hedge fund with over two thousand employees worldwide trading stocks, currencies and bonds. He tells me this street hosts 'two of the biggest hedge funds on the planet'. I'm in the right place. Searcher could easily be a professor: bookish, intense, well read, serious, Italian. He speaks quietly so as not to be overheard. It is difficult for him to describe what he does to someone who is outside the industry, and he's obviously long given up trying. He knows that his work is misun-derstood, widely criticized for generating inexplicably large volumes of money in arcane ways. Wearing a jacket, jeans and sneakers, he fades into the background of these opulent streets.

So, how exactly do the activities of hedge funds differ from those of the banks in the financial district? Searcher breaks it down for me, explaining that the investors or other entities (mutual, pooled funds of a number of investors) in a hedge fund range in size from a group of five people to hundreds. Mutual funds or pension funds, on the other hand, could represent thousands of people, by which point there is no difference from banks. Also, he continues, 'Theoretically, they [hedge funds] should be hedging the risk; they should have less risk than other places. Of course, that is relative. That's not necessarily the truth with some places.' Banks and hedge fund operations are differentiated but interconnected enterprises, it seems.

Hedge funds try to maximize returns and minimize risk, as Searcher says, by betting both ways: *long* on anticipated rises in the price of something and *short* on falls. Money is staked and expanded however markets move. Hedge fund investments can be in any kind of asset: land, real estate, derivatives, currencies, diamonds or wine. In practice, hedge funds often specialize in assets they know most about, choosing to focus on gold or art, for example. Their investments might be global or they might target certain countries. They aim to profit from changes in macroeconomic variables such as global interest rates and countries' economic policies.[5] Both these Searcher tracks when looking for new opportunities. 'For the time being, I'm working on futures,' he says. He tells me he is looking for patterns in seasonal behaviour by oil products. Some of these patterns are well known, but there are also some 'exceptions to the rule', which his fund can take advantage of, because, he says, 'Some people haven't seen these things.' Searcher probes the unknown seeking undiscovered angles. This is how hedge funds make serious money. As investors pile into what is becoming a crowded investment space, so returns diminish and the quest for asset value becomes a search for ever more unusual angles and one-off opportunities to grow money.

As private investments open only to financial institutions or wealthy individuals, hedge funds specialize in risky and aggressive manoeuvres. Their investments can be difficult to value and hard to sell. Knowledgeable investors often take a different view to the markets, and this underpins hedge funds' riskiness and profitability – returns of 18 per cent or higher are not uncommon. Investors must also be able to afford to lose their money *and* to pay the fees that hedge funds charge, typically the '2 and 20' that Quant described. Substantial investments involve substantial risks. And risks are amplified when investors borrow the money they invest in the hope of increased returns. Hedge-fund manager John Paulson said that when returns are good and assets grow the fees 'just pour out of the sky'.[6] And, as a private equity investor I call Cake will tell me later, this is 'a zero-sum game'. If a hedge fund makes a lot of money, say, several hundred million, then someone else hasn't. I notice a maroon Rolls-Royce parked outside Cojean on Berkeley Street with a licence plate that reads RR08 LON. And I wonder whether this is Rob from London's car or Rob's London car – though it also suggests an unintentional reference to popular perceptions of how Rob acquired the money to buy the car, by robbing London.

I am not surprised that Searcher doesn't accept the view underpinning the 'casino capitalism' theory that private equity and hedge funds are complex upscale betting syndicates. He argues that his research reduces uncertainty, drawing the game away from gambling. His financial-engineering background in robotics and machine learning have trained him to apply mathematical models to financial problems, and his intensive, scholarly reading of the latest research enables him to forecast which way investments will move. Here is another finely trained mind bending itself to the demands of money. As in other hedge fund operations, his team consists of a researcher, a trader and a portfolio manager. His data arms portfolio managers with information used to instruct traders to buy and sell. 'In my case,' he says, 'it's a lot of experimentation. It's almost like working in academia, just without being able to publish ... because you're not allowed to publish.' He is certainly not. His data is valuable proprietary information not to be shared, but used instead to gain advantage and profit over others.

The sheer scale of the potential rewards means that Searcher doesn't always have to pull off highly lucrative manoeuvres. 'If someone wants to sell something and you have done the research, more than anyone else, you have spent months and you know that something will rise, so you can buy cheap and sell – you know, you're rich, you make money.' By his estimate, 'Even if you are correct 1 per cent of the time, that 1 per cent is enough that you will make money. You don't have to be, you know, 90 per cent correct. It's only about mathematics and knowledge.' He crunches the numbers, creates models and runs them repeatedly: 'I try again and try again.' I order us more coffee.

Money is paramount: 'Your first responsibility is to your client's money.' Money also often demands long working hours that intrude on family and personal life, he tells me – Searcher and his wife have a young child. Money movers are judged by results. 'It's about whether you can do it.' Oxford doesn't open these doors. 'We tend to give [applicants] an assignment and we say, "You have one week on something that you have never done in your life. Go and learn for yourself and do it", and then you see people who tend to be clever and pick up things by themselves.' He notices 'people that come from very average circumstances', who are 'the ones that really try hard' and 'the people that persevere'. Searcher thinks hedge funds favour people from multidisciplinary backgrounds, who have worked across different scientific areas: 'You may not be the best mathematician, but if you can do the mathematics, and you are a good programmer, you tend to survive.' Hedge fund bosses expect a return on their human as well as financial assets, and this means hiring people with a relentless determination to succeed, a broad range of skills and a talent for creative thinking.

Stakes are high and losses are swiftly punished. 'If the team loses money, all of us are out the same day.' Searcher explains that, because of non-compete clauses, which mean that former employees have to wait for a set period before working for competitors, and the time it takes to find a new job, 'Even though you have high salaries, you have to take into consideration that, sometimes, if you lose your job, you may be out of a job for a year-and-a-half, two years.' The hedge fund world doesn't offer the same seniority, progression and exit strategies as the banks. Success and failure are instant; wealth and unemployment sudden. It is a highly competitive niche – not quite as aggressive, he jokes, as the Jubilee Underground line at rush hour, but not far off.

I wonder if the regulatory apparatus vested in the Financial Conduct Authority to protect investors is more relaxed in hedge funds than in banks? Are there fewer restrictions on ways of expanding money? No, Searcher tells me, the restrictions are just different: 'Especially since the [2008] crisis, the regulation has gone super-strict.

Simple things, like your phone calls are being recorded. When you go out with one of your counterparts who's in a bank that deals with you ... if the bank takes you to a dinner, anything above a certain amount, you cannot do it, you cannot accept gifts. If you have any meeting with any bank, you have to report it.' He and his colleagues bemoan the extra administration of better regulation: 'There's a form that you have to fill every single time. It used to be providers would just send you Christmas presents. Now we don't want them, because we just don't want to fill forms. Every few months we have revision training to always keep us updated, because nowadays, it's not only the fund that can be fined, it's also the individual, so people don't want to get in any trouble.' This may be so, but stricter rules protect the public investing with a bank more than the wealthy, knowing investors in a hedge fund, and this leaves hedge funds and private equity quite a bit freer to take risks and generate high returns. Hedge funds are also less integral to the financial system than banks, and so are not subject to the same capital requirements. I leave Searcher to finish his lunch and get back to work.

Hedge fund owners are even more reluctant than their employees to disclose the inner workings of their organization. But sometimes they have no choice. Financial settlements surrounding divorce are one of those times,[7] and divorce judgements are public records. Tipped off that this was the case by the judge Wig, I dug out the 2014 divorce judgement of a hedge fund owner I will call Genius, a term used by the judge deciding his divorce settlement to describe him, which gave deeper insight into the business of expanding money than I had managed to coax from Searcher. Genius owns a hedge fund valued at $1.2 billion. Divisible assets of $6 billion are on the table with the dissolution of his seventeen-year marriage. The legal debate is over the post-separation accrual of income and whether it results from his extraordinary efforts alone or should be shared with his wife. In determining a fair outcome, the judge presses Genius on how he plies his craft. 'The husband,' the judgement notes, 'describes his investment strategy as a direct result of his "personal, intellectual and emotional make-up". The judge likens the husband's abilities to those of an expert chess player who is able to recognize patterns. This ability, he says, when combined with "an appetite for financial risk, determination in business and a contrarian approach" are the keys to his success.' She continues, 'He describes his ability to pick stocks as not being driven by formulae or data but as coming from within his head: "It is subjective, not mechanical; an art rather than a science."'

Describing himself as an 'activist investor', Genius provides examples of how he makes money. He identifies and buys a stake in 'companies experiencing dramatic change'. In one case where he owned only 1 per cent of the shares in a bank he put a motion to its Annual General Meeting to offer the entire bank up for sale. 'The management said, "You should go to hell,"' he recalls, but he replied, '"Well it's my legal right. You have been underperforming." 70 per cent of the shareholders voted for my motion and the bank was sold for $100 billion, virtually all cash, in a hostile break-up by three financial institutions and the fund made $1 billion on that investment.' On another occasion, he got a CEO sacked and the share price rose. He identifies what he calls 'activist investment ideas', like proposing companies sell off one of their divisions. Shares rise by 90 per cent. Genius tells the court: 'One way or another, virtually all of our investments are actively managed. We work hard to create change in companies; it is not passive. That is what produces these dramatic returns which are far in excess of what normal people can receive by investing in the stock market. That is how we justify what are very high fees.' As what the judge describes as an 'extremely aggressive player in the field', his reputation for high returns brings investors to his fund. He says there are investors offering $700 million waiting to join the fund, but he restricts access, to keep the returns of existing investors high. In 2014, his personal profits from the fund were estimated at $150 million. Exceptionality, instinct, a contrarian approach, bold assertiveness, appetite for risk and traditional masculine aggression are Genius's tactics for acquiring vast sums of money.

The judge summarizes: 'His particular talent (some might call it financial genius) lies in his ability to identify particular ideas or commercial opportunities, to take significant and often very high-risk positions with a limited number of entities, to "work them" (often from the "inside out") and to "exit" on behalf of his investors at the optimum moment for maximum return. It is precisely the opposite stratagem to conservative, long term investment.' His is 'a change for profit agenda', says the judge. This enables him to 'generate wealth on an exceptional scale'. Why? Because he can. Genius himself says, 'I do not need the money.' While the purpose of the fund is to 'compound my capital', he claims, 'I do not really care about money.' Although he's still not keen to give his ex-wife any more than the court requires. What, then, is the money for? Is it a measure of masculinity, a way of keeping score in a rich man's dick-swinging contest?

Emerging from Cojean back on to Berkeley Street, I notice the number of luxury cars parked around. Land Rovers hover around the streets as drivers wait to collect people they earlier dropped off. Land Rover, Rolls-Royce, Ferrari, Bentley and Porsche showrooms offer a way to spend sudden windfalls, with prices starting at a hundred thousand pounds. There are luxury restaurants nearby too: the Japanese restaurants Nobu and Sexy Fish, and the Michelin-starred Indian restaurant Benares, are just some of the dining options. From there diners can move on to Annabel's, the exclusive private members and celebrity nightclub on the west side of Berkeley Square, which sits slightly incongruously next to the house where, in the eighteenth century, Clive of India – whose administrative failings led to the Bengal famine – lived. The Hop On Hop Off bus trundles past again and tourists take photos. The doormen at Annabel's wear techno-coloured, patterned outfits, suggesting iconic 1960s London cool, perhaps ironically: or perhaps not.

At the north end of Berkeley Square, the art gallery and auction house Phillips occupies a prime spot. When I visit, they are displaying paintings by William Kentridge, Damien Hirst and Eddie Martinez, for sale by auction. Nearby, the Palm Beach Casino and the female body-service centre Nails & Brows wait for customers amid a constant stream of deliveries. A pair of brown brogues, I imagine to be stepping out of old money, march past me as I linger in the square. A man in a fur coat and brilliant white pointed-toe boots, a man-bag slung across his body, walks with a rock-star swagger in the opposite direction. A group of East European motorcyclist deliverymen, sitting on motorbikes waiting for their next assignments, laugh and take selfies: the May Fair rolls on.

Mayfair is the home of private equity, too, and I am keen to know more. I find a private equity dealer willing to talk to me, though he wants to meet north of Mayfair, at the Chiltern Firehouse. Once a working fire station, this is one of the West End's most fashionable places, modelled on Soho House, which draws young Londoners to the private members' club scene. North of Mayfair, sitting between Oxford Street to the south and Baker Street to the north, Chiltern Firehouse is a few roads over from Marylebone High Street, which once offered refuge for those who couldn't afford Mayfair. Its neighbourhood amenities are now superior to Mayfair's, and with its local village feel Marylebone is popular with wealthy people and shaped around their needs. There are (expensive) independent shops, cafés, restaurants and delis. Daunt Books is a popular haunt. So too are Conran and Skandium, designer shops selling furniture and household accessories.

I call the private equity man Cake, because cake is a part of his repertoire. Cake is a relaxed, mischievous, 70-year-old with a dry wit, who lives off Marylebone High Street. Successfully navigating his way through the banking and insurance industries, he was executive director of a FTSE 100 company by the age of 45. Although formally 'retired', he is clearly anything but. He specializes in the zone where finance and technology meet, commonly called fintech. Mobile payment systems like PayPal, systems everyone uses to spend the digital money in their bank accounts, are an example of the kinds of fintech he works with.

As we sink into deep sofas next to a roaring fire, he explains that if you want a 'proper return on investments' – say, a return north of 10 per cent – there is no point in investing with banks. Like hedge funds, private equity – the private, often pooled funds of wealthy and institutional investors – buys equity stakes (shares) in start-ups that cannot raise capital elsewhere, and in underperforming companies that, with the right kind of management, can make better returns for investors. Where hedge funds will sometimes actively undermine businesses, betting on them to fail, private equity seeks to bring them back to life. Equity stakes bring an active approach to management, as Genius described. Cake, who now lends his management experience to getting things back on track, calls this 'putting a grown-up in the room'. That is, someone like him, an experienced manager who can better 'look after the money'. 'Everyone knows why you are there,' he says.

'You can argue about the morals, but that's another matter.' Helping failing businesses often means firing people. This is his routine. 'I take them for a coffee. They've figured it out. If I buy them a piece of cake they are going to be fired. If I don't buy them a piece of cake, I just want to chat.'

He tells me that over a five-year cycle the original funds invested in a company being rescued get used up and provide returns, so new investors are invited into the private pool party. They, too, take equity shares in the company in exchange for lending their money. 'My friend bought 10 per cent of a company' – which he wanted me not to name. 'You may think it is only 10 per cent, but for 10 per cent you pretty much get a total say in what is going on in the company.' Cake's friend has a private equity company managing £750 million, with a good reputation for growing money. 'At the end of five years the company changes again; other investors come in. Someone like [the fintech] Worldpay, who see it as a key element in their offering, might buy the company. Apple might buy the company. It becomes something else again.' Money morphs and moves and expands.

Cake explains that these kinds of investments are not driven by profits, as I had assumed, but the smoke and mirrors of indeterminate value. 'Spotify, which was valued on Wall Street recently at $26 million, has never made a profit.' What is more important is 'the perceived value of the company *if you sold it*'. Cake gives the example of Amazon, now one of the most valuable companies in the world, which has only become really profitable in the last few years. 'Amazon's value is driven by revenue growth, and the *perceived* value of its (hard to value) technology.' Tech companies especially often bet on growth in market share, and future rather than current profits. In this they take a long view. Companies that are difficult to value invite just these kinds of speculation, and this, too, is how money expands.

As a private equity investor, Cake is drawn to the technologies that shift money. He likes fintechs because they disrupt existing financial arrangements and create new ones. They provide the latest IT solutions and programs that enable banks to move digital money, a landscape that is constantly changing. Worldpay, which connects customers with their bank accounts when they are buying goods and services, is a good example. Banks don't want to invest in constantly changing technologies for shifting money, so they rent them through highly profitable licensing agreements from fintech companies instead.

Software licence fees are a major source of fintech profits. 'Our biggest banking partner,' Cake tells me, 'pays us £50,000 a month, without us writing a single line [of code]. That's simply to use the software. Then, every time they write a loan, we get a slice of the margin on the loan. That's how this business is put together.' Cake says he stabilizes revenue streams by regularly renegotiating and ramping-up existing software licence fees: a particularly lucrative kind of rent-seeking. He gives me another example of how he makes money on loans: 'Two weeks ago we processed 6,000 mobile phone loans in a night.' This loan occurs when people pay for their phone over the life of their contract with the network provider, rather than buying the phone outright and paying just to use the network. 'The lender – often a bank – sends the money to the mobile phone company. We sit in the middle, between the lender, the phone company and the customer. We get a cut. Not a very big cut, but we don't care, because there are so many of them.' Serious money is made this way. Cake is a master of understatement. Between licensing fees and overnight deals on 6,000 mobile phones, he says, 'These days before we get out of bed we know we are not going to lose money.' Large-scale skimming has made him a multi-millionaire.

I leave Cake to his coffee in the Chiltern Firehouse and wander along Marylebone High Street, threading my way south until I reach Oxford Street, the northern boundary of Mayfair. As day turns to night there are other Mayfairs to explore.

4
Mayfair Nights

Mayfair at night is another place. Reasoning that luxury hotels are a good spot for a foot-loose researcher to closely observe the comings and goings of the night, I hover outside The Dorchester on Park Lane watching taxis drop off and pick up guests. I stand nervously beside Doorman, in his dark green tailcoat and top hat, meeting and greeting arrivals, and helping them out of taxis: 'Welcome back, Sir', 'Welcome back, Madam'. Gathering my courage, I take a deep breath and tail the next wave of arrivals in through the art deco revolving doors of The Dorchester and spin into the lobby. I stop abruptly in front of several security men guarding the entrance and a phalanx of smiling women on the reception desk who greet me: 'Welcome back, Madam.' Back! I'm pretty sure I've not been here before: I'd have remembered and not felt quite so intimidated. 'Can I help you, Madam?' I had learned from talking to one of my contacts that 'Can I help you, Madam?' actually means, 'Who are you and what are you doing here?' Nodding towards the receptionists, I stride confidently towards the only thing I can see from the lobby, the Promenade Bar, set back from the reception area. I am transported to the first decade of the twentieth century. Potted palms, pale-pink marble pillars, enormous fresh-flower arrangements in Grecian urns, cosy armchairs and sofas, around little tables set with teapots and china teacups: Edwardian drawing-room pastiche. Middle Eastern men in suits and traditional robes look up from their tea and quiet conversation as I sweep past, looking for a place to sit and watch the night unfold.

In Mayfair after dark, the business of finance and luxury retail veer into the varied businesses of pleasure. My night in fact began earlier, in the yellow street light, with an elephant made of China: another inhabitant of an over-lit and meticulously curated cabinet of curiosities, this time on Mount Street. Standing tall in a shop window, above glittering crystal glasses, bone china plates and cups so fine they were almost translucent, the white elephant was about three feet high, and mounted on a mahogany and green tile plinth. It was dressed in royal finery: gold bangles around its ankles, an embroidered and jewelled (ceramic) blanket over its back, and a howdah on top waiting for a regal behind. Who buys these things?

This thought prompted me to walk back to South Audley Street, a few streets away, to re-examine a large poster in an estate agent's window I had noticed earlier. Over an enlarged aerial photograph of the area was a question: *Who lives in Mayfair?* It was answered by a series of local 'facts' printed over the image: *Local resident average spend is more than twice that of a non-resident Bond Street customer*. I suppose this includes ornamental elephants and stuffed zebras. The estate agent is selling the neighbourhood as well as its properties, to those who can afford it of course.

Early evening. Just around the corner from Berkeley Square, The Footman pub was heaving with suits that didn't make it home after work. Some of the drinkers were more casually dressed, perhaps because they lived close enough to change into their play clothes before coming out again. A lively crowd had decided to stay for a few more drinks at the pub. Others moved to restaurants, or retreated to the tranquillity of someone's private club, or opted for a night in one of Mayfair's many hotel bars and restaurants. Mayfair's 85,000 workers, who shift in and out of its streets each day, vastly outnumber its 5,100 residents.[1] Sitting in the corner of the pub at a small table, I noticed that the stories told by after-work drinkers centre around numbers too, these tales of deals and titbits of finance gossip. Once most of the women in the pub had left, climbing into Ubers clutching designer handbags, the men's stories turned to heroic feats of drinking and all-night partying. The estate agent's window display had informed me, *55% of Mayfair households are single*. They are also primarily under 45 and made up of forty-two different nationalities. Mayfair is London's most fluid and exotic neighbourhood: flats rather than houses, a high proportion of them rental with high turnovers in tenants.[2] According to the estate agent, *45% of residents are employed in financial, real estate and professional services*, an unusually high percentage for a London neighbourhood, and they often rent or own a pied-à-terre where they live from Monday to Thursday. A fifty-something asset manager that I had met some months earlier told me that Mayfair is where you 'play' not where you live your 'real life'. Real life, he suggested, is lived in a 'community' in the shires in a large house, with equally prosperous neighbours. For some, Mayfair provides an alternative life; its possibilities are wrapped around work and separated from life-lived-elsewhere in more conventional arrangements. As I left The Footman, middle-aged men were standing outside to smoke and make phone calls. Were they calling families? Making arrangements for the rest of the night? Mayfair is all about latitude.

I walked past several restaurants with famous chefs and Michelin stars, some of them in hotels. According to the estate agent's poster, *28% of London's Michelin starred restaurants are in Mayfair*. The estate agent also claimed, *The restaurant ratio [of potential diners per restaurant] in Mayfair is 31:1*. This compares favourably with the *prime London ratio of 319:1*. Mayfair restaurants, one of the pleasures of the night, are better and less crowded than elsewhere in the city. Novikov, the Asian restaurant on Berkeley Street, was doing brisk business as I walked past. A party of 'thirty-something' Russian men with shaved heads and expensive suits were standing outside smoking. More black Range Rovers and their drivers hovered, waiting to transport diners to homes and hotels.

At night, Mayfair is a land of bars, nightclubs, restaurants and casinos. In Mayfair, high life and low life have long coincided, the one penetrating the other, blurring the usual social boundaries between toffs and the rest. Close to Novikov, two security men stood outside the Palm Beach Casino. I walked past Aspinalls, a private members' club that boasts, 'an exceptional gaming experience', which 'combines traditional elegance with the contemporary flair of a luxurious Crown Resorts property', according to its website. Here were more security men in dark coats and with earpieces. Bars, nightclubs and casinos all have security, and the sheer density of these establishments creates in turn highly securitized streets. Between these hotspots of the night-time economy and a cluster of embassies, this is arguably one of the most closely guarded corners of London.

Some days later, I will arrange to meet with the head of security at one of the area's most famous hotels. Cop – who used to be in the Metropolitan Police – is in his early forties. He has three young kids, and says he doesn't 'take for granted' the gleaming marble floors and elaborate flower displays of his new working environment, despite their contrast with police stations. He doesn't look like security either. In a beautifully cut dark-blue suit with a light-blue shirt and red silk tie, a slight cockney intonation in his voice, he could be one of the guests.

Cop says the Underground and bus bombings of 7 July 2005 'changed the security dynamic' in London and its high-end hotels for good, and subsequent terror attacks consolidated these changes. Thereafter, the people he describes as 'high-net-worths', especially Americans and international corporate clients who favour this hotel, changed their priorities: they became less concerned about the breakfast and the size of the rooms, and more focused on hotel security. This 'brought my world into the revenue side of the business', as security became a selling point emphasized by the marketing team. As a result, Cop says, 'The head of security can override anything else in the hotel. Yesterday we had a session on what to do if anyone comes into the hotel with a gun. I've had three security updates today already.' He still works closely with the Met Police. London's image as an elite destination is closely linked to the general security situation, and hotel security measures in particular. The state and tax payers, through the police, underwrite plutocrat security and comfort.

Cop's other job is to keep the street out of the hotel. Unlike banks with impassable security systems, a hotel's front of house is open to the public, and almost anyone can wander in. 'London has a huge rough-sleeping problem. You see it all around you. They may not be coming in to commit crime – they may be coming to use the toilet – but it's still something we cannot allow in a private business.' Few rough sleepers would wander into such an exclusive hotel, but, if they did, they would be quickly escorted out again. Yet, he acknowledges, 'Gone are the days when you had to be in a suit and tie to come in here. So, we cannot stereotype on appearance.' Other risks include 'low-level crimes' like scams and bag theft, given the rich pickings for thieves offered by the concentration of wealthy people in one place.

Hotels are an important hinge to the Mayfair night. They are places to eat, dine, or rent rooms for private functions, and for other, still more private pleasures. Mayfair has 4,000 luxury hotel beds at eye-watering prices, with guests paying up to £10,000 a night for a suite at Claridge's. In hotels, the paths of Mayfair's visitors and residents cross. And hotel workers have a front-row seat for the spectacles of the night. On finishing my drink at The Footman, I headed to one of London's most exclusive hotels in order to see what I could learn about how they operate in the ecologies of the Mayfair night. I was meeting Night Manager, who had worked in a number of elite hotels before the one where I tracked him down. Silenced by strict codes of confidentiality, he could lose his job if I reveal which hotel he runs at night. Inscrutable, charming, polite, grey suited, in his early forties, Night Manager worked his way up through the hospitality industry from the bottom by being exceptionally good at his job. The perfect plutocrats' servant, he reminded me of a butler.

He knows who stays where and why, who expects what levels of luxury service and attention: the hotel's clients are a mix of wealthy tourists and locals on business. He sketched out the Mayfair hotel scene for me. Claridge's, its cheapest rooms starting at £840 a night, is generally regarded as the pinnacle of luxury. The Connaught, a shade cheaper, is next. The Dorchester – owned by a consortium headed by the Sultan of Brunei – attracts the 'Philip Greens of the world and that type of thing' (by which I think he meant the brash but wealthy end of the corporate world), as well as what he described as 'the Middle Eastern market'. Night Manager told me that clients from the Middle East divide along gender lines. 'They don't necessarily stay together with their spouses and the kids and nannies and all that. They separate. The men will stay at The Dorchester – their toys [cars flown in] on the forecourt.' The women choose Claridge's or The Mandarin in Knightsbridge, because they're more 'feminine': 'The families [children] and staff will go to The Hilton.' Like Cop, he said that it is difficult to distinguish who is and who isn't wealthy. 'Your wealthiest are not necessarily the best dressed. If you read the labels on their clothes, then you would know, but they're not Prada and that all the time. They're very basic; they tend to be very understated. I just describe them as Yahs. You have your Yahs and then you have your new money, and in Mayfair it's more Yah.'

It was Night Manager who urged me to visit The Dorchester. After my anxious and faltering entry, I loiter for a while in the Edwardian fantasy of the Promenade Bar. Unable to eavesdrop, because I don't understand Arabic, after a while I give up and follow a sign from the reception to The Bar. The Bar is small, intimate and dark, everything decorated in dark browns and swirls. The sound track is the low piped music you might hear in an elevator. I've moved from the 1910s into the 1970s. The bar itself, where a barman is mixing drinks, runs the length of the narrow room. A waiter, who turns out to be from Paris, instantly materializes to take my order. Both the waiter and his Italian boss – the bar manager – check in with me regularly, gently gathering information: Who am I, and what I am doing alone in The Bar? Their attentions interrupt my note-taking. But they are friendly and present me with a random free gift: a tube of clear lip gloss that lights up as I remove the applicator, presumably so that I can make my lips look shiny in the dark. I feel awkward, scrutinized. Later, when I check back in with Night Manager to relay my Dorchester stories, he tells me that my notebook makes me look like a hotel critic. Apparently, if security wanted to read what I was writing they could easily have done so, as their CCTV zooms in when they want to take a close look at something. Here am I, watching the goings on in the hotel at night; in the process, I become part of the night I am watching; and the hotel is watching me watching it. My assumed position as outside observer collapses.

In between chatting to the waiter and his manager – who has to cycle home to a south-eastern suburb after his shift – I tune in to the conversations on either side of me, trying to get a sense of the clientele and atmosphere of the bar. On one side is a man wearing a grey suit, in his late forties, gently stroking the hand of a beautiful woman in her twenties wearing a diaphanous white dress and gold shoes. As they drink, the gap between their bodies slowly narrows. I am too far away to catch their whispered conversation, but their movements pick up the story instead. On the other side, three glamorous Nigerian women have parked their designer handbags on the table while they drink strawberry margaritas. One wears a short black dress, the others designer jeans and blouses; all display expensive watches and diamond jewellery. They are discussing intimate relationships: 'I am going to say to him, do you want someone else to keep you happy? I don't want a central control system.' They all laugh. 'My father's property, he has quite a lot of it actually, but don't make a noise about it.' They are sassy and confident. One of them mentions passing her exams at Imperial College: wealthy students.

After midnight, The Bar is emptying when two young women arrive, dressed to attract attention. It works – we all turn and look at them. One wears a white trouser suit and glittery high heeled shoes, the other a short dress and knee-high boots. Their style of dress suggests, although ambiguously, erotic possibilities: perhaps one of the most important aspects of the Mayfair night. As the historian Frank Mort says, erotic pleasure has always been about wider networks of sensuous delight in dining, drinking and entertainment,[3] and these combine in Mayfair. Night Manager, drawing on his experience at one of the city's most luxurious hotels, had earlier described to me the prospectors who work the sexual economies of high-end hotel bars. 'Never, ever mention escorts, prostitution, ladies of the night,' he advised. 'No bar wants them coming in looking for business. Generally, you can spot them from their habits. Green tea. They always drink green tea.' In court cases involving escorts, the owners of The Dorchester have strongly denied that they are knowingly allowed into the hotel. The waiter and his manager are on high alert. This is an impossible judgement call. The women's dress and demeanour are easily misinterpreted. The two women sit at a little table in the centre of the bar, as though they were the cabaret; they laugh loudly and order drinks. At the other end of the bar, the gap between the suit and the diaphanous dress narrows still further, as he moves in to kiss her neck; he calls for the bill, and they leave in a conspiratorial huddle.

Night Manager said that hotels prefer discreet agency-booked prostitutes and escorts who slip in and out of rooms to walk-in prospectors. Upscale prostitutes and escorts, both male and female, are young, beautiful, expensively dressed, and, sometimes, flown in to London from Eastern Europe and former Soviet republics. They command rates in line with what exclusive five-star hotels charge their guests, in the region of £12,000 a night.[4] Of course, there are local services too. Sex work is an unspoken part of the elite service culture of hotels. As Night Manager put it, 'If someone is paying ten grand a night, no hotel is going to tell them what they can and can't do, and let's be honest, if a guy wants to have three "friends" in the room for the evening, no hotel – providing he's discreet and not disturbing other guests – will say no.' Because 'There's an unwritten rule: the hotel turns a blind eye. You don't talk about it.' This is how high-end hotels justify their fees: 'That's why guests don't mind paying ten grand a night, for the discretion, because they know if their boss phones or their wife phones or whatever', the hotel will cover for them. 'Who isn't at it?' Night Manager shrugged. Sex work is hinted at and brushed over.

Night Manager told me about a full-scale peep show for Middle Eastern guests at another top Mayfair hotel he worked at. 'All the boys will get together in a suite and hire ten prostitutes or whatever, just to have sex in front of them. They won't get involved. They just sit there like an audience with a live show. Everything's at their disposal. I think they're bored. In Mayfair, you see a lot of boredom, a lot of really lonely people.' As he sees it: 'At two o'clock in the morning, the world over, men are men. They want exactly the same thing. It doesn't matter whether you are with the government of Qatar or a builder from Braintree [Essex], men are the same and you are paying for discretion.' He suggested I ask a hotel concierge how often do they get asked to go out and buy condoms: 'The billionaire who goes to the concierge, "Here's fifty quid. Thanks for the restaurant booking and can you go get 300 condoms?" He isn't going to say no, is he?' I thought it best to let the 300 condoms pass without enquiry. Mayfair's erotic possibilities and spectacles, as Night Manager described them, are ultimately empty, mechanistic, uninteresting, bought like everything else, and fiercely protected by elite-hotel codes of secrecy.

Sex, security and service, it seems, underpin the Mayfair night, and express the unequal power that excessive money confers: rich people can demand whatever they want from those who serve them, however risqué or absurd their requests. I follow up on this sometime later with a 35-year-old Colombian woman with impeccable credentials in VIP service in luxury London hotels. VIP Service works closely with

Big Spender. Big Spender can be anyone; spending money is the prime guest qualification for VIP treatment, in what she describes as a 'yes culture': 'Anything they want they can have.' She tells me the story of a guest demanding a jacuzzi be installed in his suite, and another about a Russian who brought his own fridge, chef and food-tasters, because he was afraid of being poisoned. Are there no limits? She says she once had to rebuff an American man who offered to pay her for sex, ever so politely threatening to call security. On another occasion, she continues, 'I said, "no" to a request to turn the floor of one suite into grass, because the guest was bringing their dog and the dog would only use the toilet on real grass.' 'I'm not joking,' she adds, seeing the look on my face. 'The dog was the one I remember most, because the dog also had a menu and we had to send it to the chef. The chef was furious.' Money confers on the rich just this kind of authority: the authority to humiliate those who serve them.

It is after midnight when I spin back through the doors of The Dorchester. The streets are more subdued and empty now. The activities of the night are either drawing to a close or have moved off the streets, out of sight, where I can't follow. I stop briefly in the night air. Despite everything I have learned about the Mayfair night, I still feel the lingering excitement of the bright lights, the city's delights, the thrill of the gaudy 'May Fair', the awe and wonder that make cities exciting. I catch a taxi east and home to bed.

5

Milking Fish

'It's not just about making money by any means,' Legacy insists. I thought it was. I had begun to understand from my conversations with Cake and my (virtual) encounter with Genius's divorce papers that private equity was driven by the relentless expansion of money, whatever the consequences. So, I'm surprised to hear this alternative view expressed in the well-appointed office of a private international investment group. I stare at the polished table and sip my glass of water, unsure how to develop this conversation. What else could it be about? Legacy tells me it is about 'the *art* of business'. This, he says, is what drives investors like him. He means older, successful business-men, former chief executives of Fortune 100 companies, Lords and restless billionaires, men who have made all the money they are ever going to need, but don't quite know how to stop. Why don't they stop and enjoy a life of wealthy leisure? I am starting to wonder what happened to the leisure class often associated with wealth. I certainly haven't met them. Is making money addictive? I want to know more.

So, I am back in Mayfair after the excitement of my night-time encounters. Having fought my way through the crowds around Green Park Underground Station and The Ritz hotel once more, and dodged the practised choreographies of hotel guests, tourists and homeless encampments that are daily restaged here, I crossed Piccadilly, skirted around Berkeley Square and headed for an adjoining street, to Legacy's office, to probe private equity a bit more. To see if I can get under its skin, to discover what makes investors tick, besides the vacuous rapa-ciousness of outwitting other investors and piling up money, which is all I have heard so far in the town houses of Mayfair and the glass towers of the City banks. I want to know if there are other purposes.

I want to know how successful investors think about what they do and what gives their lives meaning. Reasoning that older men, who are no longer in the daily scrum of expanding money, might have time to think about these things, I follow up on a contact's contact and eventually manage to meet Legacy. The *art* of business indeed. Whatever can he mean?

I navigated the usual entry-controlled barricades with the help of yet another smiling woman receptionist – what a burden all this smiling must be – and was directed to a comfortable, well-appointed reception area to wait. Legacy came downstairs promptly to fetch me: early fifties, wispy blond hair, his open-necked shirt and well-cut suit suggesting a carefully curated corporate-yet-relaxed style. His greeting was warm and generous. The meeting room where he has taken me for our discussion is like all the others in the world of corporate finance: polished wood table, smart chairs, water, glasses, restrained yet expensive.

I started by probing his version of private equity. Legacy insisted that the principles and timescales by which his group operate distinguish them from other kinds of private investors. Private equity, he said, is usually about 'short-term investments' and 'making money by any means'. It is driven by a philosophy of pure expansion and the demands of quarterly reporting cycles.[1] This much I had understood. Life at his office, on the other hand, he insisted, obeys different imperatives. Its investors are well established. They 'have built, in their time, massive businesses'. They have already made all the money they can ever spend, but they are driven to keep on working, practising what he calls their 'art', putting their accumulated expertise to work alongside their money.

What exactly do they do? What is this art? 'We identify a company that we think has good prospects and is well positioned for whatever we feel is going to be the next development in the sector or area of growth.' If the company passes their due diligence checks, the investment group will take a stake in it, large enough to be active investors with a few seats on the board. They'll agree a strategy to improve the company's prospects, and then play the long game. As Legacy says, 'Some things take time to develop, to come to fruition. Long-term investing is really about buying and building a company that in ten, fifteen, twenty years becomes something which is well known and a *legacy asset*.' Legacy-building is a more patient, and by implication more worthwhile and morally worthy, enterprise than grabbing money by whatever means. This is what he means by art. It also sounds like a plutocrat's version of retirement. Unable to stop, they simply shift into a lower gear and keep going.

I wonder what motivates the legacy asset investor who is already very rich? Legacy finds that his colleagues will inevitably tell him, '"The bit I loved most in my career, was when I had my first business." There is an element there of really loving starting up and growing something', a feeling that gets lost as businesses expand and become institutionalized. As successful businesspeople move out of frontline building operations into governance and high-level leadership, 'The energy that built their business is no longer necessary. I mean, look at this country.' Legacy's voice sounds a new note of conviction: 'We're built on pioneers, people all around the world opening up trade routes and trying to find the North-West Passage and discovering America. Most people here work all day and night because they love it; it's the *art of business*. They love it. They want to be part of something which starts something up.' The art of business, the pioneering instincts driving the start-up, are eroded by wealth and success. Legacy-building, on the other hand, preserves the energy and vision he associates with a pioneering impulse. This is how money can live beyond the plutocrat's grave, a shot at immortality. In the process, in Legacy's estimation, it is elevated to an art form, a noble calling, to be aligned with British 'nation-building', through 'discovery' or, as I think of it, through appropriation of other people's land and resources. I wonder, to myself, what motivates this bid for moral worth and higher purpose. Hubris? Justification of activities of dubious social value? The eternal quest to secure a sense of masculinity?

Still turning these rather surprising thoughts about the art of business over, I leave Legacy, cross Piccadilly again and keep heading south down St James's Street to Mayfair's annex: the area of St James's. I am heading to another successful businessman, on my quest to penetrate the motivations of private equity. On the way, I explore a landscape encrusted with old money. The buildings of St James's are grandly imposing, royal treasure long buried in these streets. At the end of St James's Street is St James's Palace, where the street bends into a right angle at Pall Mall, which forms its southern boundary, stopping just short of the Mall and Buckingham Palace. Pall Mall, which runs parallel to the Mall itself, displays the grand designs of Victorian architects; its buildings intended for important activities and people of substance. Impressive imperial-looking buildings host a cluster of old-school gentlemen's clubs, with discreet brass number plates, not names, at the door. Solid, imposing substance: no sign here of the 'May Fair's' frivolity. I walk past London Yacht Brokers, advertising its services in buying, selling, chartering and managing yachts, and Berry Brothers and Rudd, the upscale wine merchant. This seems a good place to stop and browse before I head for The Wine Club, a private members' club on Pall Mall, where I am to meet Sturgeon.

The Wine Club, unsurprisingly, is for connoisseurs of fine wine. It boasts a 'wine library' and a well-stocked cellar: there are 800 top wines available by the glass, a staggering number by the bottle, plus a top sommelier on hand at all times for consultations. Some wealthy people build collections for sale as well as use. A pleasure that has been turned into an asset, wine gains value if the right stocks are bought at the right price. The Wine Club is housed in the rambling Victorian premises of a former banking hall. Dropping Sturgeon's name at reception gets me onto the main floor where I am given a glass of water and a seat at a small table. He's in another room and another meeting. Unlike the traditional gentlemen's clubs of Pall Mall, which discourage or even prohibit work, beyond the subtleties of networking and informal influence, here it is expected, promoted in the arrangement of space. Toil and leisure sit side by side, with little rooms off the main sitting room set aside for meetings and working on laptops. The Wine Club supports the habits of today's work-driven plutocrat.

Sturgeon tells me mischievously that The Wine Club is his London office. Balding, short, energetic, friendly, open, in his mid-fifties, he moves towards my table with speed and purpose, and speaks English with a heavy Russian accent. Although he has owned a family home in London since 2007, it was until recently just a weekend retreat from life in Moscow. Now their house in Moscow is the weekend and holiday home, maintained 'for the kids because we'd like to keep their

Russian language'. Since he has already made a large amount of money, his Moscow businesses no longer need his constant attention. They have a large house in South Kensington, and, he tells me, he loves everything about London: the culture, the history, the schools, and the proximity to their third home in Saint-Tropez, for school holidays and better weather.

Sturgeon's day begins with a two-hour gym session. Today, he went home after his session to tackle a two-day backlog of emails, accumulated because yesterday he'd taken the 7 a.m. flight to Geneva to deal with one of his businesses, only returning late at night. No private plane, I note. No home gym. By the time of our mid-morning conversation, he is already on his third meeting. How much does he work? 'A lot,' he concedes. 'I should spend more time for myself and for the family. When I come home, I usually spend some time in front of the computer working until eleven or twelve o'clock.' Does he eat at home? 'Yes. No. It depends if I have business dinners.' He qualifies that 'I try to spend the evening, at least, with my family and kids. They should at least see their father.' His wife works too, mostly for his businesses. A nanny and a housekeeper keep domestic life on track.

I never directly ask the wealthy people I meet about money. I am convinced that asking 'Exactly how much are you worth then?' would abruptly end our delicate conversation. Money is always the bejewelled porcelain elephant in the room, and I leave it there. But the subject of money is often introduced, if obliquely, by wealthy people themselves. When I was building up contacts and collecting stories, I interviewed an elderly couple with a house in Hampstead and a flat in St James's, not far from James Dyson's home. Dyson is number four on the 2021 *Sunday Times* Rich List with an estimated fortune of over £16 billion, and I was reminded of him as I was walking through his neighbourhood – or one of them. The elderly couple dropped into our conversation that they had sold one of their companies for £300 million. I was trying to understand how they thought about London. 'We are London,' they told me rather starchily. The St James's flat was bought, I suspect, to use a pile of money they otherwise had no use for, and, as they admitted, in case they wanted to go to the theatre without the inconvenience of driving the six miles back to

Hampstead. Of course, their flat is also an asset that will likely appreciate in value. Similarly, Sturgeon wants me to know that he is a billionaire; referring to only one of his companies, a technology business, he says: 'I grew that one-person company to now over a billion dollars. Now the major sales are in Russia. I'm not an operational manager there any more. I'm just on the board of directors. I try to visit quite often, maybe once a month but not more often.' He is a billionaire in his fifties, taking a back seat in the money-churning machine.

Sturgeon made his money in IT and tech start-ups. Tech covers a lot of ground, so I probe. 'It's so difficult nowadays to draw the line [between] what is tech and what is not tech,' he demurs. 'It's actually all around us; it's everywhere. Even a refrigerator, now, could be connected to the internet to order the products.' What Sturgeon means by IT is 'all the disturbing tech' that disrupts existing markets and social habits. Disruption has come up several times in my conversations now, most recently with the fintech mogul, Cake, always as a virtue, a leading edge. Sturgeon lists some examples: 'Artificial Intelligence, new automobile industry needs like electric and driverless cars, cryptocurrencies and blockchain. No one knows if bitcoin will survive, but definitely the area [of cryptocurrencies] will grow very fast. The Chinese military was the first to use blockchain to keep their sensitive data.' A physical data centre is vulnerable to attack: 'In case of war, it's easy to bomb it. No data, no communication. If you have a distributed-data system [blockchain], the same data could be anywhere in the world. It's just impossible to destroy it.' Blockchain is an algorithm that knows what is where. It controls little blocks of data that are linked together rather than stored in one place. Sturgeon still hunts for 'very, very, good IT start-ups' to invest in. Much as Legacy described, his wealth is the outcome of pioneering (and mountaineering) inclinations: he is driven by the challenges of building something new, as well as the energy demanded by the climb.

I ask Sturgeon about his background. 'I graduated from school during the Soviet Union. We had quite a large apartment in Moscow. We were quite a wealthy family.' His grandfather was a general in the Russian army, and his father was a professor, who had communist sympathies: 'All of his life he was a communist, not because he liked

them [the Party] ... because he doesn't like what's going on now.'
Like other well-heeled Russian intellectuals and businesspeople, he
says his family are not Putin supporters. Putin does his best to be
popular with the masses of the Russian Federation. But Sturgeon hails
from Soviet intellectual aristocracy. He graduated from the elite Soviet
Military Space Academy, where he acquired high-level technical and
scientific skills, and elite social connections. While not originally
intended for money-making purposes, his education and inclinations
made him a billionaire, as Yeltsin's economic reforms allowed a
minority of former Soviet citizens to become very wealthy.[2]

Sturgeon has invested some of his billions in his experimental sustainable caviar business, which he describes as 'a nice hobby'. He says,
'It's a business in terms of the money we invested, but in terms of outcome it's more a passion and a hobby than a business. We are proud
of what we are doing. Usually the caviar producer just kills the [stur-
geon] fish.' Sturgeon doesn't. He milks them. First they anaesthetize
the fish and then massage them to extract the eggs. 'It's quite expensive technology,' he says, developed in collaboration with a big-brand
global food producer. It is a hobby because it is not (yet) economically
viable but an experiment, and – therefore – more interesting to him.
'We built this mixture of technology and food,' Sturgeon tells me
enthusiastically. 'Our farm is very automated. We have just seven
people for the whole farm. Feeding, temperature control, oxygen,
everything is done by machines.' Each fish is implanted with a chip,
connected via Wi-Fi to a central system, which allows the 'fish master'
to track its temperature and tell when it is ready to be milked. After
milking, the fish are placed in a special pool to recover, 'because the
procedure is quite stressful for the fish'. Sustainable caviar taps into
the current zeitgeist for luxury products with sustainable credentials.
He doesn't need to work or make more money: both are hobbies
and hard-to-break habits. How else to fill a life with purposeful and
challenging activity, but pursue projects that pique his intellectual
curiosity?

I leave Sturgeon to his fourth meeting, as I set out from The Wine
Club to walk back across Piccadilly into Mayfair. I'm thinking about
pioneering energy and adrenalin, the fix, supplied by the art of business: the satisfaction of intellectual curiosity, the quest for new

(business) territories, building immortality and sustaining masculinity. And also about insisting on the higher purpose, aesthetics and skill that the term *art* usually describes. All are counterpoints to the altogether grubbier, predatory business of asset stripping other enterprises and piling up money. Art itself has many uses, and Mayfair, of course, is focused on the business of art, too. I counted twenty private Mayfair galleries, plus the Royal Academy of Art, Mayfair's major public gallery. Art lives next door to private equity. Berkeley Square – private equity HQ – has a dense concentration of private galleries. In fact, they compete for space. Galleries have big footprints. I walk into the private gallery Phillips, on the north side of the square. It takes up an entire block, stretching around the corner into Davies Street. Its large, white rooms are watched over by amiable African security guards. (I keep coming across this scenario – African men guarding London's treasures.) I wander around Phillips's wide wooden-plank floor and acres of white wall. I stop before a canvas by Ed Ruscha: *God Knows Where* is stencilled in large white letters across a desert floor, white rocks and a blue sky. The painting is expected to fetch between £2.5 million and £3.5 million, plus buyer's premium and VAT, naturally. Keith Haring's *Untitled 1981*, an abstract figure in bold yellow, red and black on a piece of tarpaulin, is thought to be worth between £3 million and £4 million. Under the Young British Artists (YBA) banner, decked out in acid colours, work by one of their teachers at Goldsmiths, Michael Craig-Martin, titled *Full* is expected to fetch a more modest £80,000 to £120,000. His student Damien Hirst offers *Summer Breeze*, a painting of blue sky with white butterflies. Nearby, one of Hirst's medicine cabinets invites bids of between £1.2 million and £1.8 million. Next to Hirst, lesser-known artists Gilbert and George are hawking their giant composition *City Fairies*, which I later discover sold at auction for over £156,000. Art is serious money too.

On Davies Street, I pass one of Mayfair's most famous galleries, the Gagosian. *Live in Your Head* is stencilled in thick black letters across the main window, through which I can see another African security guard in a dark suit playing with his phone, sitting in the middle of the exhibition, titled *Richard Artschwager's Cabinet of Curiosities*, as if he were one of the exhibits. The Gagosian is part of a global network of fifteen galleries owned by Larry Gagosian, an American art dealer reported to be worth $600 million. Its locations – New York City, Singapore, Hong Kong – are also the locations of global finance, so closely are they connected. The Gagosian is one of art's most expansive global enterprises and stages museum-quality exhibitions; yet it operates in the secondary market for art, the private resale of works between collectors and institutions. In an interview with Larry Gagosian, the art critic Peter M. Bryant calls this market 'a part of the art business that remains a point of near-constant speculation, if only because it occurs largely behind the scenes and thus encourages debate as to who is selling what and why'.[3] Gagosian himself is widely considered to be 'secretive'.[4] Private galleries are major players in making art markets, brokering connections, turning money into art and art into money. They sell what they show, and this distinguishes them from public galleries displaying art, such as the Royal Academy.

The art auction house Sotheby's is one of the most influential intermediaries in Mayfair's art and money game. But Sotheby's is impossible to read. There is no problem getting in; it is open to the public. I stand in the bustling entranceway, where Sotheby's employees dressed in black usher in potential buyers, their anticipation palpable. There is an Impressionist and Surrealist art sale under way in the main hall, where those sitting in the audience maintain poker faces, determinedly not showing interest in coveted paintings. A young woman auctioneer in a bright red dress is on the podium talking smoothly, picking up invisible signals; in front of her, a row of Sotheby's attendants sit on phones taking bids from unseen bidders calling from who knows where. Very few members of the audience make a bid – the main business is on the phone. 'Yours Julian on the phone', or, occasionally, 'Yours Crispin in the room,' says the auctioneer. A Van Gogh drawing, *Peasant Digging Potatoes*, sells on the phone for £400,000, without betrayal of any hint of irony. Other works in this sale are priced between £1 million and £2 million – money spent in split-second decisions. This is art sale as spectacle – if few 'in the room' are actually bidding, then they are the audience. Such is the opacity of Mayfair's art world. Even when it is hung on walls and traded in public places, money manages to hide.

I meet Arty back at the Gagosian, hoping he can shed some light on Sotheby's. Arty is an urbane, casually dressed curator in his fifties, who ran a top Mayfair gallery. His mandate was to revamp it, to show living artists of the future in place of the classics of the dead. Now his work is largely consultancy: he guides those who want to build private collections, and sits on advisory boards in the world of public art. As we walk through the streets together, he tells me that the public and private art worlds have become 'embedded within each other' over the last thirty years, because of the lack of public funding and resulting reliance of major public galleries on private patronage. Private art collections and collectors shape art institutions, and it was this that made London's most significant public gallery, Tate Modern, possible, says Arty. 'The thing that pushed Tate Modern over the line was a driving art scene, which was fuelled by a steady circulation of capital,' he says. 'London, always a centre for connoisseurship embedded in old money, shifted towards collecting, the rich and the international scene.' London's (finance) money responded to the very same influences.

Arty suggests that the auction house is the 'ultimate democracy', because if you leave your hand up long enough you can get it. 'Before there was a kind of code, there was a club.' A democracy of sorts, I suppose, but a democracy of the wealthy in which the coffers of new money skew the playing field. Although it doesn't rival New York City as an art market, London is important. 'All the major galleries in the world have galleries in London, even if they don't make much money from them, because they want to have access to those clients.' 'Those clients' are 'a community of people from elsewhere', seeking 'a kind of [financial and political] stability that even other European countries don't have'. London is a safe harbour for the kinds of money that mixes with art, and galleries are a 'natural extension of that'. London's political and financial regime is amenable to art speculation. Although art is a taxable benefit, it can be warehoused offshore in free ports or in non-EU locations like Switzerland. This allows its owners to avoid paying VAT – 20 per cent in the United Kingdom – a substantial saving on art worth over a million pounds. Arty thinks that a large contingent of wealthy buyers forgo the pleasure of actually looking at their art in order to save on tax. Like fine wine, art is a pleasure that has been turned into an asset.

'Art never used to be seen as an asset,' Arty tells me. 'It used to be the little cherry on the top of the super wealthy.' Now art has become more tradeable, more liquid and much more international. Before, Arty argues, art was the domain of old money. 'If you owned a painting, you probably owned it for a long time. Now, it's like being in a start-up. It's the same kind of thing. If you bought that painting for £100 and over ten years that became £1 million, that's kind of mind blowing.' Wealthy people collect because 'They all fantasize about these rising values.' But they also collect to belong, Arty thinks. This exclusive club of art collectors generates its own anxieties. 'There's a looking over your shoulder, what have *they* got?' Of course, this is not the case for everyone. He remembers, 'The first person I ever advised said, "Well, I want to tell a story." And I thought, "That's a really nice thing to say." They actually saw their collection as a way of stabilizing who they were.' In this vision, a collection could be 'a manifestation of my desires and my interests and my passions'. Whatever the reason, according to Arty, collectors are 'seeking to define themselves through their collection, either in a sophisticated way or in a very blunt way, in terms of what my public persona is'. Art conveys important messages about the wealth and tastes of its owners.

In the business of art, Arty's job is to make sure that his clients 'pay only the right price'. What is the right price? Databases track what a work of art has been sold for in an auction house. But as Arty puts it, 'Value is what some people pay for it.' Not so different from value in the world of finance, then. 'Value is something to do with monetary value, but also something to do with cultural value. Cultural value and monetary value are very often moving in parallel, but sometimes one moves ahead.' The market struggles to accommodate works that may not be expensive now, but could have future significance. Like private equity, art collecting is all about taking a well-researched gamble on a hunch.

Arty gives me an example of one of his clients at a Sotheby's auction. The client rarely cared if he bought something he didn't really like; what upset him was the art that got away: '"I could have had that." "Yes, but you didn't."' Arty had seen an important painting that he thought had been undervalued in an auction, and advised his client to bid for it. The asking price was £1 million to £1.5 million; his client gave him permission to go up to £1.3 million and asked to go with him to the auction. 'So, we went to the auction together,' Arty says. 'I can see immediately whom I'm bidding against. My heart sinks, because I know that guy represents a very wealthy guy and I know he's got deep pockets. The bid at £1.3 million is with him.' He turned to his client to ask permission to pay another £100,000. His client shrugged. 'To my regret, I didn't bid. I should have bid more. I should have pushed it. I should have got him a painting that's now worth ten times what he would have paid for it.'

His story reveals what I *hadn't* seen at Sotheby's. 'You won't really see a collector on the frontline, even if the collector is in the room,' he explains. 'Auction rooms are much less revelatory than they used to be. My technique, actually, when I was buying for a private person, anyway, would always be to be on the phone even if I was in the room.' That way, no one would know that he was bidding. 'I could be on the phone to someone next to me, or I could have my client next to me, and I could be on the phone to the guy in Sotheby's who's sitting six feet away from me.' Art journalist Jan Dalley points out that, unlike for shares and property, there is no register of owners of artworks. In fact, she says, we don't even know where some of the world's most famous pictures are held. Leonardo da Vinci's *Salvator Mundi*, which sold for a record $450 million, 'appears to have gone AWOL'. She adds that: 'Since the art market relies heavily on advisers, agents and intermediaries, including foreign and offshore companies, questions of ownership become even more opaque.'[5] And, once again, there is money to be made for intermediaries by skimming small percentages from large sums. The business of art is a highly profitable and covert activity.

It also extends beyond the actual purchase of artworks. Arty says, 'There is much more money in art than the price of a painting.' Auction houses like Sotheby's often involve private finance to back a price guarantee. Arty elaborates: 'Let's say you have got a Giacometti that you think is worth £100 million and you won't sell it for less than £100 million.' Sotheby's will guarantee the £100 million, but in return they will keep anything above the £100 million that the

Giacometti fetches at auction. But Sotheby's may not be able to afford to stump up £100 million. Instead, 'They go to a third party who's normally a financier who will promise to buy the Giacometti for £100 million.' If it doesn't reach £100 million in the auction, 'The financier pays the £100 million to the seller and keeps the art.' But if it goes for £101 million, the buyer takes the art and the financier takes 50 per cent of the extra £1 million. Arty says, 'It's another way of participating in the art world, which has nothing, really, to do with art.'

The ripples of art money extend beyond Mayfair. It hikes property values throughout the city, indirectly shaping the lives of all Londoners. The urban scholar Sharon Zukin describes artists as the storm troopers of gentrification.[6] Gentrification involves the beautification and restoration of previously neglected and run-down neighbourhoods. Unfortunately, these improvements also push up real estate values and rents, pricing those with limited means out of the area. It was the arrival of artists and private galleries in Shoreditch and neighbouring Hoxton that created the modern face of the Ditch and bars like Looking Glass. Arty describes the transformation of this area: 'Within a decade, it's become some of the most prized real estate in London.' Hoxton and Shoreditch were briefly understood as rivals to Mayfair's art scene. This didn't last, for the simple reason that art is entangled with broader luxury markets, like fashion, and very wealthy people. Arty says: 'Money doesn't go East, not shopping money at least.' Art quickly reconsolidated itself in Mayfair, leaving just the higher rents and property prices behind in Shoreditch. There is a reason that Damien Hirst is selling in Mayfair not Shoreditch, he continues. 'If you want to define the centre of the art world in the UK, you put a pin in your map at Claridge's, and if it takes longer than five minutes to walk, it's off pitch.' He describes Berkeley Square as the 'optimum location' for art. There aren't many buildings in Mayfair large enough to house galleries. Instead gallery owners will knock through the walls of several buildings to create the right kind of space. This is only viable for a certain kind of gallery now dominating the area: a gallery with a 'larger turnover' that can afford to pay. The business of art combines certain kinds of display and concealment. It consolidates the changing face of Mayfair and refashions other parts of London, like Shoreditch and Hoxton, as well as Brixton, as artists move in and then move on in search of affordable studio space.

Art markets are ideally suited to money laundering. Transparency International refers to the United Kingdom as a 'safe haven' for money laundering, especially its luxury sectors, in which art along with property plays a prominent role. It suggests that such dubious transactions in the art world may total billions of pounds. A *Financial Times* columnist described the response of someone she refers to as a 'senior gallerist' to recent EU regulations to combat money laundering as: 'Panic. Absolute bloody panic.'[7] In 2018, the US government charged the British art dealer Matthew Green, co-director of Mayfair Fine Art Gallery, with using a Picasso painting to launder more than $9 million, allegedly from a stock exchange scam. Beaufort Securities Investment Managers, who were involved in the case, explained to an undercover FBI agent that art is the 'only market that is unregulated', and that art is a profitable investment, because of its money-laundering potential.[8] Art is a flexible and so potentially criminal source of money. It links Mayfair to international mafias and corporate or state crime: an unseemly underworld, out of keeping with art's urbanity and cultural credentials.

The moneyed Mayfair I have found is subtler and more complex than the predatory dealings of private equity and hedge funds. In this rarefied world of fine wines and fine art, money is – in the eyes of its makers and spenders – elevated, becomes something more worthy, the foundation of a legacy and even a nation. As money accumulates, it struts in the clothes of high culture. By insisting on the artfulness of business, the money machine's Mayfair operatives and beneficiaries valorize their profits while downplaying their rapaciousness. Culture and finance share the streets of Mayfair, where they jostle with each other for space. Behind elegant architectural facades, both work by obscuring what they really are and how they operate.

6

A Game of Clubs and Monopoly

Walking through Mayfair and St James's, I am searching for private members' clubs, or gentlemen's clubs, as they are sometimes called. These are a long-established feature of plutocratic London, and, having visited The Wine Club to speak to Sturgeon, I am eager to explore some more. Instead of name plates announcing this or that club, I encounter instead only numbers on discreet brass door plates. I stop in front of 106 Pall Mall. Anyone could walk past and notice nothing. But I have persuaded an old friend from university to invite me to his club. It occupies a grand palazzo building, built in 1832 and designed by Charles Barry, who also designed the Houses of Parliament. It is only because of my friend's instruction that I know I am standing outside The Travellers Club. His choice of club had always amused me: among my friends, he is least inclined to travel. But his name gets me past a porter who wouldn't look out of place in an Oxford college and into the main lounge on the ground floor. Its chandeliers, high ceilings, cornicing, elaborate and slightly shabby furniture give it the air of a rundown palace. The Duke of Edinburgh was, in fact, a former member.

Even if I could afford it and was able to convince several members to propose me, I could never be a member of The Travellers: the club doesn't allow women members, although, according to their website, 'Ladies are welcome as guests.' I discover when I try to wander into the library that, as a 'lady guest', I am barred from all areas of the club except the lounge and the dining room. The women's bathroom isn't signposted – like the club itself, guests must know where it is. With few other women guests on this particular night, it strikes me that women are intended to feel out of place here. The club exists for men of a certain age to congregate, read or doze – or to dine, alone or at the common table. It was originally a 'meeting place for gentlemen who have travelled abroad, their foreign visitors and diplomats posted in London' – travellers of a certain stripe. Today, club etiquette limits the use of mobile phones, insists that work papers not be openly displayed, and confines business to rooms booked for that purpose: all rules reflecting a time when gentlemen-explorers didn't work. The dress code is jacket and tie, and: 'Ladies are expected to dress to a similar standard.' My friend and I had discussed whether I could wear smart casual trousers, or should dig out a frock. I dug out a frock. Rumours suggest The Travellers is favoured by former spies. Whether this is true or not, some of the talks given by members suggest they have journeyed down roads less travelled. After one of the talks, I stay for dinner and sit at the common table. The talk has been on Myanmar, before it became a tourist destination and then a no-go area on human-rights grounds. The speaker's photographs suggested he wasn't a tourist. When I ask what line of work the men sitting around me are in, one of them mumbles 'Information Technology', in a way that discourages further questions.

I leave The Travellers to explore further. I don't have to go far. Next door at 107 is The Athenæum. The Athenæum was founded in 1824 in association with several learned societies, and its members are university vice chancellors, ranking church figures and notables in the worlds of science, arts and culture, who come for intelligent conversation and to make use of its three beautiful libraries. As its members include fellow academics, it wasn't too difficult to get invited here for lunch on one occasion and dinner on another. The dining room feels like a cross between a five-star hotel and a stately home. Small groups of men and women at small tables are deep in conversation about university politics. An off-duty bishop sits dozing after lunch in an armchair. The Athenæum is splendid, opulent, chandeliered and high-ceilinged, shinier and better maintained than The Travellers, with a spectacular pillared stairwell and art deco lights. The building is an architectural gem designed by Victorian architect Decimus Burton in the Greek revival style. A Greek frieze runs around the top of the exterior, above the top floor windows and wrought-iron balconies: it seems sometimes only classical empires are grand enough. Private members' clubs occupy some of London's most beautiful historic buildings.

Like The Athenæum and The Travellers, most clubs specialize in elite niches. The RAF Club (Piccadilly), The Army & Navy Club (Pall Mall) and The In and Out Club (St James's Square) were once exclusively the domain of high-ranking military officers. Today The Army & Navy tries to attract non-military members, emphasizing its five-star hotel, and dining and spa facilities. The men-only Whites on St James's Street claims to be the oldest gentlemen's club in London and lists the princes Charles and William among its patrons. In Mayfair, Marks, on Charles Street, occupies a beautiful old Mayfair town house, accepts women members and offers itself as an *alternative* to the gentlemen's clubs of St James's. Curiously, its dress code – *elegant* – specifically prohibits cowboy boots. Morton's, in a Grade II listed Georgian building on Berkeley Square, in among the private equity firms and private galleries, cultivates a younger, more contemporary, more relaxed image. It has an in-house nightclub, targeting under-thirties wearing smart jeans and heels. Its website description captures the essence of a private members' club as a 'place to see and be seen by some of the most important individuals in the capital, with an impressive – if discreet – membership base'. Membership in most of these traditional clubs is guarded, not by fees, which are sometimes comparatively modest – by which I mean in the region of £1,500 to £3,000 a year – but by nomination and scrutiny of applicants by existing members: procedures that restrict membership to a small circle of members' contacts.

As nods to youth culture and adjustments to tradition suggest, the capital's club scene is in flux. More recent arrivals on the scene have redrawn the clubbing map beyond the traditional heartlands of Mayfair and St James's, to Soho and Chelsea – and even to East London, with the arrival of Shoreditch House. Stuffy rules and ancient furniture are replaced with high-spec interior design, top-notch facilities, flexibility, and work-friendly environments aimed at young freelance entrepreneurs. And restaurant-quality food has replaced the school dinners style of the old clubs. Modelled on five-star hotels, available to anyone who can afford them, not just the entitled, these clubs have democratized luxury, at least for new and young money. As a journalist at the *Economist* noted, clubs are competing to attract 'women, businesses and the global moneyed elite who increasingly make London their home'.[1]

The Club at Café Royal – a private members' club in a five-star hotel on Regent Street on Mayfair's eastern edge – exemplifies these developments in 'clubland'. From the grand marble entranceway of the hotel, a doorman in a sharp black uniform shows me to The Club on the first floor; its windows overlook the elegant crescent of Regent Street, designed by John Nash. Sinking into an armchair, I soak up the atmosphere. The large open-plan room is gently humming with laptops and subdued meetings. Two men in their thirties discuss a television show they hope to produce – thirty episodes on fashion design, following existing TV offerings on competitive cooking. They are concerned about 'making the right introductions'. A female television producer joins them, first kissing the (strikingly handsome) turbaned waiter on both cheeks. He hovers next to the party, awaiting its order: a bottle of red wine. Their conversation about fashion continues: I hear snatches on financial support for milliners, Alexander McQueen, the Fashion Council – making 'the business of fashion' work. Two women on the next table are planning a new charity. A backpack and cycle helmet walk past on the way to the bar. I learn later that the man sitting next to me in jeans just sold his multimedia production company for millions. The Club curates a cultural programme for its members, including talks by writers, designers and artists: it is a world away from The Travellers and The Athenæum, where members doze off on leather sofas after a good lunch. But, counter-intuitively, these seemingly modernizing, democratizing nods to popular culture, in a club that admits anyone who can pay its comparatively modest fees, reaffirm exclusivity, if in new forms. Members are still wealthy and successful: they are just new money and a fair bit younger.

Later, in the early evening, I am a short walk away from the Café Royal. Standing outside London's most exclusive private members' club, 5 Hertford Street, an unremarkable eighteenth-century Mayfair town house, I wonder what all the fuss is about. I am outside because I was refused entry: the privacy of guests mustn't be compromised by researchers, I have been told. Hertford Street was set up as a more exclusive alternative to the nightclub Annabel's in Berkeley Square, after Annabel's owner, Mark Birley, expanded it into a new luxury site, adding restaurants, bars, a gym and a spa to attract a broader spectrum of members. Birley's son with Annabel Goldsmith, Robin, founded Hertford Street after his father fired him from Annabel's. Breathless journalists report its extraordinary social exclusiveness, membership quality – A-list celebrities – and the legendary length of its waiting list, shrouded in rumour and secrecy. A *Spectator* journalist spotted leading Tory politicians and hedge fund owners and a smaller crowd of attractive young women on a visit there. He described the club as, 'staking out ground where the information/communication elite intersect with the world of politics and finance'.[2] Robin Birley is as secretive as his club. But *The Times* reported his financial contributions to the United Kingdom Independence Party (UKIP),[3] and the *Sunday Times* noted Robin Birley's support for Chilean General Pinochet while he was in London awaiting the decision of a Spanish extradition request for crimes against humanity.[4] I can only imagine that conversations at Hertford Street are highly politically significant and not particularly progressive.

Luckily, I found another way to take a brief look inside Hertford Street. My young lawyer friend, Investigator, who works in a private banking and wealth management operation in the old financial district, has a colleague who is a member. Investigator's colleague is her age (36), equally blonde and attractive, a whizz in investment with a PhD from a top university, and she invited her along one Saturday night. Investigator's colleague's intentions make Investigator a little uneasy: she is looking for a rich husband, preferably before this year's membership expires and she has to pay to renew it. I ask Investigator how her colleague managed to land membership of such a prestigious and exclusive club. Apparently, their boss put in a good word for her. There is a sexual economy at work here; being an attractive, intelligent, single woman provides a shortcut to membership, suggesting the women are bait intended to lure male members. She is both a member and part of the club's offer. Slender, beautiful and wide-eyed, in a short, classy black dress and fishnet tights, Investigator's colleague tells me her plan when I meet her in a bar beforehand, with an unguarded directness that makes her seem vulnerable, naive even, rather than predatory. Investigator is anxious about the mission, but eager to see inside the club, and promises to report back. Off they go into Saturday night, looking stunning.

I suggest Investigator WhatsApp me at convenient intervals with whatever she notices about the people and the club. Her first messages are downbeat: the interior decor, the people and the food are all surprisingly 'frumpy', by which she means pitched at an older demographic, and 'tasteless'. Apparently, it is overly elaborate, lacking a simpler elegance, descending at times into expensive chintz. There is, she says, lots of patterned carpet. Her messages detail brief encounters. 'We met a beautiful 37-year-old family-office owner who complained that her boyfriend had just dumped her. He felt that his life was too hectic for a relationship, even though he worked the same hours as she did.' (Family offices administer the affairs – financial and sometimes other – of wealthy families.) Investigator adds that he was probably threatened by her success. 'Two middle-aged American women in the toilets both in black cocktail dresses. One complains that her husband thinks she has loads of free time. She does more at home than he realizes. She feels guilty about eating carbs at restaurants with her kids.' Wealthy men can be demanding at home as well as at work; and women find it difficult as they age to keep in the required shape. 'Just met a Lord who brought his two dogs with him. He is ugly and quite old, but he dates women my age. My colleague says there are no good-looking men. This rich Italian guy in his late forties replied, "Their looks aren't their best asset." Of the women in the club he said, "Their money isn't their best asset."' The play is clear: sexual and financial assets stare each other down. Investigator signs off, apologizing for typos and saying she has only had two drinks, as they are too expensive to buy any more.

My clubbing quest continues. I am thrilled when Blazer, another contact's contact, suggests we meet at George, his club, in Mayfair's Mount Street. A serious 'clubber', Blazer is a member of eight different clubs. Clearly he is an inveterate networker, and I wonder how he finds the time to fit them all in. On the day of our meeting, he phones to bring our discussion forward, making it impossible for me to get there in time. I move fast and arrive flustered in a taxi, only to find he has already left. He lives in Mayfair, but has left instructions with one of George's waiters that he will be back and I should wait in the downstairs bar. My interactions with him in the run-up to our meeting have been difficult. He scrutinized the certificate of ethical responsibility from my university, which confirms the ethics of my research practice. He questioned the appropriateness of my research methods, and insisted that I hadn't done a thorough enough job in checking him out before arranging to meet him. I head down the steps, noticing that the main (restaurant) level is hung with David Hockney paintings. In the cosy, dimly lit atmosphere of the basement bar, I try to get a sense of the place through the people and conversations around me. An Italian man in his thirties is trying to sell his think tank's services to a posh English man who is dissatisfied with the 'one size fits all approach' of think tanks. The sound of their debate merges with the voices of another: one of the parliamentary debates on the United Kingdom's relationship with the European Union is being shown on the television in the corner of the room.

I try to imagine George conversations past. On one September day in 2009, on the eve of the general election that swept David Cameron's Conservative Party back into power, James Murdoch, the then chairman of News International, and Cameron sat together in this room. James told Cameron at this meeting that his father, media mogul Rupert Murdoch, had switched the editorial stance of the populist *Sun* newspaper, from Labour to Conservative. This was to prove a crucial and timely intervention which helped tip the election in the Conservatives' favour. A *Guardian* journalist suggests that George is favoured over glitzier venues by billionaires and FTSE 100 regulars, for its 'deathly quiet'.[5] In the near-silence, George evidently hosts secluded conversations with far-reaching consequences, in changing the course of nation states and people's lives.

Blazer arrives silently from behind me. In his late fifties, he is carefully put together – sharply pressed beige trousers, navy blazer, shirt, and a tie with the same paisley pattern as his neatly folded pocket handkerchief: the look of an off-duty officer of the Raj. His family were part of the native elite of one of Britain's former colonies; his respect for the British establishment, particularly the royal family, is total. The royals, he says, 'know how to treat their subjects'. Bearing and etiquette are important to him. He sits down opposite me and tells me he has just left the House of Commons debate, still rumbling on the TV in the corner. He supports Britain's departure from the European Union, but is disappointed that the Conservative Party doesn't have a credible plan for how to go about it.

Blazer and his wife moved to Mayfair eighteen years ago, because 'It was the most expensive property on the Monopoly board.' They got to know the area beforehand in frequent visits and liked the restaurants. He says Mayfair is not suitable for families, because it is 'a playground for adults'; Blazer and his wife have no children. 'We were lucky,' he recalls, 'the ideal home came on the market, we saw it, fell in love with it and we bought it – it's a beautiful six-storey house with about 7,000 feet of space. We're very happy with it and we love the neighbourhood.' He is pleased with the redevelopment of the American Embassy into a five-star hotel around the corner in Grosvenor Square, likewise the renovated Four Seasons Hotel opposite. He credits the landowner, the Duke of Westminster (to whom I will return later), for his influence in restoring the area to its 'past glory' as a place for 'respectable, high-net-worth families, people like us, all living comfortably', conveniently surrounded by boutiques, restaurants and cafés. He and his wife have a country home too: 30,000 feet in 60 acres, complete with horses, stables, a swimming pool and tennis courts.

Blazer is reluctant to speak about his wealth. He made his fortune in private equity, during the dot-com boom, between 1996 and 2004, when 'Everything you touched turned to gold.' Companies were being valued purely on the basis of web traffic, or 'eyeballs', as Blazer puts it. The more people visited the website, the more it was worth. 'It was a crazy time, we were just lucky,' Blazer says: this is the second time he has used that word. Lucky in his house, and lucky in his job. 'We were there at the right time and the right place. It was hugely exciting, the deal-making was phenomenal, the newspapers described me as the most prolific deal-maker of my generation and I had the privilege again of leading some very, very important big transactions.' He doesn't want to say what they were. His deal-making life is over: 'I don't do much for profit now.' Instead, through his foundation, he gives his money away, which he sees as 'doing something meaningful, having a purpose and giving back to society for the wonderful privileges that we have been able to enjoy'. He is an enthusiastic advocate of ethical and socially responsible business. 'I think private equity, venture (start-up) capital and the big asset owners are now slowly starting to realize that their approach to owning businesses will need to be ethical.' Blazer is critical of the current standard business model, which prioritizes shareholder enrichment over social responsibility, and thinks the objectives of individual accumulation and social need should be brought into a better balance. Of course, he can now afford these principles.

For a Conservative Party donor, he takes a surprisingly radical stance on London's vast concentrations of wealth. He thinks 'foreigners' like him living in £100 million mansions don't pay enough tax. Instead they take advantage of the creative accounting that London offers. He suggests that tax breaks should be given only to those who invest in ways that contribute to collective wealth creation and decent jobs. 'Those are the people that should get the best tax breaks,' he argues, 'not the people who can hire the best law firms and organize the best trusts and foundations and hide everything where nobody can ever touch it.' He is optimistic that things are moving in this more progressive direction. Tax loopholes are being slowly plugged. 'If we want to be citizens here and take advantage of what this country has to offer, then we've got to bridge the rich–poor divide. Because if we don't, the poor are going to rise up one day and demand what is rightfully theirs.' Spoken like a former colonial subject! Even if Blazer's stance on social inequality is motivated by pragmatism, anxiety about the potential restlessness of the natives, and the fact that he has already accumulated his wealth, it is socially progressive, self-aware, and in this regard quite different from other plutocrats I have encountered on my walks. The uber-wealthy come in all varieties, as I am gradually discovering.

I am interested in Blazer's philanthropy. A wealthy progressive woman and patron of the arts I spoke to a few weeks earlier in north London's Highgate told me of the importance of philanthropy among the rich. She argued, 'An awful lot of rich people get a lot of pleasure from giving money away as well as spending it. It's how you are as a person.' She suggested that philanthropy is an extension of who wealthy people are, or, perhaps, how they want to be seen. Sociologist Rachel Sherman's study of wealthy New Yorkers similarly notes the importance they attach to philanthropy as a sign of being morally worthy.[6] Yet there are other benefits too. Like private members' clubs, charitable giving offers a means to meet other rich and influential people, to 'get on in society'. Patronage of the arts brings social prestige, invitations to events where donors mix with artists and other wealthy patrons. My Highgate contact is involved in a £600 million charitable trust, formerly run by her late husband, which gives money to less popular causes. 'We never support anything to do with animals,' she explained, 'because animals find it very easy to raise money. Every donkey in the country has God knows how much money.' Contrary to popular opinion, she argued, 'Giving money away well is just as hard as making money. It's very easy to spray money around, but, if you are a good businessman like he [her husband] was, you don't want to waste money and you can waste money giving charitably as much as you can spending it on handbags.' She pointed out that 40 per cent of charitable donations are denied to public finances, because of the tax incentive: 'I think it needs to be done responsibly.' Philanthropy benefits the wealthy and their chosen recipients, and diminishes the tax take.

I ask Blazer about how he gives his money away. He says that philanthropy 'starts with the heart and ends with the heart, and in between it is controlled by the mind'. For him, it is about feeling sufficiently emotionally engaged with something to want to give money to it. That's the heart part. 'However, very quickly they [philanthropists] realize that while it is true that every small change can make a big change, most of these issues that the world faces are systemic issues where no one person can move the needle.' In this scenario, says Blazer, 'That's where the mind comes in, so you start to become a bit more strategic at looking at the impact of what you do.' Between touching lives and actually changing them, he thinks, 'There is a big difference.' He prefers to fund big systemic projects: building sustainable communities, education and inclusive capitalism. In terms of the amounts involved, donations below £50,000 indicate, 'You don't really care', and he just hopes recipients spend it well. 'Anything between £50,000 and £250,000, you need to have some sort of role, whether it's an advisory board role or some sort of oversight . . . you really need a proper seat at the table to ensure that the money you

have been giving is being spent properly and there is proper accountability for it.'

'Properly' means reviewing what is going into overheads and what
goes to the cause itself. 'Between 5 and 10 per cent is a reasonable
overhead', taking salaries, rent and administrative fees into account.
Any more is 'inefficient'. In that case Blazer applies what he calls the
'what if?' test: 'If you had not intervened, where would they be in contrast to where they are now?' Outcomes must be quantifiable to justify
large donations: how many more girls are going to school as a result
of the intervention? Money isn't freely given to appealing causes.
Where it is given and the conditions in which it is given are as
complex as the business and investment affairs through which the
benefactor's money is made in the first place. Philanthropy too has its
business models and strategies.

As our conversation draws to a close, I am struck by Blazer's dis-
avowal of the private equity that made him wealthy, as well as his
implicit acknowledgement of the damage it does financially and
socially. There is a stark contrast between the ways in which he made
his money, in the dog-eat-dog arenas of private finance, and his reinvention as a philanthropist and businessman who is concerned about
social justice and equality. Is he seeking redemption for past sins? Is
this a nifty piece of reputation laundering? Or a road to Damascus
conversion? Even so, Blazer is not about to give up his position and
influence. Despite being a foreign resident, he navigates old, establishment circles at the highest levels, partly thanks to the exclusive, elite
networks of private members' clubs. As Blazer is a founding member
of 5 Hertford Street, I ask, 'Do you think Robin Birley would speak to
me?' 'I doubt it,' he replies, dismissing me. Undeterred, I leave George
and wander off to have a look at how the Four Seasons Hotel, Mayfair's largest building site, is coming along. The Duke of Westminster
owns much of Mayfair, including the land on which the Four Seasons
and the former US Embassy stand, and his estates are where I am
heading next.

7

His Grace's Bees

I am on the trail of the aristocracy. Victoria Station seems an appropriate starting point, not least because I am convinced that the aristocracy rarely use it. Commuters shift in and out, their footsteps beating the everyday rhythms connecting work and home. Some may have been on longer journeys; Victoria Station is London's portal to the south coast and Gatwick Airport. The vaulted ceiling of the train station echoes with a continuous stream of departure and delay announcements. On the ground, there is the humming mundane world of everyday commerce, of Boots, Pret a Manger, Accessorize and Dorothy Perkins. Along the road outside, buses gather at the bus terminus, from where they are routed across Britain and Europe; Eastern European migrants begin new lives in London here, or end them and head home. The bus is the people's transport: cheap, inconvenient, moving at a pace that requires resignation and the suspension of expectation.

Having left the station, I walk along Buckingham Palace Road. As I turn onto Eccleston Street, a different kind of world gradually comes into view: a shop selling wedding dresses; two or three independent restaurants, waiters outside catching a quick smoke. Walking north along Eccleston Street, I am suddenly in a surreal place of matching magnolia stucco houses and neat well-tended garden squares: Belgravia. Belgravia stretches from Hyde Park on its northern boundary, between Knightsbridge and Hyde Park Corner Underground stations, down southwards almost to the Thames at Chelsea Bridge, with Sloane Square on its western border and Victoria Station to the east. A self-important residential repetitiveness reigns in these streets: black metal railings, their spear-like heads standing to attention; pillars adorning gateways; substantial, identical, black front doors. Even the planters are a uniform black, and I would not be surprised if the vegetation itself were regulated. Stiff, miniature evergreen bushes are trimmed into regular shapes; some are artificial, with all maintenance and risk removed. Balconies over porticoed doorways, planted with olive trees, bring a hint of the Mediterranean. Down the side streets, there is the occasional mews, once the stables of grand town houses, now the humbler dwellings of Belgravia – or maybe not so humble, as the Maseratis parked outside suggest serious money. The sage-green signs over the arched entrances leave me in no doubt as to whose land I am on: the Grosvenor Estate, owned by the Duke of Westminster.

London has many graces, but today I am looking for the titled kind: His Grace The Duke of Westminster. Hugh Grosvenor became the 7th Duke of Westminster aged just 27, when his father died in the summer of 2016. As the rules of primogeniture direct, despite his having two elder sisters, the young Duke inherited the Grosvenor Estate and an estimated £9 billion fortune. Walking around Mayfair and Belgravia without stepping on His Grace's estate is impossible; these streets are his, the squares and the statuary. I cannot meet the man himself to talk about this – a millennial aristocrat has no desire to answer a researcher's questions – but thanks to yet another contact's contact, his people have generously agreed to see me. And the best way to approach His Grace, I have decided, is to meander through his ancestral lands towards the office of the Grosvenor Estate in Mayfair.

I follow His Grace's land through to Eaton Square. Stucco spreads from house to house, through rows of terraces, entire blocks: a world coated in a fine aggregate render, painted in off-white magnolia. Master builder Thomas Cubitt built much of this district between the 1820s and the 1850s, making it early Victorian, now Grade II listed, a prestige tag that carries all manner of restrictions on remodelling and maintenance. The building work was commissioned by the 2nd Marquess, who developed the family's land, earlier expanded in the seventeenth century by the dowry of heiress Mary Davies. Davies's dowry was the land on which Mayfair and Belgravia stand today. Originally built as town houses, many buildings were converted into elegant flats in the 1950s, some stretching laterally across more than one house. A vast oblong-shaped garden occupies the centre of Eaton Square, an impressive third of a mile long. The garden is, of course, reserved for the private use of residents. Through the railings on the east side of the square, the view resembles the manicured grounds of a stately home. On the west side of the square, there is a tennis court.

There is an oddly rural tranquillity to this square: it doesn't feel like part of the city. Expensive cars are parked in the street. Concierges stand at intervals in pinstriped trousers, black jackets, long black coats with military buttons, black bowler hats, and, a contemporary addition, earpieces that connect them with estate security. They wander up and down the street and stand in pairs to chat. One of them tells me how quiet it is at weekends and during holidays, as residents retreat to other homes. He says the square is kept pristine by the Grosvenor 'requirement', presumably embedded in leases, that the exterior is repainted in the stipulated magnolia every five years. The Grosvenor family have their London home in this square. Who else lives here now? According to Seamus Wylie of Ayrton Wylie Estate Agents, this 'jewel in the crown of Belgravia' is occupied by 'captains of industry and hedge fund guys', including advertising mogul and art collector Charles Saatchi, formerly married to Nigella Lawson.

Proximity to Parliament and the royal court ensured Eaton Square was the neighbourhood of choice for high-ranking state officials and aristocrats in the nineteenth and early twentieth centuries. The list of past residents reads like a roll call of political influence: George Peabody, philanthropist; Edward Wood, 1st Earl of Halifax, one-time foreign secretary and viceroy of India during Jawaharlal Nehru's civil disobedience campaigns; Stanley Baldwin, Earl of Bewdley, who was prime minister; and Neville Chamberlain, another prime minister. Enoch Powell, the notorious racist rabble-rouser, Conservative MP and minister, later moved in at number 33, a few doors down from Chamberlain's former residence; unlike his celebrated neighbours, Powell is not commemorated with a blue plaque. Lord Robert Boothby, Conservative politician; Vivien Leigh, actress; and Nye Bevan, Labour politician and architect of the National Health Service, together with his wife Jennie, Baroness Lee of Asheridge, also an MP: all lived in Eaton Square. The square swarmed with influential elite residents, people who shaped society and politics in the United Kingdom, and, sometimes, in other countries too.

On I walk to yet another square – Belgrave Square. This, too, is a masterpiece of identikit five-storey stucco houses surrounding a gated black metal-railed garden. I try the gate but it's locked. The notice says *Private*, and underneath, *All dogs must be registered with Grosvenor*. I spot a (presumably registered) dog in the distance, on the other side of the square: a pale skinny greyhound, alternately running around its walker and shivering in the cold.

Belgrave Square is dotted with statues that memorialize people of significance. At the southern end, where I am standing watching the dog, is a statue of Christopher Columbus; a scrolled map in his right hand, he points into the distance, suggesting, I presume, unseen places to 'discover'. I think of Legacy. I walk anticlockwise around the square past the Serbian Embassy – this is embassy central – and the Saudi Cultural Centre. A blue plaque honours the residence (1920 to 1926) of Field Marshal Viscount Gort, commander at Dunkirk. Somewhat incongruously, a statue of Simón Bolívar (1783–1830), the Venezuelan military and political leader who was instrumental in revolutions against the Spanish Empire, stands near Gort. Past the Embassy of Trinidad and Tobago is the Turkish Embassy, guarded by police in flak jackets with automatic weapons. Next to it is the Malaysian High Commission and, on the corner, the Mexican Embassy, grander than the others, with pillars embedded in the walls and entrance. His Grace is the world's landlord. An elite version of history, shaped by elite concerns, is here given substance in stone.

His Grace is history's landlord too. At the north end of the square I stop to look at the statue of Sir Robert Grosvenor, the 1st Marquess of Westminster (1767–1845), founder of the dynasty. On the plinth beneath him is a quote from John Ruskin, suggesting the 1st Marquess's philosophy on city-making: *When we build let us think we build for ever*. The plinth sketches the Grosvenor family history and heraldry, which includes a now extinct breed of hunting dog (Talbot) and a wheatsheaf, to symbolize the family's rural connections. Tracing their land rights to ancient conquest, the inscription on the plinth declares that their ancestors came to England with William the Conqueror. Eleven centuries of wealth and privilege later their

140,000-acre estate in Lancaster, extended to Mayfair (100 acres) and Belgravia (200 acres), still stands. When the rich build, they build for ever.

Walking along Lanesborough Place, I stop to take a look at the Peninsula Hotel, a joint venture between the Grosvenor Estate and the hotel chain, at this point still under construction: the ancient estate is still expanding into new luxury. The hotel will command one of London's most iconic views, near Decimus Burton's Wellington Arch and the statue of Achilles, the Greek hero of the Trojan wars, built to memorialize the military campaigns in France of the 1st Duke of Wellington (1769–1852). The arch stands between two royal parks, Hyde Park and Green Park: the grandeur of His Grace's London is painted in both magnolia and shades of green.

As I skirt around the back of Buckingham Palace and onto the Mall, I walk across the ancestral lands of an even higher-level institution – the Crown Estates. This land comes with the office of the monarchy, and is separate from the vast tracts of land owned personally by the Queen and other members of the royal family, like the Duchy of Cornwall. The Crown Estates are a £14.3 billion UK real estate business with substantial holdings overseas. Crown Estates own half of all the retail, residential and office buildings in St James's and almost the entire crescent of John Nash's Regent Street, between Piccadilly and Oxford Circus. In this part of the city their property includes three palaces – Buckingham Palace, the Queen's official London residence; Kensington Palace, where the Duke and Duchess of Cambridge live when they are in London; and St James's Palace, which comprises various residences, providing a London base for an assortment of top-ranking royals. I head down the Mall, and up the steps leading to another stucco Nash creation, Carlton House Terrace. The mansion at number 13, reputedly worth £500 million, is owned by British Indian-born investors, the Hinduja Brothers, number three on the *Sunday Times* (2021) Rich List with an estimated fortune of £17 billion. The uber-rich pay a high price for proximity to royalty. I walk past The Athenæum and cross Piccadilly, leaving St James's for Mayfair.

As I am early for my appointment with His Grace's people, I wind my way slowly though Mayfair towards his offices. Berkeley Square was once the grounds of another aristocratic house, built for the first Lord Berkeley of Stratton and demolished in the eighteenth century.[1] But the aristocracy have rivals. New land grabs are under way. The square's ten acres and one hundred properties were bought by the British Petroleum pension fund in 1967, and sold in 2001 to a consortium led by the House of Saud for £345 million. This bid was led by no less than Prince Alwaleed Bin Talal Bin Abdul Aziz, with additional Middle Eastern money joining anonymously. It was reported at the time, from sources inside His Grace's operation, that they were the losing bidder, despite having £335 million on the table.[2] Oil money, it seems, sometimes trumps ancient power.

Just around the corner, on Charles Street, is the Saudi Embassy. It is housed in an elegant detached Georgian mansion, Crewe House, set back from the street behind black metal railings. A row of men and women are standing outside holding poster-sized photographs of Saudi political prisoners. 'Free Ashraf Fayadh' is their rallying cry. Fayadh is a Palestinian poet who in 2016 was sentenced in Saudi Arabia to eight years in prison and 800 lashes for 'apostasy' and promoting atheism. Just as in London you are supposedly never more than six feet away from a rat, in Mayfair you are rarely far from a serious human rights violation.

I walk past the Egyptian Embassy on South Street, guarded by two armed police: a global politics makes its presence felt with guns in London doorways. I stop in front of the window of Harrods Estate Agents, on the corner of South Street and Park Lane, and review properties for sale with price tags ranging from £3 million to £34 million, in Mayfair but also in Dubai. Mayfair's Wetherell Property Agents describe the Middle Eastern influence on this and other West End neighbourhoods like Knightsbridge as *intense*. The Dorchester itself is owned by a consortium headed by the Sultan of Brunei. The iconic Knightsbridge department store Harrods is now owned by the Qatari Investment Authority, linked with the Qatar royal family, who bought it from its previous owner Egyptian businessman Mohamed Al Fayed. Middle Eastern buyers, according to Wetherell, consistently account for 10 per cent of residential sales in Mayfair, where the lands of ancient aristocracies are invisibly underpinned by money syphoned from fossil fuels. London property acts as a safe deposit box for oil profits, which could otherwise be invested in diversifying the currently carbon-based economies of the Middle East or providing welfare, education and other social benefits for their people. Spending vast quantities of money on properties and other luxuries in London keeps the money of the super-rich hidden from those at home. The ruling family of Abu Dhabi is Mayfair's second-largest investor after the Duke.[3] Plutocratic London is Middle Eastern as well as British. Ancient privilege and global oil money interweave, and nowhere is this strange tapestry more visible than in the streets of Mayfair and Belgravia. Given the ways in which Britain intervened in the Middle East to control oil and politics in the early twentieth century, Middle Eastern appropriation of prime London real estate seems oddly apposite.

I walk along Grosvenor Street to number 70 and take in the 1960s HQ of the Grosvenor Estate. I like the contemporary riff on Victorian metal balconies, and the concept of encasing an ancient operation in modern architecture. For a family firm, it also looks a little corporate. The two are not mutually exclusive, as I discover. I walk through sliding glass doors towards a minimalist reception desk, staffed by a young woman and an older man. He gives me a pass that gets me through the barriers to the waiting area, where I am invited to take a seat on a low, modern sofa. On the marble coffee table is an arrangement of orchid heads and leaves; at the other side of the waiting area is a tall vase of orange bird of paradise flowers. Behind the reception desk, there are a series of small meeting rooms with circular tables and chairs, intimate and anonymous at the same time, much like a bank. Yet the walls are hung with family portraits. A recent portrait of the young Duke is positioned next to three from an earlier period – one of a woman in the centre, with those of a father and a son on either side. Smart but casually dressed employees arrive, exchanging pleasantries with the receptionists. The atmosphere is one of elegance, efficiency and polite, restrained conviviality.

His Grace's Buffer, who fends off requests like mine to see the young aristocrat, appears in a suit and tie, the epitome of urbanity. A smart, city-savvy estate professional: in a different context, I might mistake him for a friendly professor of urban studies. He ushers me into a small meeting room, where we sit, my notebook and recorder on a large polished table between us. He tells me that 300 people work for

the estate from these offices, the headquarters of Grosvenor Britain &
Ireland.

Among the many privileges of working for what he describes as one
of the 'great estates' is the prerogative of a long view: 'We've had it for
300 years and we hope we will have it for another 300 years, and
we've been proud of it for that time.' Neighbouring great estates
include the Cadogan Estate in the adjacent area of Kensington and
Chelsea, also 300 years old, but small in comparison to Grosvenor.
Buffer suggests the 'stewardship' of the estate means responsibility for
its history and architectural heritage, as well as an ethic of care – this
distinguishes it from operations based on short-term commercial
considerations. 'I mean clearly we're here to make money,' he
acknowledges. 'We are an estate, not a charity, but there is a great deal
of charitable work here on the estate.' This branch of the activities of
an ancient aristocratic family is one of Britain's most successful property developers; the estate is part of the modern city, with an obligation
to the family to evolve in ways that 'keep it prosperous', while observing the responsibilities of history. Might the continued prosperity of
His Grace's family firm conflict with public good? Buffer thinks not:
obligations to history and the public good are perfectly compatible
with serious money and the modern city.

Buffer confirms what I already suspected; the estate has consider-
able control over 'any substantive change' in the built landscape. Even
in Eaton Place, where they don't have the freeholds any more, 'We do
have the power to ensure that it is painted a uniform magnolia colour,
that the woodwork is the same, so it looks harmonious, it looks as it
always would have done.' Through regulation and magnolia paint,
the estate preserves, as in a time capsule, a nineteenth-century aesthetic in the built environment of a modern city that is otherwise ever
changing. Its 'close working relationship' with the City of Westminster, the London Borough on which most of Grosvenor's urban land
stands, ensures magnolia stucco in perpetuity. I suspect they have less
of a say in the redevelopment of the American Embassy. He says: 'We
own the freehold. It's on a very long lease, which the Americans sold
to Qatari Diar, but we've still got the land', and this gives the estate 'a
say' in the development. Qatari Diar is the sovereign wealth fund of
the State of Qatar – more fossil fuel money. This doesn't inhibit the

estate's website from proclaiming its 'sustainable' development credentials. They are, Buffer says, 'absolutely thrilled' to have the Peninsula Hotel on the estate too, and they are working with a global chain of private clinics and hospitals who want to establish their London administrative offices there. In this part of the city, the interests of a modern aristocracy and contemporary city-development are aligned.

Ironically, given the uniformity of its appearance, 'mix' is the word Buffer uses most to describe the estate's vision for the city. He is referring to building-use and public access. 'Community space, cultural space, we're a bit short on,' he admits. 'The main public buildings in Belgravia are churches and Mayfair Library, which does very well in terms of community use. We want to promote these churches as part of our cultural offering.' He recognizes the benefit of creating space that is *not* entirely monetized, not designed with revenue extraction in mind. And he understands the need to attract a more diverse crowd to the area than simply those who can afford to live there. Pubs, along with repurposed churches, carry the estate's ambitions for social mixing. Buffer reels off their names: The Cubitt, The Orange, The Tennyson. 'They are definitely pubs, but they've got nice . . . not gastro, restaurants attached to them. Again, we think that keeps the mix going.' Mix is about creating what is missing from these streets – the vitality of popular life that might animate them.

More controlled kinds of vitality are curated instead. For example, the estate is involved with the Chelsea Flower Show through Belgravia in Bloom: 'We encourage all of our tenants to dress up for the Chelsea Flower Show, to cover their shops or their houses in flowers, displays, and we have a competition for the best Belgravia in Bloom.' These kinds of community awards are supposed to counter the 'sense that it's full of very rich people who don't live here all the time': 'That's something we do feel quite strongly about.' Buffer argues that 'Belgravia has always been like that.' Historically there was 'the season', when rich people would come to London, but the rest of the year was spent in the countryside. The image 'which the press like to peddle sometimes', of silent streets with all the lights off, and no one at home, is 'a bit extreme'. 'Yes, if you drive through Eaton Square at night it can be quiet, but you drive into Elizabeth Street, Chester Row, and it's busy, the pubs are busy . . . the pubs in Belgravia actually are permanently packed.'

New commercial developments are intended to generate vitality too. Buffer tells me about a development in Eccleston Yards: 'Something quite new for us. A bit of land completely hidden away.' It is a former industrial site, variously used for ice-making and electricity workshops. Now it contains Barry's Bootcamp, a 'boutique fitness concept', as well as smaller office spaces for hire. 'We've got dress designers there,' Buffer says, 'who can hire rack spaces by the yard, just to give them a real start-up – and organic restaurants, open air events and, again, yes, very much appealing to that, sort of, twenties, thirties crowd. That's the audience we want there, without, of course, putting off the Belgravia audience, and I think we've got a good mix.' It's a mix of sorts, 'hidden away', expensive and highly aesthetically regulated.

His Grace is a millennial: the generation born between 1981 and 1996, widely credited with prompting a sea change in conventional values. This is the generation that has firm views on sustainability, climate change and the wastefulness of consumption. In most of London, it is the generation least likely to own property, or to hold a steady full-time job. I ask if Buffer thinks being a millennial will make a difference to His Grace's relationship to his money? He wrestles with my question, which he considers either nonsensical or stupid, although he is too gracious to say so. He patiently explains that the Grosvenor ancestral money and the new directions it takes are not matters of individual whim. There is a board of trustees. 'So, his relatively new Grace, the 7th Duke, is clearly one of the trustees, but there is a very clear structure', steering a massive global property empire centred on London and the family firm. 'One of the pleasures of working for Grosvenor is that you do still get that feeling that you are working for a family company and the family are quite visible in London. They live in Belgravia.' The trustees have a background in property or finance, and, Buffer assures me, are all 'exceptionally agreeable and pleasant people'. Strategic change, change that impacts the direction of the estate, he explains, would come from the top, from the Board of Trustees. He doubts whether 'one person could change significantly the course of the estate to move with the times or actually shape the times'.

Why would anyone want to change it? Part of the estate's job is to preserve what Buffer calls 'that, sort of, lovely hush' that exists in Belgravia: 'As somebody once said, it's the sort of hush which only lots of money can buy, and I think that's probably true. So, I'd be wary of thinking that because there is a 28-, 29-year-old ostensibly at the helm that would make a significant change.' I press on the sustainability question. 'We already have those values because, clearly, the Wheatsheaf branch of Grosvenor is entirely devoted to enhancing the environment, to researching food sustainability,' he retorts. He suggests that although sustainability is a popular theme, Grosvenor's efforts on this front are not widely reported in the press. 'But it's very, very important to us. We try to ensure that all our new and retrofitted buildings are as green-compliant as possible. It's something we're passionate about. It's one of our business values, one of our core values.' And he concedes, 'That probably is very millennial, but it's also something we want to do. We keep bees on the roof here.' So, this is a modern aristocracy? 'It's a very modern approach, but what I am not keen to talk about is the individual role of His Grace in running the estate.' Time to walk on.

8

Keeping It in the Family

The Grosvenor Estate is a family office, and family offices are how some plutocrats run their money. Wig, a judge whom I will later meet on this walk, tells me: 'Through having an entry-level ocean-going yacht ... then you work your way up to bigger ocean-going yachts. Then you get into one of the private-jet-sharing schemes, where you get so many flying hours a year, and at some point, you get a private jet of your own.' At this point, in serious oligarch territory, 'You get an ocean-going yacht with a helipad on it. But somewhere along the line, you get a private office, and that, like these other things, in its way, is a mark of showing ... you have made it to another level.' Having a family office is a signal to those in the know that a family has serious money.

My meeting with the Grosvenor Estate underlined the importance of inherited money still pervading these streets. So, I am following it to its handling stations: family offices, the private companies that manage the wealth of super-rich families. They are a key piece of the infrastructure for consolidating and transmitting money to future generations. The demand for these services is only increasing. In the last ten years, their numbers have exploded, alongside significant increases in individual wealth. *Forbes Magazine* reports that globally there has been a tenfold increase in single-family offices alone since the 2008 financial crash. Austerity accelerated inequality, and French economist Thomas Piketty argues that as wealth becomes ever more concentrated into fewer hands, the significance of dynastic wealth transmission increases.[1] Globally, there are an estimated 10,000 family offices operating today. With assets under management in excess of

$4 trillion,[2] they control a sizeable chunk of the world's wealth, and their operations have implications for national economies.

My departure point for this last Mayfair walk is The Connaught Hotel, as good an example as any of money on display: positioned on a little pedestrianized circus at Carlos Place. A large tree outside is periodically misted by a fountain; a Union Jack flag flies over an African doorman standing below in a top-hat uniform. I walk along Mount Street, pausing to review handbags in the window of Valextra – average price £2,500 – just opposite the Porsche dealership – average price, don't even bother. I mooch along Brook Street, Mayfair's most northerly main artery, also Grosvenor land. Claridge's, grander still than The Connaught, sits on the corner with Davies Street – the soft pink brick is shaded by a green awning. I pass Sunseeker, a leading distributor of second-hand yachts; the model boats in the window evoke in miniature a world of floating luxury at sea. Outside the rug shop Sahrai, I watch a uniformed chauffeur cleaning the wheels of a Rolls-Royce with a tiny brush: both busy and waiting.

My research has revealed a concentration of family offices around Davies Street, but I can't find them. The brass plates and rows of buttons on the front doors give only numbers, and, sometimes, the names of companies, but no hint as to the kind of business. From the street, family offices are as opaque as all other instruments of serious money accumulation. Instead, a green plaque on the wall of one town house announces that Barry, Robin and Maurice Gibb – aka the Bee Gees – lived and composed their songs here, from 1968 to 1980.

On Charles Street, flanked by nineteenth-century town-house offices, the manager of a family office has agreed to meet me. Runner – who runs the office and the money management – is an investment expert from the world of private banking. He recalls a time when, a little like private members' clubs cultivating exclusivity, private banks looked down their noses at potential clients, evaluating the reputational risk of taking them on. A family coming into disrepute or banking money derived from less than impeccable sources would reflect badly on the bank. They are no longer so discriminating. The rise and rise of the super-rich has led to a burgeoning asset management industry. What exactly does Runner's family office do? 'We do a bit of asset management, we have a hedge fund, but it's really a family office, owned by a high-net-worth family.' Runner simplifies for me. 'All it is, is families who have a lot of money set up an office to help them manage it. It's as simple as that.' It is not as simple as that, though. What is it that they manage? 'It might be investing in hedge funds,' he says. 'It might be investing directly in a company start-up [private equity]. It might be all kinds of things, but the point is, let's say you're actually in the billionaire class, it's worth your while to actually employ a group of people to help you run that money.' Serious money needs looking after and putting to work. Runner joins the dots for me: hedge funds, private equity firms and family offices are interlocking infrastructures that expand, consolidate and transfer money. It is not unusual for a hedge fund to downsize and morph into a family office, as it gives up managing the money of several other entities to focus solely on one or two clients.

Whose money does Runner run? He is understandably reluctant to say, having doubtless signed a non-disclosure agreement. But he hints, and later admits, that he specializes in Middle Eastern royalty, and, I suspect, this describes the clients of this family office, although he doesn't confirm it. Instead he says: 'These Arab royal families are very grand. I mean they are not just rich; the Abu Dhabi royal family are rich beyond imagination.' Very serious money indeed. I am left to draw my own conclusions.

The skills he has mastered while working for rich families have enriched Runner in turn. Runner is much more willing to talk to me about his spin-off property development business than he is about family offices, and so I let the conversation move in this direction for a while, to see where it might lead. He and his wife run a business that specializes in providing the flawless perfection required by ultra-high-net-worth buyers. They currently have a big project in Notting Hill, he says. His customers come in waves: Middle Eastern, Russian and, more recently, Chinese, as well as a few locals. Research by the economist Christobel Young reveals that, while plutocrats are not especially geographically mobile, those who move to cities like London come from poorer or more authoritarian home regimes, or, as in the case of Middle Eastern potentates, *are* the regime. The UK government doesn't ask difficult questions about the social inequalities of oil economies, or the human rights abuses of autocratic governments.

Runner says the market for properties around the £50 million mark is hot with overseas buyers. He volunteers without my prompting that this market has been negatively affected by new anti-money-laundering regulations that came into force on 1 January 2020, and so, unexpectedly, takes me to the issues at the heart of the London property market. He reasons, 'Whether all that money is clean, who knows? Some of it is and some of it isn't, I guess.' London property is a safe place to store money, and his admission that some of it comes through criminal activity is confirmed by recent reports of investigative journalists.[3] As one CNBC report put it, 'London property is a compelling choice for criminals looking to make dirty money clean.'[4] But Runner needn't worry too much: London real estate agents are struggling to implement the new anti-money-laundering regulations. In July 2020, the 'Russia Report' of the UK parliamentary Intelligence and Security Committee raised concerns about the extent of Russian money and influence. Is London a Russian laundromat? Ironically, Runner suggests that London is valued for its rule of law. The United Kingdom has a strong legal apparatus that can be used to defend assets – *however they are accumulated*, potentially including the gains of mafia, drug and criminal activity – with due process. The lines separating illicit and legal money are fuzzier than might be imagined, and family offices do their best to keep them that way. Distinction between what is legal, ethical and possible are kept deliberately blurred by those who are served by this obscurity.

The secrecy that hides such illegal activities as crime and tax evasion also enables legal, if morally dubious, purposes like tax avoidance. London is internationally renowned for its expertise in hiding money. The Panama Papers, the files of the Panamanian law firm Mossack Fonseca, leaked in 2016, exposed this.[5] These files reveal that Mossack specialized in advising clients how to hide their wealth through sequences of shell companies and offshore jurisdictions, making it effectively untraceable. The International Consortium of Investigative Journalists (ICIJ) reports that the United Kingdom – London – is high on a list of intermediary countries that facilitate these processes with banking, legal and other services, supporting clients of Mossack looking to set up trusts and make use of offshore money hideaways. The ICIJ declared that 'the UK boasts an unrivalled tax-avoidance industry'[6].

On the UK land registry list of overseas property-owners, 2,800 Mossack clients appear. Among them are associates of Bashar al-Assad, the Syrian president who unleashed a bloody civil war on his citizens.[7] By 2016, as many as 36,342 high-end London properties were held by offshore registered companies.[8] Subsequent investigations released as the Paradise Papers (2017) and the Pandora Papers (2021) only serve to consolidate this reputation, with still more damning evidence and examples of complicity by politicians. From his desk at the family office and his property company, Runner is witnessing just the tip of an iceberg.

Runner certainly does not knowingly manage money on the run looking for a safe harbour, but other property developers may be less discriminating. Nevertheless, expensive properties that keep rising in value are a crucial piece in the infrastructure underpinning plutocratic life in London for the local and international elite alike. For foreign buyers, legal questions aside, part of the appeal is what Runner calls the 'dream of English country life': 'English aristocratic life has an enduring appeal. The rich have always had big estates.' I think about the mannequins in tweed in the Mayfair shop window. Maybe even plutocrats want something to aspire to, although the nineteenth century seems an odd choice. And grand estates need grand families to fill them, and, in turn, family offices to run them.

I try to turn our conversation back to Runner's day job, but what few leads I have run into a wall of confidentiality. He just manages money for a rich family: end of story. He invests it to make it grow. Family offices are a private wealth advisory service to the superwealthy. It is as simple as that. Or it is as murky and complicated as that. I will need to search elsewhere to find out more. As I leave Runner's office, a thought is forming at the back of my mind, unacknowledged. We are contemporaries. We both graduated with a PhD at the same time in the eighties when there were few academic jobs. From the same starting point, we have each ended up in radically different places. He turned these same qualifications into big money. I teach in a university and write about it. No regrets. But it surprises me that I did not even notice the pathway he took as an option. How purposeful, specific and blinkered are the routes we tread through the city.

My next contact is still less eager to speak about family offices than Runner. Meet Walker. As we sit in his Mayfair office nearby, Walker explains that no one can agree on what a family office is. They do all sorts of things in the plutocrat service sector. At its most basic level, he says, 'A family office is an in-house network of legal and financial professionals, who protect and grow money and advise on the best ways of passing it tax-efficiently to future generations.' Family offices create the next generation of plutocrats' money. Of course, wealthy families could also buy these services directly from individual specialist firms, but bringing experts in house into a family office ensures a bespoke service over which they have better control. And this is their appeal, along with higher levels of security and privacy.

Walker distinguishes multi-family offices, which run the money of several wealthy families, from single-family offices, like Runner's – and indeed His Grace's, which serves only his own wealthy family. Financial experts estimate that the entry price into multi-family offices starts at $100 million, rising to $250 million for single-family offices. Whatever their size, Walker says that the first job of the family office is to 'mind the money', to make sure it doesn't get lost or wasted. This means, among other things, keeping an eye out for predators, and potential overcharging. Is the yacht skipper on the take from suppliers? Is the art adviser getting kick-backs from the gallery? The second job of a family office is to mind the family. This is a much more complex task.

Despite the growing number of family offices, we know little about them. Anthropologist Luna Glucksberg managed to get invited to a family office conference in Switzerland, for deeper insight.[9] Glucksberg learned that the trickiest part of the job is the concierge services some family offices perform, which one of her informants referred to as 'walking the dog'. 'Walking the dog' includes packing bags for international trips to families' other homes. Glucksberg's family office informants tell her that their rich employers have as many of the same pairs of shoes as they have residences, and everything is replicated to keep the surroundings constant and familiar in the shifting landscapes of mobile lives. The same kinds of socks must be in the same drawer in each home, or even on the yacht. Other examples of 'walking the dog' Glucksberg heard included rescuing a grandmother who was taken ill on a walking tour in Nepal, and organizing legal assistance for young adult children when their wilder antics got them into trouble on a luxury holiday.

Family offices ease the path of serious money at every turn; they untangle the complex administrative details that such large amounts of money entail. They make life for the rich work smoothly, and, sometimes, this includes practical problem-solving and responding to family emergencies. Social commentator Peter York refers to family office workers as 'very superior butler types', since many of them, he says, are 'well-bred Brits'.[10] It takes more than a financial expert to run a family office. Through these personal services, Glucksberg's informants build intimate and trusting relationships with their clients. Or so they believe.

At the Swiss family office conference – which one of Glucksberg's female family officers described as 'male and pale' – attendees found that 'walking the dog' is tricky to get right and difficult to monetize. The value of these services, like so much else in wealthy lives, is indeterminate. But the greater difficulty, family officers agreed, is managing the family itself. Money and emotional life entwine; indeed, money reroutes emotion around its own imperatives and shapes how it is experienced. To better understand the families and navigate working with them, one conference presenter constructed a typology of wealthy families. The most difficult, he suggested, are families that dislike and are constantly in conflict with each other. Undoubtedly. A second type is the 'value-driven' family, who like each other and 'operate through emotion'. (Surely family life is all about emotion?) The third type, the 'vision-driven' and the 'future-facing' family, which is open to the reasoning and guidance of the family office, unsurprisingly, is the preferred type. Glucksberg doesn't comment on this, but the typology transforms families into something akin to brand identities, or perhaps operating systems, making them more interpretable to those who run their affairs. It turns wealthy families into businesses, and, indeed, for family offices, this is what wealthy families are: rapidly expanding and very profitable businesses.

UBS's 'Global Family Office Report', which claims to be the most extensive study of family office clients and service providers, finds that the average family office in 2017 spent $11 million on operational costs and investment fees: presumably this includes their own fees.[11] But UBS insists these costs – skimmed from serious money – are worth it. The report confirms that family offices are a successful way to increase family money, suggesting they secure twice the usual return on capital invested (15 per cent). This handsome profit accrued to the already rich is driven by investments in equities (shares), with private equity dominating returns, followed by real estate. Rising property values and private money – already key drivers of serious money's accumulation – are solidified through family offices and their phalanx of experts. No wonder family offices are hard to track down: they are reluctant to draw attention to the mechanisms which manage and transmit dynastic wealth so profitably.

There are aspects of families and wealth I feel I still don't understand, and I would like to learn more about the legal side of these complex operations. This takes me from the streets of Mayfair to the Inns of Court in Holborn, just over a mile away. I hop on the 98 bus to meet Wig at his office. The Inns are an oasis of calm in the heart of London, reminiscent of an Oxbridge college, with large green quadrangles. They are also a handy service centre for serious money, not far from its Mayfair engine room. Through a substantial black door with a brass knocker into a grand-looking town house, past yet another smiling woman receptionist downstairs, I climb to the top of a nineteenth-century building. Where the house narrows and the ceilings become lower, I find Wig at his desk behind an enormous pile of papers. I met Wig by chance just a few weeks earlier at a concert by a band in Islington Town Hall. Rather more hip at 70 than I imagined a Queen's Counsel (QC) and judge would be, he works with family offices on trusts and prenups.

What do family offices do from Wig's perspective? A family office, he tells me, will coordinate the activities of managing your wealth: getting the tax advice, which you will undoubtedly need on an ongoing basis, and managing a wider network of tax advisers. In addition, 'You will also have some kind of in-house investment person, who will coordinate various kinds of investment activities, and you will also probably have somebody who runs, or at least assists in running, the family foundation.' The family office, as I have already discovered, also does day-to-day admin. 'It will make sure there is money on your wife's and mistresses' credit cards; it'll pay your children's college fees, the staff of your various houses, and look after the repairs of your various houses, the repairs and servicing of your cars, your yacht and your plane.' It will 'walk the dog'. The workings of serious money are so elaborate that it takes an entire office of professionals to run them.

A family office, he continues, manages the managers. 'It means there is an additional layer of management between you and the money.' Wig tells me the story of a friend who runs a family office for an extremely wealthy Middle Eastern family. While his friend is rewarded well enough to live in a grand house in Chelsea and have a chauffeur-driven car, he is expected to be on call twenty-four hours a day. 'One of his main jobs is to make sure that the boss wasn't being ripped off. He's somebody you would trust with your grandmother's or your children's lives.'

Wig comes in as an expert in family law. He advises on the loopholes that marriage and divorce create in family trusts. Family trusts are legal ruses protecting assets from taxation. There are different kinds of trusts, but in essence they are arrangements in which a 'settlor' – the wealthy donor – gives power to a third party, a trustee, to ring-fence assets for the future use of beneficiaries, who can often only access the funds once they have reached a certain age. There are rules about how trusts can be run. But they are essentially legal and financial instruments for passing money on to future generations while avoiding inheritance tax. All sorts of moderately well-off people use them, but, as their benefits magnify with levels of wealth, they are a useful tool for preserving the money of plutocrats and keeping it in the family at the expense of public finances.

Divorce, Wig's speciality, can disrupt the smooth transmission of money. When families are setting up or restructuring trusts, he says, 'I advise on the potential for a spouse to be able to make a claim against the trust assets, in the event of the marriage of one of the beneficiaries of the trust breaking down.' He mentions a client he had a few years ago: 'I was advising a Russian, quite a complex trust structure. He had two daughters. Neither of them was actually thinking of getting married. They were student age.' But, 'He wanted to have in-depth advice about how to structure the trust, so as to minimize the risk of any spouse being able to claim against their interests in the family trust, if and when they got married.' Careful structuring can protect trusts from claims on family assets. One of Glucksberg's family officers made a joke about in-laws, or, as he put it, 'outlaws', getting their hands on the money.

Prenuptial agreements are another way of protecting family money. Wig gives me an example from a case he is currently working on. 'This couple is getting married in July.' Neither is a British national. They are both from other European countries. 'I am for [representing] the prospective husband. And again, I simply don't know what this family are worth, but I suspect we are talking in the hundreds of millions. And, you know, he is a perfectly nice young man, about the same age as my son [30 years old], but he is obsessed with preserving the family money.' This means consulting lawyers in several different countries, to see whether they can just 'increase the odds in his favour', in the event of the marriage breaking down. 'And if he can't get what he regards as a satisfactory prenup, I don't think he is going to go through with the wedding.' This is a deal-breaker then, and further insight into the complicated entanglements of money and emotion. Prenups, Wig says, are now more likely to be upheld in English courts if previous decisions and settlements create a precedent. While they are not legally binding, because they are not understood to be equivalent to a commercial contract, 'They are given much greater weight and it is much harder to get out of them than it was before.'

Trusts go further than protecting family money against claims. They can also be vehicles for everlasting life. Wig says of the Russian he described earlier: 'He was trying to achieve immortality through his trust. He wanted the money to cascade down through the generations. To set his imprint on how it would be spent.' Some of his aims were perfectly good ideas, Wig says. 'He didn't want his kids spoilt and so on. He wanted to preserve the money, and he wanted to preserve it long after his death.' He intended to die 'knowing that future generations – several future generations of his family – would look back to him as the founding patriarch, and would be obliged to spend money in ways which he, long dead, would approve of'.

Can plutocrats freely pursue these tactics of hubris and control; can they live beyond the grave through legal instruments controlling money? The money, says Wig, is actually controlled by the trustees of the trust, as I discovered with the Grosvenor Estate. The person who sets up the trust, the settlor, can write a 'letter of wishes', which doesn't force the decisions of the trustees, who retain discretion over the money, 'But in practice it gives them guidance which they are highly likely to follow,' Wig says. 'Historically one of the reasons that the whole legal structure of trusts evolved in English law was to protect family fortunes, and in particular to protect fortunes against depredations of spendthrift sons.' And so, 'In a sense this is a continuation of what trusts have always been about. Rich people can do what they want.' He gives the example of a beneficiary's heroin or gambling addiction as a valid reason for controlling the flow of funds. Trusts allow much greater control over relatives' behaviour than could usually be exercised, and provide another example of the entanglements of money and emotion.

Succession planning excites family office workers and wealth managers. The UBS's survey shows that 43 per cent of family offices have succession plans in place, and 70 per cent of offices said they expected the 'next generation' to 'take control' in the next ten years. Given the current astronomical levels of wealth under management, this is set to be the biggest transfer of wealth in history, its potential impact on cities like London yet to be understood. My question to Buffer about whether His Grace might live with his wealth differently was informed by the magnitude of this transfer and the question as to whether big social changes to life in London can be expected as a result. Or will it be business as usual? UBS suggests that what it calls 'purpose driven wealth' is on the rise, that there is increasing interest in what they call 'impact investing'. This means investments that benefit society and the environment, while, of course, seeking the usual levels of return. Investigator, the lawyer who reported from inside 5 Hertford Street, says that equity investments are usually mixed bundles, making it difficult to disentangle socially and environmentally beneficial investing from the rest. The balance in the bundle is crucial. Also, she believes, there is an argument for choosing to invest in less ethical sectors rather than abandoning them completely, that is to gain the kind of leverage that can drive change.

One of the wealthy families cited in the UBS survey said: 'Our duty is to leave something behind.' *When we build let us think we build for ever.* The language of social responsibility and environmental respect now dominates investment talk. I recall Blazer's championing of socially useful and ethical finance – once he had already made his money in private equity. Socially sensitive, ethical enterprise and notions of legacy provide a new language. This obscures the greed of finance money and insists that excessive wealth is acceptable, beneficial even, to society as a whole. Whether making the accumulation and transmission of wealth more palatable actually changes anything on the ground, driving more progressive and environmentally attuned causes, remains to be seen. These are either further obfuscations by serious money or moves in a more progressive direction. Time will tell.

Family offices feed on and manage the money raised by private equity, property speculation and hedge funds – Mayfair's inscrutable staples. Private equity and hedge funds, of course, are money-expanding games only rich people can afford to play. As I found earlier, they are predatory, they live on roadkill, on the failures and misfortunes of other enterprises. Family offices magnify these gains and in turn live on fees skimmed from money acquired in aggressive acts of accumulation. They also provide a means of growing, consolidating and transmitting dynastic wealth to future generations through careful succession planning: a string of currently perfectly legal ways of minimizing contributions to the public finances, which could be used to fund the National Health Service, education, welfare and so on. Family offices ensure that ever-growing piles of money remain in the hands of London's local–global plutocracy. Meanwhile, they also smooth the lives of people who are so rich that it takes an entire office of expert staff to manage their money. Family offices run the family and the family money. As Peter York says, unlike the Square Mile, Mayfair is transformed by finance in a far less conspicuous manner. Small companies have floors in anonymous, upgraded office blocks. They are so inconspicuous that '*Most people don't know they're there.*'[12] Well, they do now.

9

Working the Split

Wig has another story to tell me about divorce and taxes. I am still in his Lincoln's Inn office, looking down at the narrow streets, with barristers in flowing black robes, laden with documents, hurrying in, flitting in and out of doors to other offices, or heading towards the Central Criminal Court. Talking about inheritance has led us to another complication in wealthy family life. In the story, Wig's billionaire client was considering divorcing his wife. She didn't know yet, but as their relationship had been extremely difficult for many years, she must have suspected that divorce was a possibility. Wig's role was to advise him on the divorce, 'in conjunction with worldwide tax advisers'. The billionaire had to decide whether to pay the high cost involved in moving his money and his tax affairs offshore. While this would be expensive, it would also weaken the couple's connection to Britain, and this would make it more difficult for his wife to argue that their divorce petition should be heard under English law, which is comparatively generous to partners who are not directly involved in generating the money. A divorce under English law could cost him dearly. On the other hand, moving his money offshore would be costly too. Should he move his money or leave it where it was? Like worldwide tax advisers, such dilemmas only come with extreme wealth. Without wanting to diminish its emotional significance for this billionaire, divorce was a calculation with various possible financial outcomes and opportunities.

In the end, Wig's client decided that the cost of divorcing his wife was likely to be even greater than the cost of moving his tax affairs. Wig estimates that it could have cost the billionaire as much as £100 million to divorce under English law, as it adheres to the principle of fairness to both parties in division of marital assets, and takes into account money accumulated before, during and after a marriage. Taking Wig's advice, and with the steer of his international taxation experts, the billionaire moved his tax affairs offshore, potentially saving tens of millions of pounds. Because this divorce was widely reported in the UK national press at the time, Wig prefers not to name names, but intimates that he has dealt with a number of similar cases. However the billionaire's move is interpreted, his is an essentially instrumental, calculated and finance-centred approach to love and money. Large piles of money encourage – or perhaps require – self-protective calculations like these, even when there is more than enough of it to go around.

London's super-rich are no more likely to divorce than anyone else, but divorce opens oblique new angles onto their lives, revealing details that are otherwise obscured. Many of the super-rich I talk to are guarded – wary of giving too much away. Divorce leaves them exposed. It penetrates inside family homes and offices on London's wealthiest streets, stripping away the facades. The life of money is starkly revealed in the cold-blooded, forensic written judgements of the London High Court Family Division. I discovered this peculiar little treasure trove in Wig's office – and through it I found Genius and glimpsed the inner workings of a hedge fund. Wig showed me how to access divorce judgements in 'big-money cases', as one judge referred to them. And so, I got to rummage through these public documents full of small and fascinating details about the lives of London's plutocrats.

Wig specializes in the international dimensions of family law. He acts in cases where there is potential for divorce petitions to be heard in two jurisdictions, as in the case of the billionaire. His expertise responds to the realities of super-rich life, which often stretches across a global canvas. Drawn to London from all over the world, plutocrats can go jurisdiction shopping when it comes to such matters as divorce and taxes – official processes that ground most of us. Those rich enough to live in multiple homes across more than one nation state, and by extension, more than one divorce regime, use Wig's expertise in considering the jurisdictional possibilities – and the balance sheet of gains and losses – relating to divorcing in one place rather than another.

Wig explains that different countries have quite different approaches to divorce and financial settlements. Disputes arise when couples can't agree where to get divorced, because one regime is more favourable for one, and another for the other. 'In nine cases out of ten,' he says, 'the English regime will be more favourable for the claimant, which is to say, usually the wife. When I am acting for wives, I am usually trying to secure the jurisdiction in England. When I am acting for the husband, I am usually trying to secure the jurisdiction almost anywhere else in the world.' His big-money Russian clients will invariably institute divorce proceedings in Moscow rather than London, where courts are far more generous to wives. In these cases, large sums of money, sometimes hundreds of millions of pounds, are in contention.

Divorce petitions can only be heard in English courts if the parties have a substantial connection to English life. If they own property in London – in Wig's experience these are often houses in the range of £10 million to £30 million – and spend time there, then their divorce can be heard in London. But this isn't straightforward. He says London properties are often not held in the parties' own names, but by offshore companies. If a company is the owner, the property is defined as a business asset rather than a personal one, and only the basic rate of tax, that is, 20 per cent, is payable. This particular tax wheeze is available primarily to the rich. Otherwise, 'The primary test for jurisdiction in the UK and in other EU member states is habitual residence.' But, 'If somebody has got two or three or more homes around the world, the answer to that isn't always very obvious.'

Wig gives the example of a Lebanese multi-millionaire. It was obvious that his main home was in London, where he spent most of his time. However, 'He'd set up his tax affairs so that he wasn't resident in the UK for tax purposes.' His lawyers were relying on this to make the case that his divorce should be heard in Lebanon – where he also has a home, in addition to another in the south of France – and not London. Wig was 'for the wife'. He says that how people divide their time is important in establishing a substantial connection. Sometimes, there are 'telling details' which reveal 'the truth'. The Lebanese man had a shotgun certificate. This is only legal if the gun owner is resident at the address on the licence. It is a criminal offence under the Firearms Act to state that he was resident at his London address if he wasn't. Astonishingly, for a multi-millionaire, 'He also had a Freedom Pass.' This is the travel card that allows Londoners over 66 to travel free on London transport, a benefit only available to those who live in the city. Habitual residence refers to where your centre of interest is. 'Where do you keep your winter clothes in summer?' Seemingly insignificant details in fact ground lives otherwise routed through different jurisdictions and across national borders.

Even if all parties in big-money divorces agree on where the petition can be heard, fresh disputes arise over the amount of money that is up for grabs, what one judge called 'the kitty'. This complicates financial settlements, which English law requires to be 'fair' to both parties. Wig says that husbands will have a pretty clear idea about what the financial position is and may not be telling their wives or their lawyers 'the whole truth about it'. The wife 'may well have her suspicions that the husband is much richer than he is'. He may have bragged about his wealth at an earlier stage in their relationship, only to conceal it later. Wives, he has found, often don't know so much about the true financial position. 'They have often been controlled by wealthy husbands, who tend to be controlling people.' Wealthy women who stake everything on marriage and motherhood run these risks. On the other hand, the wives may want revenge, and this makes it difficult for them to advance reasonable demands. The truth about wealth, he says, is complicated. In the world of the uber-wealthy, money lacks clarity and integrity.

Offshore companies once again rescue the rich. It is difficult to accurately assess how much money there is to argue over when it is obscured by complex networks of offshore companies owned by trusts rather than people. Trusts shield beneficial owners of homes and companies from public view. 'You can have a trust in one country,' Wig explains, 'say the Cayman Islands. That trust will own a holding company, say in the British Virgin Islands. Then there will be intermediate subsidiary companies anywhere in the world. And then you've probably got, say, a Jersey company, somewhere a bit closer to home, which is the company that immediately owns the house.' As the immediate owner, it is the Jersey company that has to comply with the money-laundering regulations. He concludes that these 'fluid' and mobile business structures give the wealthy 'the maximum leverage in avoiding tax', and make them 'very experienced at shuffling money around'. This complicates following the money in uber-rich divorces.

For example, in a 2016 divorce judgement concerning a billionaire Malaysian couple resident in London, the judge described the billionaire's businesses as 'held within a spider's web of interrelated companies'. His business was made up of twenty-six main companies incorporated in Malaysia, Hong Kong, the British Virgin Islands and the United Kingdom, with smaller companies ranged below them. In the absence of hard data – which the husband failed to produce – the judge must estimate his real worth. He wants to pay £15 million in the divorce settlement. His wife wants £520 million. The judge says, 'She has never worked in the sense of "doing a job"', and that her husband exercised 'more than a normal measure of control over her'. He is controlling. She is aggrieved. Her court battle is only indirectly about the money: it is about anger, resentment and the entitlement this confers. His resistance is about losing control.

The judge describes this bitter four-year-long case as 'wasteful and extravagant litigation'. She says it has already cost £8.9 million in (UK) legal costs, quite apart from Malaysian costs, for the couple to argue about how much money they have. The judge notes, 'Whatever the precise extent of the husband's wealth, there is enough in the kitty for it to be said that they would be hard-pushed to spend it all in their lifetimes, even if they wanted to.' This is a marriage of over forty years and the couple are 70 (her) and 78 (him). Their settlement involves multiple UK properties as well as properties in other countries, in addition to what the judge calls the husband's 'business empire'. The opacity surrounding the money makes the wife suspicious that he has warehoused assets where they cannot be found. Shifting money around and hiding it might bring tax benefits and the benefits of secrecy. But it also breeds unease and mistrust in wealthy families, and divorce starkly reveals this.

Divorce further brings to light the extraordinary amounts of money and the luxurious lifestyles London plutocrats enjoy. The financial settlement of the long-term London-domiciled American wife of a Saudi billionaire, who lives between Riyadh and London, as well as places in between, gives a glimpse into excessive expenditure. She is her husband's second wife, a 54-year-old former model, who gave up work when she married ten years earlier. The billionaire's soon-to-be third wife is much younger, as was this wife when she replaced the first. In accordance with English law she argues that her divorce settlement should reflect the lifestyle she enjoyed during the marriage. This is how she describes it in court: 'It is difficult to convey the extraordinary level of luxury and opulence we were fortunate enough to enjoy. [Our lifestyle] was one that, because of the sheer expense required to maintain it, is only open to a very small number of families, even within the global ultra-wealthy.'

The court requires her to itemize this lifestyle, along with its cost. The judge suggests that she has no idea what her lifestyle costs as she's clearly never had to concern herself with actual money, which explains why she employs the accounting firm PWC to estimate it for her. They begin with her annual travel budget, which the judge says is in excess of £2.1 million per annum, including nearly £600,000 per annum for private jet charters. 'She is claiming nearly half a million pounds to rent a yacht for two weeks, just under £145,000 to provision it during the charter and a little short of £5,000 to tip the crew.' The judge continues, 'She plans to spend the October half term this year in Paris staying in the Presidential Suite at The Ritz at a cost of just under £250,000, plus a further £74,000 for the nanny's room. She is claiming a further £103,000 for two weeks in the south of France at the Hotel du Cap-Eden-Roc and a further £30,000-odd for the nanny's room on that holiday.' Only famous luxury hotels and travel by private yachts and planes will suffice.

The wife's next expense is personal maintenance, as required of a billionaire woman. The judge again: 'Her budget for clothing and jewellery is in excess of £1.02 million per annum including £40,000 for a new fur coat every year; £83,000 for fifteen new cocktail dresses every year; £80,000 for a special gown annually; £109,000 for seven haute couture dresses annually; £197,000 for two white-tie jewellery sets every year; and £79,000 on cocktail-dress jewellery sets every year.' The judge ploughs on: 'In addition, she seeks £58,000 for two luxury handbags every year; £23,000 for six casual handbags every year; and £35,000 on ten clutch handbags every year. Sunglasses will cost a further £4,000 per annum (fifteen new pairs every year). She has budgeted for two new sets of skiwear every season (including new helmets every year).' And then there are the shoes. 'She envisages buying fifty-four pairs of shoes a year, seven of which (for white tie events) will cost an annual sum just under £21,000.' And jewellery: 'A further £39,000 is needed for two new watches every year (to add to her existing collection of 43 valuable watches). She claims to need three new suitcases every year at a total cost of just under £15,000 and five new silk dressing gowns each year.' Plutocratic femininity doesn't come cheap, but fifty-four pairs of new shoes a year does seem a bit much. And wasteful: the judge wonders what happens to last year's stuff. The wife's body maintenance bill is pretty steep too. 'Her beauty costs include a sum of just under £94,000 per annum for treatments and £22,812 on products, including £9,400 per annum on four bottles of face cream.'

To support this lifestyle the billionaire woman needs a full complement of serving staff. The judge finds: 'Her staff costs are exceptionally high at £335,558 per annum. She claims to need in her London home a live-in butler, housekeeper, nanny and chauffeur.' This in turn means, 'Her London property will need a separate annex or wing to accommodate these staff.' Her live-out staff include two cleaners, a chef, a reserve nanny and an office manager. 'She has budgeted for two live-in cleaners at the home in Henley, which she wishes to purchase despite planning to spend only forty-three days a year in the property.' Her budget includes 'staff at her Beverly Hills home, where she claims to need three housekeepers and extra staff when the family visits'. The billionaire wife anticipates keeping three fully staffed homes, even though two of them are only for occasional use.

There is more. 'Her mobile telephone is estimated at £26,000 per annum.' Her leisure and entertaining budget includes '£50,000 for Christmas lunch and a further £50,000 for each of her and her daughter's birthday parties every year; [and] £21,000 for theatres and shows'. She needs £28,000 for Wimbledon tickets and £18,000 for a box at Ascot, as well as '£10,000 per annum to attend Elton John's White Tie Ball'. Who knew that Elton John represented an essential part of billionaire entertainment? The wife estimates the cost of a London property is £68 million, in addition to another in Henley, just 40 miles away. Billionaire life requires five cars and three houses. The judge awards her a settlement including maintenance of £53 million.

This is much less than the £500 million plus she asked for. And it was much more than her husband wanted to give: he was keen to maintain some sort of parity with his first wife's settlement. In deciding on the settlement, the judge rules that standards of living enjoyed during the marriage are 'relevant but not decisive'. The judge – otherwise cold and factual in her pronouncements – finds it hard to suppress her incredulity at the sheer waste and extravagance of the itemized lifestyle she is presented with.

Of course, this is an extreme example. But it provides a rough guide to billionaire and multi-millionaire life in London: multiple houses, teams of staff, yachts, complex beauty regimes, excessive consumption. Such divorce judgements also complicate the idea that the rich live unusually mobile lives.[1] While their movements are not confined by monetary considerations, as most people's are, and they often own multiple homes and travel frequently in private luxury, they remain grounded by the same everyday mechanisms as everyone else. They get divorced – as well as send their children to schools, join gyms, obtain shotgun licences, acquire travel passes and pay taxes when they must – in a jurisdiction. Yet, even if the rich themselves are grounded, their money is not. Divorce shows how difficult it is to follow money and assess how much of it there is, when it is concealed in cascades of shell companies or through other offshore manoeuvres. Money is slippery and scheming. It covers its tracks. And it calculates comparative advantage, protecting itself in divorce, even when, as described, there is more of it than anyone can spend in a lifetime. In this way, extreme wealth brings mistrust and the constant possibility of betrayal into intimate relationships. Love and money are fatally entangled in wealthy lives. With these thoughts, I finally leave Wig's office, descending the steep stairs, and walk back into the still-quiet streets of London's legal quarter and plutocrat service centre.

Notting Hill and North Kensington

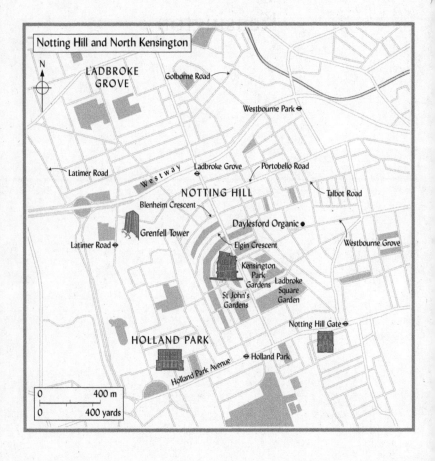

Notting Hill and North Kensington

N

LADBROKE GROVE

Golborne Road

Westbourne Park ⊖

Latimer Road

W e s t w a y

Ladbroke Grove ⊖

Portobello Road

NOTTING HILL

Talbot Road

Blenheim Crescent

Daylesford Organic ●

Grenfell Tower

Elgin Crescent

Westbourne Grove

Latimer Road ⊖

Kensington Park Gardens

Ladbroke Square Garden

St John's Gardens

Notting Hill Gate ⊖

HOLLAND PARK

⊖ Holland Park

Holland Park Avenue

0   400 m

0   400 yards

10

The Burning Tower

I first caught sight of it in the distance. Surprised, because I didn't know it was visible from the train I was on, the westbound Overground train to Clapham, just outside Shepherd's Bush. I was looking out of the window, thinking about something else. I'd resisted going to look at it up-close, even though it was in a part of plutocratic London I intended to walk around and write about, after my walks in Mayfair. I didn't want to appear ghoulish, or a sightseer, or a chronicler of tragedies, so I stayed away. But there it was – unmistakable. Grenfell Tower, black and charred at the top, like a partially decayed tooth, rising from streets I could barely make out from the train as it moved west.

Few neighbourhoods reveal themselves as suddenly and dramatically as Grenfell Tower and the North Kensington area of Notting Hill. The Tower, consumed by flames on the night of 14 June 2017, cracked open to the sky and to the streets below. It provided a rare, raw and intimate view of this deprived splinter in one of London's wealthiest neighbourhoods. Residents able to escape, many abruptly awakened from sleep in the early hours, had to scramble through the stairwell filled with smoke, bodies, firefighters, hoses and general pandemonium, emerging into the street, and into the spotlight of local and global media.

Grenfell Tower was built in 1974, as social housing, in the north end of the Royal Borough of Kensington and Chelsea, on Latimer Road, next to the elevated Westway motorway. The Tower was only ever a meagre instalment in social housing, intended to mollify locals struggling against dilapidation and overcrowding in the area, dating back to the 1940s. It was in this landscape that the infamous slum landlord Peter Rachman built his property empire in the 1950s, on the crumbling foundations of Notting Hill's decaying housing stock. By subdividing houses into single-room apartments and letting them furnished, to put them beyond the rent controls that operated at the time, Rachman created a squalid, overcrowded and extremely valuable property portfolio.[1] The story of Grenfell Tower is part of an ongoing legacy of extreme housing inequalities, shortages, exploitation and neglect.

Seventy-one residents died from burns and asphyxiation in the early hours of 14 June. Survivors were temporarily rehoused, some in hotels, while the Royal Borough scrambled to conceive and implement long-term solutions. Theresa May, the then prime minister, ordered a public inquiry, as controversy raged about what had happened, why and, most importantly, who was to blame. Angry, grieving residents, supported by local housing campaigners and activists, fought for justice from a local authority who had been refusing for years to respond adequately to their concerns about fire safety and the governance of the building.[2] Against this highly charged and charred backdrop, I began walking Notting Hill in the months following the fire. Grenfell Tower was emblematic – it epitomized London's housing polarities.

Less than four miles north-west of Mayfair, Notting Hill is, 'an area of the UK with the highest discrepancy in wealth distribution', acknowledged one of the local charities at the forefront of the Grenfell relief effort. This assessment is repeated many times in my discussions with wealthy people who live in this area. The Royal Borough has London's highest discrepancy in income, followed by the Borough of Westminster,[3] which hosts His Grace's acres. Wealth, of course, is different from income, which is just one source of wealth, but it is not calculated by borough, so income is all we have to go on. Everyone knew about Notting Hill's deep inequalities – the gaping chasm in the neighbourhood – but the burning Tower illuminates it in such a way that it can no longer be ignored and has to be confronted, if briefly.

Because these walks follow the money, my focus is on Notting Hill's wealthiest residents, and not the low-income community that lived in and around Grenfell. I make contact with several wealthy women at the local community centre, where they volunteer. Together with other charities and churches with premises near the Tower, the centre opened before dawn on 14 June as a refuge and recuperation stop for shocked and grief-stricken neighbours, so suddenly made homeless, with just the clothes they stood up in. The Tower is part of every conversation we have; it is what everybody is talking about in the weeks and months following the fire. One wealthy volunteer agrees to talk about it some more, and I sit waiting for her in Daylesford Deli and Café on Westbourne Grove, a Notting Hill staple on its main drag. It is a place to stock up on posh cheese, charcuterie and olive oil, or pause for a freshly brewed pot of leaf tea or coffee, lunch, or a cold pressed juice on the way home from yoga. Dads and mums with strollers, dressed casually, fill the café with syncopated conversation, as they navigate the competing requirements of adult talk and the demands of their tiny charges.

Palace – because she is descended from ancestors who lived in one – arrives in a rush, apologizing for being 'disorganized'. I'm sure she isn't. She is in her early forties but looks much younger. With a blonde ponytail and intense blue eyes, she's wearing a blue denim pencil skirt, a white broderie anglaise blouse and flat suede shoes in an expensive shade of burnt orange. She is open and warm, solicitous, kind, perhaps sensing that I am a bit nervous about talking to her. I hadn't expected her to be so modest and ordinary; perhaps humility is easier to cultivate with an aristocratic lineage.

Palace describes the burning Tower as the 'defining story' of the area. 'I think how other people live within the community was brought into stark relief,' she says. 'It made a lot of people feel very uncomfortable and very guilty. Everything about it was complicated and goes on being complicated.' She says she more or less moved into the community centre for about a month. 'And I felt really privileged and lucky that I was there. It was an extraordinary experience. I have never felt closer to everyone that lived around me, and everyone who went through what they went through.' Grenfell was a brief moment when 'Everyone put down what they were doing and went to see what they could do to help. It was really magical actually, in the face of obvious destruction and horror.' She describes it as a 'life-affirming' experience – a time of connection, in an intense, emotionally charged atmosphere she shared daily with bereaved neighbours. Of course, Palace already understood the social fault lines that ran through her neighbourhood; but she would not have lived with them intimately without the fire, nor gained such a sense of obligation to her neighbours in difficult circumstances.

In the days after the fire, Palace ran the 'shop' that distributed clothes and other items crucial to daily survival. 'In pure Notting Hill style, everyone wanted to help,' she remembers. But most of the donations were inappropriate: 'There is only so much a large lady of Muslim origin can do with a tiny Gucci handbag or dirty socks.' They stopped the donations and bought new clothes instead. To free herself from her usual duties on the home front, Palace enlisted 'extra help' with her four small children. Her husband was dispatched to the Oxford Street branch of Primark to buy 150 new bras. 'One woman said to me in disgust "I don't want someone else's clothes".' It was then Palace realized that these were not 'refugees' begging. 'They were people who had jobs, houses, belongings, and they were very proud of them. And they didn't want someone else's shit.' First lesson: the poor, too, have dignity. Yet her refugee reference is not entirely misplaced. Many of those who scrambled to escape the flames on that night had originally arrived in London as asylum seekers from the Middle East, North and East Africa, and Afghanistan, according to the official inquiry into the fire, which praised 'a vibrant community with a strong sense of identity and social cohesion'.[4] This was the inquiry's way of saying that these are 'good', integrated and hence deserving migrants, to distinguish them from other kinds of migrants – the sort who might arrive in boats, criticized in the tabloid newspapers and made to feel unwelcome.

The online clothing store Boden, owned by Palace's friends, donated clothes. New T-shirts and leggings arrived to dress people dispossessed, with nothing but their nightwear. Local business-owners sent white goods and other essentials for temporary homes. Financial donations were used to buy Sainsbury's cash cards, which could be exchanged for 'knickers' and other essentials. 'But they [the survivors] were traumatized', which makes it hard to shop. Phone chargers were in high demand. Everyone had someone they needed to call, to convey reassurance or bad news. Hijabs were supplied by the local mosque – with cruel timing, the fire was during the holy month of Ramadan. With the Tower continuing to burn for another day and night, Palace says it was chaos: 'People were just wailing in the streets.'

In Palace's story, the burning Tower was an indelible moment of trauma and social awareness. It brought neighbours she and her friends rarely encountered – abruptly, fleetingly, and vividly – into the fabric of their lives. On this night, the parallel tramlines of the rich and poor, along which the neighbourhood normally ran, suddenly, dramatically and momentarily crossed, as millionaires, billionaires and aristocrats came face to face with social tenants over the fire, its causes and implications. The experience, devastating for so many, gave wealthy volunteers their first practical experience of the social diversities of their neighbourhood.

Palace and her husband own a house just streets away from the Tower, close to the Blenheim estate and its social tenants, not the most upmarket end of the neighbourhood. On the night of the fire, she jumped out of bed when she saw the flames from her window and heard the helicopters circling overhead, and went to see what she could do to help those who had 'lost everything'. She spoke to a woman in a brown dressing gown, who lived with her family on the ninth floor. The woman was disoriented, having found her way down the stairs but lost track of her husband on the way. She kept asking Palace if her husband could be at the top of the building, and would he be rescued? He wasn't. Palace says, 'I kept in touch with her for a bit, but I don't think she really wanted me to.' The chasm between rich and poor narrowed in the immediate aftermath of the fire, as lives entwined; and then reopened as social inequalities as usual were resumed.

While Palace affirms, 'I've never been more proud and pleased to be part of this neighbourhood,' she also knows, 'I am a part of the very fabric of a lot of what the anger is directed towards.' If this anger was previously suppressed in the daily life of the area, the fire quickly revealed it. From all directions, Notting Hill's most privileged became a legitimate target for grief and anger. Her kids' private school was about to take over a local public building when the fire broke out. 'The optics on that looked so bad that we backed out of the deal,' she states baldly. 'So we do feel anger in that way, the privileged versus the non-privileged. But my experience of dealing with people from Grenfell Tower was not that at all.' Not everyone shared in her in-this-together outlook. Local housing activists with long experience of struggling against the Royal Borough blamed their fatal carelessness, cutting corners and costs by refurbishing the Tower using dangerous flammable cladding. National and international media repeated this analysis in different ways. On 17 June 2017, *The Sun* newspaper headline stated, 'It was murder.' Even the conservative *Daily Telegraph* said the fire was a 'disaster waiting to happen'.

Second lesson. The rich are popularly perceived as the living embodiment of wealth inequality and thus become the focus of public anger. Housing activists characterize them as posh white English toffs with double-barrelled names.[5] They elect Conservative local councils and governments that choose to neglect social housing. Their comparatively modest council-tax bills in relation to their wealth, opens them to the accusation that they are beneficiaries of the Royal Borough's unsafe, cheap social-housing refurbishments, as well as the cause of artificially inflated house prices in the area. Finding themselves at the centre of this political storm creates uneasiness among some of the more liberal-minded wealthy residents, who recognize the gaping disparities between neighbours, and their own part in generating them. However, this uneasiness has yet to translate into action, beyond volunteering.

Palace's brief, but significant, encounter with 'the other side of the neighbourhood', the side that she sees as 'deeply impoverished', has only increased her attachment to the area. She appreciates Notting Hill's 'social mix'. Social housing estates are part of this. Some of these properties are owned by the Notting Hill Housing Trust, which incidentally often houses its social tenants east to the London Borough of Hackney, where properties are cheaper. These out-of-borough housing investments are either a nifty piece of pragmatism or a sinister form of social cleansing, depending on how they are interpreted politically. Either way, social tenants are seen to provide social balance, which many of the women I spoke to appreciate. It is residents who are not wealthy who turn a plutocratic village into a 'normal' area. What Palace likes about 'the greatest neighbourhood in London' is buying vegetables on Portobello Road, dropping her children off at a local (private) primary school, going to the gym and 'having a generally lovely time'. Notting Hill is a great place to live, and the social tenants displaced by the fire agree with her.[6] They love it too, and they loved their flats, which were spacious by contemporary standards. When I push her on what goes into the Notting Hill 'mix', she reaches for occupational diversity: web developers, lawyers. 'There's a judge, there's an economist, there's writers, there's film-makers, restaurateurs.' 'Mixed' means a diverse combination of wealthy people and social housing tenants, with the poor lending authenticity to what would otherwise be a sterile plutocratic bubble.

Palace and her husband moved into the area in the late 1990s. She says this was just before the 'bankers discovered it'. She tells me that they are a part of the area's gentrification, a source of remorse but also pleasure: their house was a good investment. She isn't wrong, but, like the Boy in Shoreditch, she has elided several waves of gentrification into one.

Low-paid professionals, including teachers and social workers, moved out of the area as Palace moved in. First arriving in the 1970s, when it was affordable, these low-paid professionals set up nurseries and community projects like playgrounds. They were often feminists and other kinds of activists – supporters of progressive causes. In an earlier, 2012–15, sociological study (referenced in the Prelude) my colleagues and I interviewed some of them. These former residents praised housing activists and initiatives that developed the Royal Borough's social housing, creating the main bulwark against 'plutocratification'. Today 25 per cent of households in the Royal Borough live in social housing,[7] and some of this proportion is due to their efforts. They complained at the changes wealthier residents brought to the neighbourhood, at the invasion of Range Rovers and basement digs. And they sneered at 'investment bankers', while selling them their houses and shifting their own equity to other areas. These middle-class sales and renovations had themselves displaced poorer neighbours, who often lived in rented properties without an equity stake to cash in.

This dynamic is not exclusive to Notting Hill. Research by geographers Loretta Lees and Phil Hubbard reveals wide-scale displacement of social tenants across London, resisted by tenants' organizations, sometimes successfully.[8] Plans to 'redevelop' – demolish – 462 socially rented units on Sutton Estate near King's Road in Chelsea, and replace them with private homes, were challenged by the estate's tenants in 2019. The local council, perhaps still feeling the reverberations of the Tower, rejected the redevelopment plans proposed by Clarion Housing, the country's largest social housing association and property developer. Despite these grassroots efforts, Lees says that since 1997 54,263 units have been demolished, or slated for demolition, on social housing estates across London,[9] adding to what is already a crisis of affordable housing. Thus, the poor and those with modest incomes are edged out of the city on a tide of rising real estate and rental values. Whether in Notting Hill or Shoreditch, gentrification allows the rich to make the city in their own image, displacing the poor and tearing down their houses. It monetizes social inequalities through building and property development: the outcome of a housing market with no political constraints and no rent controls, which were removed in 1988.

Palace is one of the beneficiaries of this shift. After university, she worked as a freelance journalist until she married and had children; the youngest is still a baby. Her wedding was a society event. Her husband's job as a high-ranking legal professional limits his contribution to childcare and domestic life. That's down to Palace. She resents it a bit, but says, 'I've always had help and that has been lovely.' The help is a Filipina housekeeper to whom she subcontracts the domestic work she prefers not to do, while she focuses on her children, doing the school run, cooking and homework. 'It's lovely, but it only works if you're there, doing everything to do with the children, then *they* [the housekeeper] are there; picking up the slack.' To justify more domestic staff, she would need a job that earned enough to finance it.

While we are still talking, Palace receives a text from someone she is supposed to be meeting at the same time as me. Alongside her various parental and civic responsibilities, she is a local school governor, and there are many demands on her time. As we finish our tea, she leaves in the same flurry she arrived in, chastising herself again for being 'disorganized', for forgetting the appointment, and runs off to her other meeting. It is time to go and do what I have been dreading: stand beside the Tower and its sad stories.

From the Daylesford deli to Grenfell Tower is less than a mile. I walk along Westbourne Grove, past local boutiques and the chain clothes shops Paul Smith and AllSaints, then an estate agent offering rentals. I turn right onto the northern end of Portobello Road, a local tourism hotspot, complete with tacky souvenir shops and East Asian visitors taking photos. I go past a striking young woman wearing a black bowler hat, and turquoise satin skin-tight trousers and jacket. The streets have a young, funky, carnivalesque feel, a sense of performance and even celebrity. In many conversations about the area, women I spoke to would reel off the names of local celebrities they had spotted walking these streets – from Stella McCartney to Robbie Williams. This starry Notting Hill contrasts starkly with its deprived mid-twentieth-century past.

Then, Portobello Road and Golborne Road were the home of self-help organizations, including a law centre, which defended the local African Caribbean population from racial violence, police harassment and other, overtly racialized acts of discrimination. In 1958, the area erupted into racist violence, with groups of white young men assaulting black residents at random, chanting, 'Go home you black bastards.'[10] Nor could Notting Hill's black community rely on the police for justice: the area was the epicentre of the struggle between black migrants and Britain's racial state. Yet the community fought back and Notting Hill also became an important centre of black activism and intellectual debate linked to the Black Power Movement in the United States throughout the 1960s. Regular police raids on the Mangrove Restaurant, where Caribbean intellectuals and activists met from the late fifties,[11] culminated in the 1971 trial of the 'Mangrove Nine' for inciting a riot during a demonstration against police harassment. The trial – which was ultimately overturned – was a high-water mark in confrontations with the police and for Black Power activism.

Throughout the 1970s, these same streets suffered heavy-handed policing as 'sus law' was used to stop and search young black men,[12] further racializing them and their neighbourhood – blackness, danger and crime became connected in the popular imagination. The Notting Hill Carnival, intended as a joyful celebration of Caribbean culture, frequently, as I witnessed myself in my student days, ended in violent battles with police as night fell. Claudia Jones, who moved to London from Harlem, founded the *West Indian Gazette* and staged the first carnival, lived on nearby Tavistock Road. On these streets, battles for racial justice, and debates about African colonial freedom, slavery and black political rights, occurred on a daily basis. Apart from the Carnival, this historic presence is largely gone. As sociologist and activist Colin Prescod says in 'The "Rebel" History of the Grove', referring to the struggles around the Mangrove Restaurant: 'Our Grove became their Notting Hill.'[13]

Few signs of 'our Grove' remain. Turning left on Blenheim Crescent and crossing Clarendon Road, I wiggle through narrower streets until I am standing outside the leisure centre facing the Tower. There are signs instructing people to respect the dead and not to take photographs. Despite this, I watch photographers with serious equipment, documenting the scene, solemnly and respectfully. On a bench an older woman of African Caribbean origin sits alone weeping quietly. Another woman arrives and puts her arms around her. I stay for a while and stare in disbelief. I've read many accounts of that fateful night, but being here, even long after the event, I feel a deep sadness.

I force myself to head south again, away from the Westway in the direction of Westbourne Grove. I am soon walking through the grandest, most spacious and elegant part of North Kensington, Kensington Park Gardens. It is jarring, after standing beneath the burnt grey Tower, to be back in the world of white stucco, black spiked railings, uniform planters and uniform plants. Grand pillars mark entranceways to houses with substantial gardens front and back, giving the area a green leafy feel. Ladbroke Square Garden is fenced off – access is only for those with keys. It looks very Belgravia, very Grosvenor Estate, and perhaps this is its model, the model for properly plutocratic streets and house prices at this end of the neighbourhood. The house of the woman I am about to visit, her friend told me – just a short walk away from a social housing estate so neglected that it burned down – is worth £30 million.

When she answers the doorbell, Desk invites me into the most spectacular entrance hall I have ever seen. I am immobilized in the doorway as I try to take it in: of course, this is precisely the reaction this entrance to the domestic world of wealthy people was designed to evoke. This is interior design with no price limit: a hallway laid with large limestone flagstones, a grand stairway leading off the hall to the upper floors, and doors leading to other elegantly furnished rooms in all directions. My ridiculous reaction is mercifully cut short as I am ushered into Desk's vast office, just off the hall. In the middle of the room is a huge stylish desk. The study, lined with books and artwork, is where she works on her 'projects' and manages her home. We sit at a small circular glass table overlooking the street. I am constantly distracted by new discoveries, and have to keep dragging my attention back to our conversation. Windows on two sides flood the study with light. On one side, the windows overlook the street; on the other, there is a beautiful Japanese garden, designed on different levels so at no point is the entire garden visible at once. Desk is as well groomed as her home; in smart-casual trousers, with short, well-cut hair, she is businesslike, a bit wary and a little sparing on details. She is in her late fifties with two grown-up children – and a vast empty nest arranged over five floors.

I am seeing the private domestic life of private equity. Desk's husband's company, described by an industry insider as 'a phenomenal success', generates serious money. So much money, in fact, that they can give large amounts of it away and still own a yacht and an enormous house. Through their family foundation, they donate to both local and far-flung global charities. In addition to being significant patrons of London's visual-arts scene – these are the kind of people Arty told me about who keep public art galleries going – they see themselves as deeply engaged with matters of social justice. These people are rich, socially aware, generous to those less fortunate and deeply implicated in the predatory operations of private equity. Their money weaves a complex moral tapestry. Private equity often dismantles other businesses to enrich investors; the collapse of the department store Debenhams after a period in the control of private equity is a good example, although it had nothing to do with Desk's husband. When firms like these are deliberately run into the ground, jobs are lost and already precarious lives, lived on low wages, are made still more uncertain. Private equity funds just the kind of high-end consumption I briefly glimpsed in Desk's £30 million home. And sometimes it alleviates the difficulties of the poor – but only on their own terms.

Desk says they moved to this house because they knew the area well and liked it; and because, in South Kensington, where they lived before, such larger homes were not on offer, only apartments. They moved here in 2000 and spent two years renovating the house. Notting Hill is, in architectural terms, 'very sympathetic', Desk says, with 'generous sized family houses' – and 'communal gardens' running along behind the houses, where children can play without too much adult supervision. Besides its family orientation, she says what she likes about Notting Hill is: 'It is a neighbourhood of two sides. Where you have extreme wealth – some of the wealthiest people in the country live around here – and you have extreme poverty.' She pinpoints the Westway as a rough dividing line. 'As you walk north-west, where it cuts through the north of there, you have got serious deprivation. It certainly has an air of reality about it, a certain grittiness. It also has a sort of West Indian Caribbean culture. Actually, that all made for a very appealing mix.'

The 'mix' makes another appearance. In addition to its poverty and social housing, Notting Hill's troubled racist and black radical past adds to its attractions as a place for wealthy people of a certain progressive orientation to live. In these extraordinary calculations, poverty and racism become neighbourhood assets. Poverty and racial diversity are at least seen as positive, rather than synonymous with neighbourhood decay and blight, but the system that creates racism and poverty is never questioned. Less surprising assets include 'a number of very good private [prep] schools', like Bassett House, Wetherby and Norland Place. The area also has 'a sort of English bedrock to it, in a way that I would say other affluent areas don't'. It's not all Middle Eastern sheikhs and Russian oligarchs. Europeans and Americans too – wealthy white folk – are immediate neighbours. Most, she says, work in finance, accounting and law, or own businesses.

Desk was a middle-class girl from the Home Counties, who worked until she married. Like Palace, 'Since then I haven't actually worked, but I have done a lot of voluntary work', raising funds for public art galleries and community work. 'I think one has to be doing something,' she says: through 'voluntary work, family, husband, children, home', she keeps busy, believes life *should* be busy, filled with purposeful activity. It is becoming apparent through these walks that the rich are not idle, though they choose how to be productive. While Desk cooks and shops, she is helped by: a housekeeper, who also walks the dog; a part-time cleaner, whose daughter lived in the Tower; and a part-time gardener. A major benefactor of the community centre, her Grenfell role involved answering the phones in the days after the fire. She is angry at what she sees as unfair criticism levelled at the local council. Some of the councillors, who attracted a storm of criticism for their cost-cutting refurbishment and slowness to act in the crisis, are her friends. She knows that they were more active behind the scenes than the media's portrayal suggests. She is also defensive about the wealthy in the borough being the targets of local housing activists' anger. I detect her profound uneasiness, and I leave the same way as I arrived, through her spectacular front hallway and back onto the street, through what had felt like the door to another world. It was.

The community centre represented such a door for Palace and Desk: a portal into a world of suffering and poverty. I go back to the centre to speak to one of its organizers, find out more about its rich benefactors, and learn of its capacity for mobilizing money and effort. I find out that being small and nimble, the centre can gather resources from several directions at once, including from the budgets of larger charities. They have 120 volunteers who are wealthy enough to have poured money on the flames at a time when it was needed most. Wealthy volunteers plugged the gap left by a steep decline in government funding. The centre was once 80 per cent local government funded. Now it is 90 per cent privately funded. In a political context where successive governments have been reluctant to tax the wealthy or curb their money-hiding activities to boost the public finances, local plutocrats both contribute to the wealth disparities of the area and provide a small-scale, privatized solution to them at the same time. Charities allow women to combine largesse and work: ways of inhabiting privilege that show moral worth, as Rachel Sherman found in her Manhattan super-rich study (referenced in Chapter 6).

Grenfell Tower's 2016 refurbishment lies at the centre of the controversy about the disaster. Aluminium panels filled with a plastic material – described by the BBC as a material popular in 'cost-conscious council refurbishment schemes'[14] – were used on the building's exterior. The official inquiry into the fire concluded that: 'The principal reason why the fire spread so rapidly, up, down and around the building, was the presence of the composite aluminium material (ACM) rainscreen panels with polyethylene cores, which acted as a source of fuel.'[15] The combustibility of the refurbishing materials combined fatally with what the official inquiry identified as a muddled and delayed reaction by the London Fire Brigade. It concluded that officers in command were not adequately trained for the challenges posed by the fire. Some of their equipment was unreliable and some didn't work at all. Funding retrenchments had cut deep into what the fire service could muster. The burning Tower exposed the lethal consequences of austerity measures that local councils were forced to implement from 2010, in the squeeze on public spending that followed the financial crisis of 2008.

The public sector's loss is always a private-sector gain, and the privatization of formerly public services also played a part in the tragedy.[16] Fire-testing materials is now subcontracted to the private Building Research Establishment (BRE), which is financially entwined with the companies whose material they test, as the state divests itself of former responsibilities. Building regulations and purview over fire safety by this time were also privatized and not properly enforced. As one letter to the *London Review of Books* put it, 'The fire was the result of a perfect neoliberal storm of self-regulation, privatization and cuts.' A weakened and divested state and a squeeze on the public finances came to a head in a neighbourhood where rich and poor live cheek-by-jowl.

If Notting Hill's wealthy residents work in finance and law, many residents in the Tower were from migrant backgrounds and worked in various serving capacities. For example, a Lebanese woman was a hairdresser, a Portuguese man was a chauffeur, a Syrian refugee worked at Harrods department store, and a Colombian woman worked as a local housekeeper. (The Colombian woman was working late on the night of 14 June, helping with a dinner party, to earn extra money, and this saved her life.) Meanwhile, an Ethiopian woman worked in a beauty salon; another Ethiopian, a man this time, was a cab driver; an Iranian man worked as a chef; and market traders sold fish and rugs.[17] Residents of the Tower and their super-wealthy neighbours didn't live quite the parallel lives I had imagined: residents were conscripted into the plutocratic service economy, one of the sources of job opportunities in the area.

Though the Royal Borough represents by no means the United Kingdom's most extreme example of poverty, it has become a beacon of national social inequality. This is amplified in London, with its crisis in housing affordability, as wages stagnate and real estate values soar. Notting Hill, especially, typified by the coexistence of social housing tenants with millionaires, billionaires and aristocrats, provides an infamous example of unequal London, unequal Britain. The burning Tower ignited a growing underlying uneasiness rooted in vast disparities in wealth. Grenfell was the moment that negligence and excess, long on a collision course, crashed into each other.

11

Living in Triangles

Writer and critic Dorothy Parker quipped that the elite early-twentieth-century Bloomsbury group, which included Virginia Woolf, lived in squares, painted in circles and loved in triangles. Life in Notting Hill, I discovered, is lived in triangles – though not the Bloomsbury kind. I have been sitting on the number 9 bus from Trafalgar Square for over an hour while it crawls through congested streets towards Notting Hill. Road closures. The traffic is a timely reminder of why country retreats have long provided refuge from London for those who can afford it. For plutocrats, country houses and pursuits are, paradoxically, an indispensable part of city life, as I saw from the mannequins in South Audley Street, and heard from Blazer, with his Gloucestershire mansion. And, as I am to discover, country life is a crucial part of rearing the next generation of plutocrats. As the bus lunges into yet another a diversion I get off and grab the first cab I can find. I have to get to Notting Hill's Talbot Road for 4 p.m. I am meeting Physics, another wealthy volunteer in the Grenfell relief effort. The taxi drops me off right outside her house in one of the streets that meet Talbot Road at a right angle.

On this quiet, tree-lined street, Physics lives in an early Victorian terraced house spread over five floors. Its exterior is a mix of stucco on the ground floor and soft pink London brick on the upper floors, which have little wrought-iron balconies. When I ring the doorbell there is no answer and the house is silent. I sit on the front step for a while and then walk up and down the road checking it out. After fifteen minutes of loitering, I decide I've been stood up, and leave the lilies I bought as a thank you on the doorstep with my business card and a cheery note. I hope this doesn't mean she's changed her mind about meeting. I wander back onto Talbot Road and then wind my way through the streets towards Royal Oak Underground Station and onto an eastbound train. I get as far as Paddington when she texts me. She'd had to 'pop out' to pick up her daughter from school. 'My housekeeper was supposed to let you in.' Would I like to return? I would.

A smartly dressed and impeccably groomed woman with short grey hair and gorgeous nails, possibly in her seventies, answers the doorbell. She speaks like the Queen, only much more warmly. Physics appears behind her and says she is 'my mother-in-law', come to the rescue because 'my housekeeper' has taken herself off to the doctor – migraines and blood tests – and Physics and her husband are due at an important function this evening. Physics is friendly and apologetic. I call her Physics because of a conversation I will hear later between her and her ten-year-old daughter about exams: Mother: 'How was physics?' Daughter: 'Easy.' Mother: 'Don't be ridiculous. Did you use those triangles [protractors] I bought you?' I sit in the kitchen for a while. Modern and gleaming, it stretches the length of the house and opens onto a raised garden at the back. Her mother-in-law sets about looking after her granddaughter's homework and teatime, while Physics and I go upstairs to the lounge. This too stretches the length of the house, windows front and back: full of light and furnished in muted, understated tones. Each of us sinks into a deep sofa. Physics is wearing black yoga leggings and a vest, with a blonde ponytail; in her late thirties, she looks younger.

The family dog joins me on the sofa and digs manicured nails into my leg. Since I have not met a manicured dog before, this is a novelty. He increases the pressure at various points, demanding attention. I am advised to be firm with him. I fail. He gouges at my leg hopefully. Physics likes Notting Hill, which she describes as 'a bit edgy' because it is 'quite eclectic and friendly and outgoing and a bit bonkers'. Also, she agrees with Desk that 'Living on a garden square is particularly amazing because when you've got tiny children everyone can run around and [it's], sort of, communal living, which is really special.' Now that her two daughters are older, 'You can go to your yoga class, or you can play bridge, or you can go to an AA meeting, I mean, everything is, sort of, on your doorstep.' She says the area changed after the 1999 Richard Curtis romantic comedy film *Notting Hill*, starring Julia Roberts and Hugh Grant, as it attracted a steady stream of tourists.

Physics was until recently taking an art history course at one of London's most prestigious art schools. But she withdrew from her studies because she had too much to do at home. 'Because we've just bought this house, there's a huge amount of work to do,' she says. 'We've got builders doing all sorts of things, and I have to coordinate all of that. Also, I try and work out what school my daughter is going to go to. My husband had quite a stressy year with his work so actually it works much better when I'm home and not stressed myself. I think if the two of us were stressed, it'd be worse than a disaster.' Now she fills her days with 'a yoga class or a Pilates class, I've started to learn to play bridge, I do all this interior design stuff, I pick up my daughter from school, organize her, and I'm around and available. And a bit bored. Also, I work with a charity around here, and I do lots of fundraising for them. So, I'm super busy. I'm always running around. But that's how I like it.' I am struck by her description of herself as simultaneously 'super busy' and 'a bit bored'. Highly groomed homes and habitats are the result of constant effort. So too are London's prime cultural spaces, like public galleries. And then there is the next generation of plutocrats to raise, perhaps the most demanding duty of all. In these circumstances, it is not hard to fill a life with constant activity, leaving no time to work in formal employment or to study art.

While Physics is telling her stories, her daughter comes up from the kitchen to ask about various schoolbooks and a possible school trip to the Lake District. She wants her mother's attention and she isn't getting it – I am. I feel bad and offer to leave. Physics says there is no need. Her daughter is being prepared for the 'common entrance' exam, the route to the private boarding and day schools that Physics is considering for her. She says, 'I'm not looking for an academically hothouse-y school. I want something gentler for her.' She will choose the right school for a child judged – by her parents – not particularly academic. A small non-selective girls' boarding school is the current front runner. Her daughter bounces into the living room once more to announce, 'Dad's on the phone.' This gets her mother's attention. The couple discuss the evening's arrangements, while the dog's sharp nails dig ever deeper into my leg. We all want Physics's attention: she is the linchpin of wealthy domestic life.

Life in Notting Hill, I discover, is just one angle of the triangle. The family live at a different angle in the countryside, a pattern replicated by their wealthy neighbours. Physics explains, 'So, our country life is very spoiling. We have a lovely house that we've just bought, and we go there for weekends and holidays and half terms.' Their house has 'a garden, so the kids can muck about. They're really into their horses, so we have horses. Yes, it's just a very nice antidote to London.' Country life is closer to the life her husband – who owns a successful manufacturing company – is accustomed to. She describes his background as 'properly rural' and rather 'traditional'. His family don't just muck about on horses: 'They hunt every Saturday. We all hunt every Saturday.' She says his family are accustomed to the most beautiful country houses, gardens and horses. The picture she paints certainly conforms to a traditional version of wealthy country life, one that apes the landed aristocracy. This second angle is distinct from city life. Doesn't managing both create extra work?

No, because Physics has 'a really lovely girl' who works half-days with her in London, Monday to Friday. At the country house, she has a housekeeper and a cook. The housekeeper will be there in the week, she continues, 'tidying it after the weekend or preparing for the next weekend. Then, she'll be there at the weekend, and she'll help with the laundry and the cooking and just generally keeping the show on the road. Which, obviously, is very, very lucky, but it just means that everything is a real pleasure.' This makes it possible to have people stay for the weekend. 'You can have people for lunch. You know, you're much freer.' The country angle of the triangle is leisure and relaxation with friends: a serving class does the support work.

When I ask where their country house is, Physics tells me, but only after I repeat my earlier assurance that our conversation will remain anonymous. Their house is in what she describes as 'a tiny village': 'There are probably, like, I don't know, twenty houses there. They are a real mix.' I suspect 'mix' means something different in the countryside than in Notting Hill. Physics says she also has some 'very significant neighbours, high-profile neighbours', but doesn't want to elaborate.

Instead she describes a coming weekend at the country house: 'I'll pick my daughter up from school – and her friend. We'll drive down with another friend's child as well, because lots of friends from round here have also got houses down there.' They'll arrive at 7.00 p.m., have a 'low-key dinner' with friends, because they are going to 'a big party' the next day. 'Saturday morning, we're all riding. Then, Saturday lunch, we've got a friend's birthday party. She's got about five families going over there for a big lunch.' Two families arrive on Saturday afternoon to stay for the weekend, followed by her elder daughter, back from boarding school. 'We'll have a kids' dinner and a grown-up dinner. Then, the next day, you know, walk and lunch and hanging out, a bit of tennis. If the pool is working, we'll go in the pool. Then I drop my elder daughter back at school on Sunday night.' She will drive back to London alone, while her husband and younger daughter will travel back by train and get a head start on homework.

Aged 12, her elder daughter has just started boarding school. Boarding schools are the third angle of the triangle. The school is a coeducational day and boarding school, housed in a nineteenth-century purpose-built baroque building set in 400 acres of parkland. The fees are £41,580 a year. Its website boasts 'stunning examination results and university outcomes that speak for themselves'. Guaranteed success, then. It stresses the 'progressiveness' of its curriculum, its 'inclusivity', its focus on the 'individual' and helping each pupil become 'the very best they can be'. It shapes its pupils via the best principles of liberal education. I want to know more about elite schools and mothering. As Physics's children are still young, she offers to introduce me to a friend who lives on nearby Elgin Crescent. Her children are older and she has more experience with this third angle of the triangle, so I hope she can help me to understand it.

As I leave Physics, I walk west along Talbot Road. It turns into Elgin Crescent in less than fifteen minutes. The houses are large Victorian terraces and even larger semis, some painted in pastel colours – yellows, pinks, blues and greens: a welcome change from the endless stucco. Elgin is married to 'a banker'. I know from my walks in the City and Mayfair that this covers a variety of financial work, but she is not keen to specify. She once worked in marketing but gave it up to manage the family instead. Her version of the triangle is similar to Physics's, but stretches over a longer period, as she is a decade older. Their Oxfordshire home is a sprawling former rectory. She has a 21-year-old daughter at an elite university; another aged 19 on a gap year in the Far East; and a son aged 17 at Eton, who is taking his A levels. The two younger children expect to follow their dad to Oxford, his alma mater. The elder of the two has deferred her place and the younger one has a conditional offer, pending exam results.

What is the boarding-school scene like? Elgin tells me about Eton. The fees are £42,501 a year, plus extras for music and other supplementary lessons. A boys' school, according to its prospectus it has a *diverse* student body: a small number of places are reserved for scholarship boys. Here again, diversity is used to validate exclusivity, and to underpin the school's charitable status. Collective life operates through its system of *houses*, into which the boys are grouped. They are prepared for *leadership* and competition.[1] Eton is, after all, the United Kingdom's most iconic elite school, a standard-bearer of the privilege it embodies and imparts to its pupils. Its distinctive, unapologetic uniform is pinstriped trousers, black tailcoats, white shirts and white bowties. Boaters and blazers grace certain occasions.

Elgin tells me: 'We tend to be less involved as they get older. Boarding schools do pull you in a little bit more from time to time because the children spend so much time together and there is a bit more of an obligation to try and get on [with other parents].' She claims again that they are 'a very mixed group', but doesn't explain. 'At our house we have a nice group of ten sets of parents from our year, and we have a few get-togethers. I'm in touch with the parents of the boys whom my son is most friendly with. That's the right thing, I think.' Even so, she says, 'I don't know how many close friends we will take from that experience.' There are significant overlaps between these two ends of the triangle, since many Notting Hill children go to Eton, and also, 'There are people that my husband works with; there are people that I've known.' Though Elgin's husband didn't go to Eton, she says, 'We do tend to know a lot of people who are following a similar path. The schools that they were at here [in Notting Hill], particularly the local nursery school and the two primary pre-preps they went to, are all linked in, and all the parents are a similar community.' A community where they are more 'at home': 'It's all of that lot that we spend time with.' Being 'at home', being 'linked in' to a 'similar community' and following a 'similar path' describes a way of moving through this world and its three angles – neighbourhood, country and school – that begins at nursery. Ultimately all three both expand and limit who rich kids can be.

In describing her son's house at Eton as 'our house', Elgin reveals the work of mothers in, firstly, creating a privileged world for their children, and, secondly, in fostering a sense of belonging in it. Shamus Rahman Khan's study of an elite boarding school in Boston suggests that privilege means learning how to be at home, how to be at ease, knowing how to carry oneself in any number of situations.[2] Sociologists use the term 'disposition' to describe this.[3] Elite schools, Khan says, teach pupils how to embody ease; they offer a style of learning that becomes a style of living, which teaches pupils how to relate to others and build connections with 'those following a similar path'. Education and parenting combine to forge an elite disposition in the children of the rich.

Knowing how to compete, how to excel in the struggle to outperform others, is an important part of this elite disposition. Along with other private schools, according to its prospectus, Eton prepares its pupils to *make their way in a competitive world*. Its entrance examinations themselves are highly competitive: wealth alone does not guarantee access. It isn't privilege unless others are excluded; and testing is the school's sorting mechanism of choice. Education operates through tests, all the way through to the public examinations – and interviews too, of course, a further opportunity to display the right disposition – guarding elite universities like Oxford and Cambridge. Sports like rugby that elite schools stress as a *vital part of their curriculum* – not just a way of keeping fit – are equally cut-throat; so too is the house system, a way of dividing boys and pitting them against each other. Competition, embedded in the world at school, is understood as the main route to individual success that demands talent and hard work. Khan's elite-school research suggests that this veneration of competition naturalizes a hierarchy of winners and losers in which hard work brings rewards. In this universe, losers have only themselves to blame and winners deserve their rewards. The idea that it is not who pupils are, but what they do, that matters can appear fairer and more meritocratic, while also concentrating pressure on rich children to succeed.

It is hardly surprising that this competition sometimes leaks into family relationships. Elgin says that she tries to leave the children to their own devices once they're at boarding school, so they can become more independent. But even so, her children have all followed similar paths to their parents and each other, as they were intended to. 'They compete,' she says. 'They're very competitive, my younger two. I suspect they've driven each other on to good things.' But sometimes this causes tensions. 'They haven't always got on, but they certainly push each other to do amazing things,' she reasons. 'So my job is managing them, I guess, and trying to help them to get the best of what they have.' This is part of the rationale for full-time motherhood. 'Because I'm around, I can organize that and make it happen for them. I've always been there.' Rich mothering is a full-time job.

They must also keep young ones on track. Elgin is wary of giving children too much money too young, having learned cautionary tales from friends. In these cases, children 'don't perform to the same level that I'm sure they could. They're quite often partying and doing other things, rather than being at school.' Boarding schools especially can provide 'leeway' for bad behaviour, according to Elgin, since children are no longer under their parents' direct supervision. And money opens many doors. 'The sky is the limit. They do all sorts of extraordinary things', and lose their focus on schoolwork. 'Some of them muck around.' She doesn't know the details, but refers vaguely to 'all sorts of parties and high living that goes on'. Elgin attributes this to the 'extraordinary money' that is available to them. 'I suspect cars are the most obvious. Travel. They seem to be able to go anywhere at the drop of a hat. Parties are paid for and alcohol is paid for. Clubs.' There is, she says, 'a huge range' in London and it is possible to spend an enormous amount of money very easily. 'Some of them are able to do that. I'm not sure we even have that [amount of money], but we certainly wouldn't make it available to the children.'

Instead, Elgin encourages her children to earn money. Her son has a job lined up for next year working in one of the prep schools. She acknowledges that, 'They wouldn't necessarily be able to get those jobs if it weren't for the network that we have, but they have gone and sought out the jobs themselves.' Also, 'They've turned up and been reliable and done what they're supposed to do. Not all of the kids do that. They are given money rather than earn it and they certainly don't do menial jobs.' Her daughter similarly worked in a café for three months, and 'had to be there at seven in the morning and wash up and the rest of it'. Having a wealthy parental safety net removes most risks from children's lives, but still there are many ways of being wealthy.

Listening to Physics and Elgin's stories, I see how mothers make the next generation of plutocrats, shaping their dispositions, their ways of being rich, while fathers appear largely absent. Wealth produces wonderful resources, which are cultivated to create certain kinds of privilege. Elite private schools are good at this. So, too, are the wealthy mothers with whom schools collaborate. Mothers work the bridge between home and school. They choose schools for their children and service the connections and privileges they bring. With significant help from a team of staff, they create homes in London and in the country. Wealthy mothers are the central point of the triangle around which everything moves.

I leave Elgin Avenue thinking about women and wealth. I am surprised at how traditional these modern educated women are: everyone I have spoken to willingly gave up their job when they married or when they started having children. They live as though their proper place is at home. It is as if the last few decades of feminist activism missed these streets completely. Elgin told me that her own mother didn't work either: 'She could have done, but she didn't. I do remember her being around.' But that is not the whole story. The work of mothering, of producing the next generation of wealthy people, is a highly valued, elaborate business in these circles, and must trump the careers inevitably cut short. The domestic duties of wealthy women are so elaborate they leave time for little else, even though they are effectively chief operating officers and all the physical labour is sub-contracted to a serving class. Anything these mothers could earn in the arts industries they generally start in would anyway be insignificant beside the pile of money their hedge fund, private equity, or captain of industry husbands pull in. Earning money is not where their value lies. It lies in cultivating wealthy lifestyles and dispositions: in producing and reproducing privilege. Being wealthy enough not to have to work is in itself a privilege and mark of distinction. Wednesday Martin's research among wealthy women in New York suggests that mothers are vital in creating the social networks that underpin wealthy life.[4] Their children's successes are the measure of their worth, the metric by which they are assessed.

Of course, there are women living in these streets who are wealthy in their own right rather than through marriage to wealthy men. We met a few women luxury asset managers and property developers during our 2012–15 study (see Prelude), and Investigator met a female manager of a family office in 5 Hertford Street (see Chapter 6). But they are exceptions: the vast majority of the super-rich are men. In 2019 it was estimated that only 12 per cent of the world's billionaires[5] and only 10 per cent of millionaires[6] are women. Women's relationship to money is nearly always secondary, accessed through others, leaving them without the fundamental power money grants men. They are born to riches and inherit; they marry money, and they divorce it. Women are mostly rich through these indirect, emotionally calibrated routes, rather than their own money-making skills. Money, it seems, enters women's lives in ways that shape how they can live it, reinforcing subordination, leaving them vulnerable in case of divorce. Martin's New York study concurs: women depend on men's money, backing and approval: a privileged but precarious place to be.

I walk along to Holland Park Avenue and stop to look at the sea of white stucco, behind a screen of mature trees set back off the street in large front gardens. On the Holland Park side, there is a noticeboard, where 'Friends of the Opera' notices suggest neighbourhood allegiances and activities. I sit on a bench outside a deli and listen to the street. A woman in her forties with a young girl in tow is complaining about a development involving Transport for London. She hopes her petition will put a stop to it. A woman in jeans and trainers passes with a boy of seven or so in a fusty-looking school uniform that looks as if it has stepped straight out of the 1950s. I watch two men, one in a blue suit, speaking with each other in Italian outside the deli. There is an Italian ice-cream shop next door. A young woman who works there, on her break, sits on the bench next to me, wearing a black mini skirt and clunky boots, inhaling a cigarette. I am waiting for Rebel.

Rebel turns up a few minutes later. In his early fifties, casually dressed in chinos and loafers, he moves with the ease of affluence. Rebel has agreed to walk with me because he wants to offer an alternative perspective on Notting Hill family life. He hates it. He thinks it is smug and awful. He knows this because his aunt lives here. 'Notting Hill is a peripheral suburb, saved only by the Central Line,' he declares. His aunt 'obviously thinks it's the centre of the world, which is what people who live in Notting Hill think'. He says, 'The upper classes all think Notting Hill is the hippest, coolest, most interesting, wonderful neck of the woods. But it's so dull. And the more I come here the more I discover the entitlement that exudes.' We set off from Clarendon Road and the deli to wander a bit more.

Walking from Holland Park Station we turn into St John's Gardens and pass one of the communal gardens. Metal railings fence it off from the street. The lawn is neatly mowed, rose bushes are planted in clusters, and mature sycamore and beech trees are dotted around. There are wooden benches for loitering and swings for children. 'I just can't stand Italianate stucco architecture.' Rebel's architectural taste inclines towards brutalism. The area is a mixture of Victorian, Georgian, art deco and modern buildings. Rebel also scoffs at the prized garden squares: 'That's what the rich like to live in.' Rebel is descended from several generations of commercial wealth and privilege dating back to the eighteenth century. He says, in the 1970s when he was a teenager, 'We had a lot of money at a time when no one did.' He continues, 'I'm not a squillionaire, but in the nineties I was a squillionaire. I'm still a member of the very rich.' Historical merchant wealth has been eclipsed by the spoils of finance and property. But he still has no need to earn a living. Instead he passes the time with what he describes as film and art 'vanity projects'.

The Notting Hill street vibe, especially on the streets around Portobello Road, is expensively bohemian. Casual linen, silk, designer jeans and trainers, discreet expensive watches and jewellery walk the streets, sometimes with a pedigree dog. As we move along Clarendon Road, we pass a middle-aged woman ushering a boy of about 11 in cricket whites, wearing a navy blazer with red piping on top of his kit. Rebel tells me he was at Eton at the same time, but not in the same year group, as ex-prime minister David Cameron and current (at the time of writing) prime minister Boris Johnson. Instead of going to Oxford with them, he 'turned on, tuned in and dropped out'. It was the 1970s, after all. What about life at Eton? Rebel remembers that being sent to prep boarding school aged eight 'really fucked me up', because he had been heavily cosseted as a child by his nanny, quite separately from his mother. 'My mum went out to the races and did her thing and was a bit depressed, but nanny loved me and held me tight.' His mother was on a number of boards and spent her time 'do-gooding' in London. His father's business meant he was only tangentially involved in family life. Child-rearing was left to nanny. This 1970s style of elite parenting – hands off to the point of neglect – is a world away from that of Palace, Desk and Elgin, who are all expected to be intimately involved in their children's lives. In contrast to his prep school, 'Eton was a sort of dream for me.' It gave Rebel access to London at weekends and a lot of freedom, aged 15, to roam the city – drinking, taking drugs and going to movies – while his parents lived the rural idyll at weekends. Rebel opted out of the country side of his parents' version of the triangle as soon as he went to Eton. Later he started exploring beyond his Chelsea habitat, discovering the arty east in Shoreditch: 'I always had a yen for the east.'

When I ask about the country angle, Rebel tells me how much he hates that too. His parents were progressive urbanites, so he finds it odd that they 'allied their desires with the English landed class'. He says that while, 'My parents ignored me more or less', they were determined that their children should 'grow up in the country', which was a 'bloody stupid idea'. He describes the weekend rituals of country life in the Cotswolds, being 'forced' to ride horses. In school holidays, he and his siblings were 'left' in the country 'to do things that upper classes do in the countryside. But my dad didn't shoot or fish because he had no idea. He was a London merchant. I've never liked the countryside ever since.' I discover later that he owns a home in Suffolk, where he bought two cottages and knocked them together, as well as two London homes. I give him the last word: 'It is a bit crazy having four houses when actually two would be quite adequate.'

Central and South
Kensington

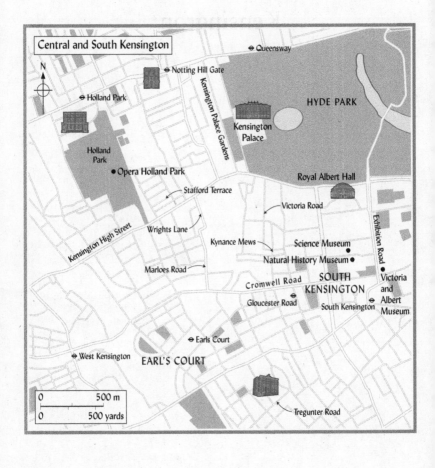

Central and South Kensington

N

Queensway

Notting Hill Gate

Holland Park

Kensington Palace Gardens

HYDE PARK

Kensington Palace

Holland Park

Royal Albert Hall

Opera Holland Park

Stafford Terrace

Victoria Road

Exhibition Road

Wrights Lane

Kynance Mews

Science Museum

Natural History Museum

Kensington High Street

Marloes Road

Cromwell Road

SOUTH KENSINGTON

Gloucester Road

South Kensington

Victoria and Albert Museum

Earls Court

West Kensington

EARL'S COURT

0   500 m
0   500 yards

Tregunter Road

12

The Way Down

It is time to meet Lady. She is a long-term resident in a street just off Kensington High Street who recalls 'the season' in London, much of it still recognizable today in updated form. As we have arranged to meet in the early evening, I take the time to walk there from Notting Hill, exploring other parts of Kensington in order to get a better sense of her neighbourhood. I move along Holland Park Avenue, which marks Notting Hill's southern border, the unofficial boundary that runs through the Royal Borough where North Kensington ends and Kensington proper begins. And proper it is. The Holland Park area lies between the avenue that takes its name, and Kensington High Street. With its cricket field and celebrated open-air summer opera, Holland Park is the daily stomping-ground of nannies and au pairs shepherding tiny children and manicured dogs. I sit for a while in the park and watch the toddlers and the dogs. Leaving the park, I wander along Kensington High Street window shopping. It has the usual upmarket chain stores: Urban Outfitters and Jigsaw for clothes, and L'Occitane for potions and perfumes. Whole Foods has an entire temperature-controlled room dedicated to cheese: its smell overpowering. An American family with young children is in the sushi section when I visit, the young children identifying their favourite raw-fishy morsels for parents to buy. The store is a cornucopia of delicacies. Well-dressed people pause to select items most grocery stores don't stock and many people wouldn't even recognize.

These central and southern areas of Kensington incorporate the Albert Memorial and the Royal Albert Hall, as well as parts of Hyde Park and Holland Park. The heart of Kensington, they include Kensington Palace, where the Duke and Duchess of Cambridge live. As I loiter around the area talking to people, I discover that locals know how long it takes to walk between their home and Kensington Palace. I'm not sure why they need to know this: most of them will never be invited. But if you live here, you live with royalty, and that means something. What could be more socially elevating than royal neighbours? The Palace, in the royal park Kensington Gardens, backs onto Kensington Palace Gardens: a street of detached mansions colloquially referred to as Billionaires' Row, a tag repeated, or perhaps it was invented, by hopeful estate agents. Properties change hands at prices starting at £40 million; £100 million and more is not unusual. They are leased from the Crown Estates, which owns the land. On this street, famous residents include Russian billionaire turned Chelsea Football Club owner Roman Abramovich, and Indian steel industrialist Lakshmi Mittal, who is perennially featured on *Forbes*' list of the world's richest 'people' – though by people, as I have discovered, they actually mean men. This street is not open to the public. I was immediately stopped by security when I tried walking along it. Armed police patrol it, and Crown Estates officials perform security checks on all entrants. Security bollards are sunk into the ground to control traffic. Surely London's most securitized street, this is a good place for those with safety concerns to live.

Kensington Palace Gardens was built in the 1840s when wealthy people ran vast homes with armies of servants. By the twentieth century, too large and expensive to run as family homes, many of these mansions became ambassadors' residences. Until a new wave of twenty-first-century billionaires rolled in and began restoring them to their former opulence and splendour: a second gilded age of excessive wealth, the evidence of which is all around me as I stand outside the security barrier trying to peer along the street. Mittal, for example, is reported to have secured the marble for his mansion from the same source as the Taj Mahal. Beyond the Gardens, the area is green and glorious, wide and elegant. And rich in an oddly secretive, security-conscious and frankly paranoiac way, as *Guardian* journalist Amelia Gentleman discovered when she tried to write about it. The Finnish Ambassador alone was willing to talk to her, and he reported that the neighbours kept very much to themselves.[1] People who choose to live on these streets rather than in Notting Hill, it seems, are reluctant to interact – even with each other – in sharp contrast to the garden squares.

As I turn south off Kensington High Street, I see that the streets are ribbed with slightly less extravagant homes: a mix of either stucco or stucco and brick five-storey Victorian terraces. Many of these substantial houses, formerly single homes, have been turned into flats. Now the area is in transition once more, as flats are turned back into single-occupancy houses. One of these streets, Stafford Terrace, is where Lady lives. When I ring the doorbell, she buzzes me in and I climb the stairs to the top of the house and her small two-bedroomed flat on the fifth floor. I am slightly out of breath as I reach her door. Lady tells me this is a problem for her too; she is 73 years old and the stairs are still more challenging with heavy shopping. High ceilings are a mixed blessing. Her lounge is small, filled with neutral beige carpets and solid antique furniture. Family photographs are displayed on top of an upright piano. Hints of blonde linger in sensible short grey hair. She offers me a glass of sherry, and I accept. It is cocktail hour, after all.

The timbre of Lady's voice is just below Queen level: not as grand as Physics's mother-in-law, but not far off. I want to hear about wealthy life in London from the perspective of an older generation, someone who remembers how things were. She tells me that she had a 'very, very privileged upbringing, hugely privileged. Absolutely. White cotton gloves. Why do you put children in white cotton gloves? Beyond me. I can't imagine why you'd want to. Had to wash the beastly things.' This seems an oddly formal approach to privilege, but privilege has many guises, as I am beginning to understand. Lady's father, sensing the direction in which the international situation was moving, enlisted as an officer in the army and did active service during the Second World War. After the war, he had no idea what to do, but ended up in advertising, as it was beginning to boom and he was good at art. He died in his early forties while Lady was still young. She remembers his talent for drawing and his sense of humour. Her mother had married for love rather than social position. Her mother's father was 'a down-to-earth practical sort of chap' – a successful businessman from the North of England who joined Churchill's wartime Cabinet and was later ennobled as a reward for his services to the nation at war. Her mother grew up around this Westminster political class. But she was widowed young with four children to support. Fortunately, there was family money.

Lady grew up in nearby Knightsbridge in genteel circumstances. Two failed marriages and two daughters, almost a generation apart in age, followed. She has moved around West London as circumstances demanded, but gravitates back to this familiar bit of Kensington where she feels at home. When I ask whether she ever worked, she says no – she got married instead. Even in the swinging sixties, it seems, married women of a certain status were still unlikely to work outside the home. Work was not part of Lady's life plan; neither was university. As her story unfolds, I learn that, in fact, she has had a number of jobs, in catering and bookkeeping. Her work stories follow a pattern. She is not looking for work. But friends or family members running businesses of various kinds need help at some point. She steps in to help as a favour, with the understanding that this is neither expected nor long-term, but a stop-gap rescue. It is unclear whether she is paid, or if she needs or wants the money. I suspect she was and she does. It transpires that she likes working. She likes getting out of the house and meeting people. Lady is a friendly and sociable woman who has spent much of her life living alone.

Lady tells me that she once owned this entire house. Houses on this street now sell for £11 million, she says, 'an absurd price'. 'How do you get a mortgage on £11 million?' As time went by and her inherited wealth dwindled, most sharply declining as a result of the 1987 stock market crash in which she was heavily invested, she started selling off bits of her house as separate flats. A friend of hers told me that Lady's wealth makes her uneasy, that she is generous to less well-off friends, often giving money away. She gradually sold the house, flat by flat, until only the top floor was left, and now she lives there stranded in old age. She says that 'the intelligent thing to have done' would have been to sell the top-floor flat first, renovate the rest of the house, sell it and move on. 'But I didn't do it, and it's too late now.' The ceilings are low at the top of the house and her flat feels cramped. This is where her younger daughter's nanny lived when Lady owned the entire house. Now it is Lady living in the servants' quarters. Above our heads, she says, 'I have an attic full of stuff that never gets used, because when I moved from downstairs, it was like putting a quart in a pint pot. And . . . there were bits where I thought well it'd be nice to keep that, you know. Books, I kept huge numbers of books', and some of her parents' furniture. A lifetime of accumulated stuff presses down on the ceiling of her reduced circumstances.

We dive deeper into the past. Proper ladies 'came out' as debutantes, even in the 1960s. Lady's cousin, who was a year older, came out the year before her, and was enlisted as her guide. 'Coming out', being introduced to the public world of elite society, involves a complex cascade of social occasions. These snowballed into ever-grander parties, culminating in a 'coming out' ball. Her cousin held one of her coming-out cocktail parties at the former home of Edward Linley Sambourne, an artist and illustrator, who was a long-time contributor to the magazine *Punch*. His house on Stafford Terrace is now a museum celebrating him. Lady explains that the Sambourne family were friends of her aunt's and are related to Antony Armstrong-Jones, who married the Queen's sister, Princess Margaret. Royal connections do count. 'Oh yes, she [the cousin] did the season in a very manic way,' Lady remembers, amused. 'And she said to me when I left school . . . "Darling, you must remember when you go to big parties, when you go to balls and things, you must remember to take liar dice or a pack of cards with you to play with your girlfriends in the loo." What!' she says in exaggerated disbelief. Games provided distraction if parties were dull, or there was a shortage of attentive, eligible young men. The purpose of these events was to find a good match, to bag a wealthy or socially significant husband.

'Coming out' as a debutante traditionally introduced young aristocratic girls to the monarch at the royal court. This ritual, acknowledging aristocratic status, gained traction in the eighteenth century and accelerated in the nineteenth century, as roads and transport gradually improved, making it easier to travel from the country to the court in London. This was linked with 'the season', the round of social events beginning in early summer, followed by the retreat to country houses in August and September for summer pursuits and autumn shooting.[2] In their straitened circumstances, after the death of her father, Lady and her 'darling mamaah' struggled to maintain the lifestyle appropriate for a young aristocrat. This made 'coming out' more significant and stressful than it might otherwise have been.

Even so, Lady tells me, 'My darling mamaah made the most enormous effort for me in order to do it right, she really did. I'm pretty certain that she probably hated every minute of it. She wasn't a terribly sociable person. She was very good at being social if she had to be, but she didn't like it very much, and especially in those days.' She explains, 'If you were widowed nobody asked you anywhere, because you were a woman on your own.' Times have changed: 'It's not the same these days, people have uneven dinner parties now.' Even so, 'My mother did the most sterling work in meeting other mothers and going to luncheons; luncheons, not lunches you understand. Luncheons.' There were coffee mornings, tea parties, dinner parties, cocktail parties – 'It was so dull, it was unbelievable,' Lady recalls. All in the aid of gathering enough contacts to have a ball, because 'Most of these people didn't know enough people to have that sort of size party.' Then there were the balls themselves. Lady ended up at one ball near Oxford because 'I was doing a cookery course with the girl involved.' The girl invited her in person before sending the invitation. 'You can't get out of something when you've said yes like that, can you? I couldn't get out of this one.' Despite her misgivings, she remembers, 'I was staying with some very civilized people; they were very nice, and the dance itself was all right. But instead of having a proper sit-down do for dinner we were given cold beef sandwiches! I drew the short straw!' The cultivation of proper etiquette – doing the right thing in the right way – wearing white gloves, not serving cold beef sandwiches, these details stand out for her all these years later. Social rules maintaining elite status – like tides – order everything.

'One of the other parties that I went to,' Lady says, 'apart from my own, was given by [finance and real estate magnate] Charlie Clore. He was the guy that bought Selfridges. He was giving it for his niece, I think.' She says most of her party invitations didn't come out of doing the season, but 'because of people that I knew anyway or who knew people that I knew'. Social networks make these events work. Lady recalls attending another party at the Duke of Buccleuch's estate, despite not knowing anybody who knew him, where she had a 'fine time'. 'He's got the most enormous place; it's just incredible.' The Duke is Scotland's largest landowner and his hospitality bestows distinction. 'That house, it's just extraordinary. Huge great long galleries with fireplaces. Fireplaces down one side, huge windows down the other side, and there's a ballroom. And they had the most ridiculous kitchens, because they're all downstairs in the basement, and the dining room's way over there. I don't know how they ever got any hot food.'

Coming out involved a surge of social events lasting between May and July, Lady confirms, because 'Everybody goes grouse shooting come August – don't be silly!' This included May balls at elite universities like Oxford and Cambridge, which are still a part of a wealthy social life. The length of the season means 'You have to stay up [in London] for ever such a long time. Even when you're very young, it's totally exhausting.' She says, 'I've no idea if people still do anything so idiotic.'[3] Of course they do. Elements of the season survive in the social calendars of the super-wealthy. But by the late twentieth century, aristocratic young women also went to university or took jobs. Princess Beatrice, the Queen's granddaughter, who half a century before might have come out, instead went to study history at Goldsmiths. The Queen ended formal court presentations in 1958. Writer Sophie Campbell suggests this was because she wanted the monarchy to look relevant to the modern world. As royalty tactically retreated from (some) displays of social status, magazines like *Tatler*, *Queen* and *Country Life*, in concert with such chroniclers of aristocratic breeding as *Debrett's* and *Burke's Peerage*, kept the season going. It was into this social landscape that Lady came out in the mid-1960s.

Lady *did* the season. As she tells it, in a self-deprecating and slightly mocking way, it seems a duty rather than a pleasure. 'I went to Ascot. I tell you I'm the most hopeless person. We went to Ascot in the Royal Enclosure because my uncle, my mother's brother, said that I ought to do this, because it was part of the season and it was part of my education. Never again,' she vows. 'It was so hot and you can't take your hat off, and mummy and I got back to the car, took our hats off and I tell you the gallons of sweat. Honestly, it's so hot and sticky, and it was absolutely horrid, and everything's in these hot sticky tents and the whole thing's a complete nightmare.' Anyway, she adds, 'I don't really want to watch horse racing very much. And I'm not addicted to betting on them either. It's just not an interest that I have.' She pauses. 'I wanted to ride very much when I was a child, but, you know, circumstances conspired against it.'

The season's roster of summer events, now as in Lady's era, includes the Chelsea Flower Show, opera at Glyndebourne in Sussex, horse racing at the Derby, the Royal Academy Summer Exhibition, more racing at Royal Ascot, the Eton v. Harrow cricket match at Lord's, tennis at Wimbledon, the Henley Royal Regatta, polo in Windsor Great Park, still more horse racing (the Queen's favourite sport) at Goodwood, and yachting at Cowes on the Isle of Wight. Contemporary music festivals, Glastonbury and Latitude among them, sometimes (ironically) staged in the grounds of stately homes, are now part of the season and one of few nods to modernity.

In these sporting and cultural events, being seen and photographed for magazines and the national press replaces being presented at court. The Queen and other royals attend Royal Ascot, Wimbledon, the Chelsea Flower Show and a host of other events. But corporate sponsorship and celebrity appearances are equally important in underpinning this new version of the season. The social distinctions they stage remain. While any member of the public who can manage to secure a ticket can now attend these events, all reserve special enclosures for VIP guests: and the frisson of elite status is reinvented along slightly different lines. The Royal Enclosure at Ascot, the preview party at the Summer Exhibition and the Stewards' Enclosure at Henley are examples. These privileges come with strict dress codes. In the Royal Enclosure at Ascot, tails and top hats for men and 'modest' – not sexy or flamboyant – clothing and hats for women are strictly enforced. The surreal world that Lady describes persists in only slightly updated ways. And the global plutocracy now joins in.

Lady's stories are a personal archive of a minor aristocrat fallen on difficult times. The aristocratic rituals she remembers, and the social distinctions they draw, resonate today, if in updated forms. Yet they are also a record of how her corner of the aristocratic world has shifted. She reveals her thinking, perhaps unwittingly, as she talks about her tenants and neighbours on Stafford Terrace. Lady is, in her own way, a rapporteur of the street, and she gives me her tour of who lives there. From her vantage point as a long-term resident, she has a view of how the street has changed over the years, and a firm belief in neighbourly conviviality and the *proper* courtesies of the street.

On the floor directly below Lady lives a man named John: 'A

lovely chap, but he's not really downstairs very much because he's eighty-something and he's married to a woman that he dislikes.' She knows, 'They only got married not very long ago. He loves her but he dislikes her, and he sees that she's really difficult. She lives in Acton, and he mostly lives in Acton, because he can't manage the stairs. He's had triple bypasses and strokes and stuff and he makes it up here about once a week.' But she hasn't seen him for ages. 'I email him occasionally to make sure he's still alive – or not, as the case may be.' John has lived in the building for about five years, having previously lived in a flat over the road years ago. He ended up in the army, and saved money, because 'The army takes care of you.' Lady continues, 'He said he just saved all his money, and he knew a builder; and he bought the properties, the builder did them up, and they sold them on, and he made his money that way. Anyway, he is a nice enough chap.' John became rich through small renovations, despite his humble origins, thanks to London's ever-rising property values.

Below John on the first floor is a couple. Lady believes the woman's family were originally from somewhere in the Middle East, though she was brought up in Spain. Lady likes them: 'She is such a nice person. And he's charming. His father bought the flat back in the mid-eighties. He lived there for a bit while he was a student and then he let it out to other people and now he's come back fifteen years later.' Below them, the basement flat 'belongs to Liz', who lets it out. 'At the moment, there's a Japanese family there, who I never see or hardly ever see. He's probably a banker.' Lady finds there are bankers all over the neighbourhood: 'Oh my God, they abound. There are huge numbers of them from all over, God knows, you didn't know there were that many banks, did you? But there are! Trust me.' I do. Liz's first tenants included 'this absolutely gorgeous little boy called Sebastian. His parents were Swiss and American, so they went back to Switzerland.' They ended up trying to return, but it was too late because Liz had found a new tenant, whom Lady describes as 'running' a credit card company. 'He's one of those guys that runs it, thinks up the system; does the whole nine yards, you know. He had a very agoraphobic wife and a very small child, and they left.' She thinks basement living didn't suit. 'It made her feel kind of dark and closed in. They moved to that Chelsea Harbour', a place I resolve to visit.

'And then after them we had the Japanese. So, in five years there've been three lots.' Lady's house is a temporary staging post: as people move in and out and on to other places. Most work in finance. Liz made a good call in buying part of Lady's house to let in an area of high rental values and corporate tenant turnover.

Lady moves on to the neighbouring houses and flats. 'There have been an awful lot of people that have come and gone', mostly 'polite and very nice' with a few 'rude and horrible' ones. She says they are 'A very eclectic bunch: they really do come from all over the place.' She lists, 'South Africa, Denmark, a whole lot of Americans, French and Italians.' Lady liked a couple, an English husband and a Japanese wife, who bought a house nearby, because 'They had a small boy who played the piano absolutely brilliantly.' They stayed for two years. She was less keen on a Canadian couple, who spent three years in London while the man was working in Brussels. 'She'd redecorated the entire place; they put a gym on the top floor, because there were only the two of them, what d'you do with all those rooms, you know? She did the whole thing in peach.' Her choice of colour scheme, it seems, wasn't the worst of it. 'She never said a word in all the three years. I think she did say a word – I think she said, "Hello", and I think she said, "Goodbye", at the end of it. He was the one that talked if you met him in the street. But he wasn't there a lot of the time; she was here. Oh, and they were building a house in Canada at the same time, for their retirement.' After they sold, there was another couple who have been her neighbours for five years, 'I think the longest occupancy almost.' Her only constant neighbour is the *Punch* museum at Sambourne House. This is a street where things are changing, where not everyone observes the civilities Lady would like them to. The churn of international money and business postings militates against building community or connections between neighbours, in contrast to the strong social networks of Lady's earlier years.

The shifting circumstances Lady describes bring flurries of refurbishment. Lady says: 'Well yes, they pull everything out, every time anybody moves everybody pulls everything out and puts it back together again.' She says, 'There used to be two houses over there, one and three, which were like single rooms let out. But they are now as whole houses again. I don't know, they come and go.' Stafford Terrace is driven by the beat of corporate life, its comings and goings observed by an elderly minor aristocrat on the way down the housing and social ladder. Lady tells me she wants to move to the south coast where she knows people, and soon after we speak she sells her flat for a handsome sum and does just that.

13
Patrol

There are many ways of walking. I prefer meandering: instead of moving straight towards something, I edge round it speculatively. But, in this next walk through Kensington, I cede control over the route and pace to my companion for the day, a high-ranking civil servant in his seventies I'll call Officer. Like Lady, he has lived in the area for decades, and watched the effects of extreme wealth take hold. Officer has done his best to slow the march of the super-rich through the area. I want to see his neighbourhood through his eyes, understand his way of thinking about it. 'Patrol' best describes the way Officer walks – at pace and with purpose. He is not an 'officer' in any official capacity, but a concerned resident, patrolling what he sees as *his* territory: safeguarding, surveilling, managing things, information-gathering, reporting on situations, and, where necessary, intervening to shift events in a different direction. When Officer takes me on patrol, and we reconnoitre his territory, he makes me think of a kindly colonial district officer, who knows his patch intimately and takes a paternalistic responsibility for it. Patrol is about management, oversight, asserting control over competing forces and regimes. What exactly these forces are is as yet unclear. What makes it *his* territory anyway?

I meet Officer at his five-storey house just off Victoria Road, near Kensington Road, the eastward extension of Kensington High Street that wraps itself around the southern end of Kensington Palace. Walking time to the Palace? Seven minutes. His house is an elegant early Victorian villa built in the 1850s. We meet in his basement kitchen-diner. It is shabby and lived in and under the absolute command of his wife, whose orders on the domestic front also shape our neighbourhood patrol. Various items must be collected from Kensington High Street. We set off at a clip.

As I admire his house he says: 'The one thing I can't live down is that I live in Kensington and Chelsea. Now, many of the people who live around here would never understand, because they think it is their natural birthright to be living here.' His neighbours behave as if they owned the place, he says, whereas: 'I don't own the place but I do feel a strong sense of ownership *of* the place.' His relationship to his neighbourhood is through a strong sense of guardianship rather than the entitlement conferred by the wealth that is necessary to buy into it, and this distinguishes him from his neighbours, who strut their rights along the streets. He says that he 'runs' it. As we start off walking, he draws the boundaries of his area: 'It's really one big cul-de-sac', the roads configured to discourage drivers from using it to cut-through between main streets and avoid the traffic. 'It's a very quiet area and outside most people's knowledge', because while someone can drive out of it easily enough, it is hard to drive into unless you know how. Officer and his wife worked their way up to buying this house forty years ago, with family help. They traded in a flat nearby, which his wife's parents originally bought for her and her sisters. Eventually Officer moved into the flat and the sisters moved on. A bequest from his wife's parents made it possible to buy their house. A civil servant could not otherwise afford to live in this area.

As we walk and talk, he points to some neighbouring streets and says, 'That's another country.' I gradually understand that his responsibility, as he sees it, extends over a limited territory – the Kensington cul-de-sac, a block of twenty-seven streets that make up the residents' association of which he is an active member. The residents' association was formed in 1982. It grew out of a group of neighbours who got to know each other at a street party for the Queen's Silver Jubilee in 1977, followed by a second street party for 'no good reason' in 1980. It took two more years to consolidate into a community organization, because no one wanted to run it or be over-familiar, all keen to keep the appropriate social distance, and reluctant to 'be in each other's pockets'.

These reservations were overcome when a local hotel next door to the home of one of the street-party participants applied for planning permission to add two extra floors. The neighbours united in their objections, and the residents' association was formed. The association's mission remains to 'preserve and enhance the character of this attractive part of Kensington'. It extends south of Kensington Road. Kensington Palace is immediately to the north; south from Palace Gate is its eastern boundary, and Kynance Mews its southern extent. These boundaries coincide with an existing conservation area of historical and architectural interest, providing a well-established basis on which to object to changes to the neighbourhood. Each street has a representative, invited to attend regular meetings on matters of community interest.

We walk along Kensington High Street. 'My vision,' Officer says, 'was to try and get it back, for the streets to look as near to as they were before.' By 'before', I realize, he is thinking of much earlier times, which he does not specify. In practice this means activities like negotiating for parking signs to be placed on walls and railings, rather than on poles on the pavement: all part of the Kensington High Street improvement scheme. 'I was involved in that,' Officer tells me with pride, 'trying to clear all the clutter, get high-quality, simple design, and that's been extended from here [Kensington High Street] to Palace Gate.' This battle is motivated by respect for the aesthetics and historical integrity of these streets, and antipathy towards the visual pollution of unnecessary traffic controls. Otherwise, the association 'tries to negotiate [with the council] for improvements wherever we could get them', and wrest some measure of control back from them.

He notes that the strategy – 'if there was any strategy' – was in his head, and involved a mixture of taking opportunities as they came, winning over the local council or simply refusing to budge. At certain points, Officer says, 'We just dug our heels in', over issues ranging from the parking-scheme hours to saving building facades. 'So we basically don't take anything lying down.' Not taking anything lying down demands constant vigilance; patrolling the streets as well as the Royal Borough's Planning Committee, watching as things unfold on the ground and organizing collective action among neighbours to challenge them. As well as watching for the demolition of historical facades, Officer keeps an eye on the 'construction-traffic management plans'. These manage the extra traffic that comes with construction throughout the course of the area's many domestic renovations. 'My vision is that this is a skip-free zone', so that waste is kept on site until it is removed. With so much renovation, skips and their building waste are a local scourge.

Planning permission applications, home renovation building sites, street security, tree planting and maintenance, traffic controls: these are residents' association staples and reasons for patrol, for keeping active watch and challenging violations and nuisance. Only recently, the association tried to block the former Jesuit Heythrop College in Kensington Square from being turned into a luxury retirement complex where apartments will cost £156,000 a year to rent. One local resident, writing on the association's website, describes this development as 'a building for oligarchs dressed up as a retirement home'. The chair of one of the other local residents' societies said that the building should not 'become an exclusive ghetto for [Kensington's] richest residents'. They lost.

Domestic renovations focus the most frequent battles. As we walk back towards his house, Officer points some out to me. He tells me about the people next door, who extended their kitchen out into the garden as a glass-covered dining area. 'That actually is modest,' he says, compared to nearby Albert Place, where basements are being built at numbers 2, 3 and 4. At number 5 is a Russian owner, whose house has been 'totally demolished and rebuilt behind a front facade, including the basement'. Number 7 was going to build a basement 'underneath the library', but the owner ended up selling instead. Luckily, Officer's street has escaped the worst of the building, 'partly because it's very narrow, and partly because the gardens aren't big enough'. Elsewhere, there is only one force that constrains basement building: 'Some places you're not going to get basements because the Underground (Tube) tunnel runs across it.' I'm relieved to hear that basements do not (yet) open directly onto the London Underground.

Home renovations, particularly the rash of digs for basements, rapidly spreading through the streets, are extensive, expensive and disrupt the area. Digs take a year or even two, causing noise and traffic disruption, as materials are delivered, and, sometimes, damage to adjoining walls, which are compromised or may collapse entirely. It can be hell for the neighbours. Officer says that basements are just 'places to dump money'. At number 16, 'He bought it, gutted the place, took the roof off, and put a car lift in, before he built a basement with a swimming pool going under the garden, and he really didn't care.' Either way, 'It's at a critical point along this road where all the traffic comes, and it was very disruptive.' Worse still: 'I don't think he spends much of his time there; he's a senior person in a big international bank. I think he's French, or Algerian or something, originally. The problem is that most of these people are not part of the community.' I ask what makes a resident 'part of the community'. Did the banker's national origins or ethnicity make him an outsider? No, he says, echoing Lady, it's people that don't join in, that keep to themselves; so tenuous is their investment in the life of the neighbourhood. Being part of the community, he says, involves more continuous residence and a more open and considerate attitude towards neighbours, especially when it comes to renovation. Too many renovations are pursued entirely through the official apparatus of planning, architects and solicitors, rather than through face-to-face neighbourly civility. Civility cannot be patrolled, but it matters. Rich people, I learn, are poor neighbours when it comes to pursuing their own interests at the expense of those who share their space.

As I leave Officer to finish his patrol, I think about the diggers, the little orange machines with small driver's cabs that scoop out the earth beneath people's houses. Journalists report that builders leave them buried rather than retrieve them from a dig.[1] Builders I spoke to confirmed this. Hiring a crane and blocking off the street to recover a £5,000 or £6,000 digger is not cost-effective in a multi-million-pound renovation. Consequently, dozens of them are buried in the foundations of houses in the area. Some of these basement digs are up to three storeys deep and require the expertise of mining engineers. I met one young man, who, on completing his course at Camborne School of Mining and failing to get a job overseas, where mining is in higher demand, fell upon basement digs as a lucrative alternative. On a few occasions, I've convinced builders to let me have a look while they are working. I saw diggers and other bits of kit, worked by armies of Eastern European builders, and the gaping holes beneath houses, exposed to the air. All in the cause of enhancing the already luxurious houses of the super-rich, one basement, house and street at a time.

I walk around the corner from Officer's house at my own more leisurely pace. Backtracking onto Kensington High Street near the Underground station I take a small road off it to find a series of purpose-built blocks of red-brick mansion flats built between 1897 and 1902. Entering one of them, I take the cage lift to the fourth floor to meet Officer's friend, Historian, a retired conservation architect and mainstay of the Kensington Historical Society. The building is in silence, broken only by my knock on the door. The flat he shares with his wife has polished wooden floors and rooms leading off both sides of a central corridor, flooding it with natural light. We settle into a large lounge filled with solid antique furniture and family photographs. Historian and his wife Opera – she's a staunch friend of Opera Holland Park – moved here five years ago after selling their suburban West London family home when their children moved on. Flats in this block range from £3 million to £7 million, a cheaper option in an area where most houses cost between £10 million and £20 million. The divide between the two is a fault line the couple see running through the neighbourhood. People who live in the cheaper flats are, in their eyes, more sensitive to the area's history. People who live in the houses have serious money and care little about the area.

Historian has more basement stories. Basements are de rigueur. Friends of his who were selling their house reported that the first questions a prospective buyer asks are: 'Have you got a basement? What's the potential? Is there a basement next door?' Apparently, Historian says, 'They all come along with their architects or engineers. One must have a swimming pool, and one must have a gym.' Basement disaster stories also abound. In one, raw sewage runs through a neighbour's flat. Historian thinks expanded basements distort houses – creating icebergs with almost as much space below ground as above. Limited ventilation and natural light prevent basements being used as living space. They only house 'gyms, music rooms, media rooms, swimming pools', and so on. 'It's only really people who can afford to have surplus accommodation that can afford to buy them. So, you're changing the whole nature of the people who will live here.' He concludes, 'We change our buildings, then our buildings are going to change us, and this community will change as part of that, I am quite convinced.' Expanded basements are creating new kinds of neighbours, who have private access to what might otherwise have been public activities like swimming, watching movies and working out.

Historian knows people who don't even want a basement, but still apply for planning permission because it will increase the value of their property, and they are worried about missing out if the council tightens regulations. Maximizing and monetizing space in this way conceives of a house as an asset rather than a place to live: an underground extension improves an existing asset, yielding additional house value. The Historical Society are alarmed because 'Quite a number of basement companies have taken a very aggressive stance and are employing leading QCs to fight their case.' The wealthy clients of developers have deeper pockets than the Royal Borough, the Historical Society and the residents' associations. And developers are slippery to deal with. In some cases, each dig is set up as a separate company, limiting liabilities for damages if clients, or neighbours with cracking walls, sue. The basement builders have 'suddenly seen there's serious money to be made out of this', Historian believes, but they have 'varying degrees of expertise' and some of them are frankly 'dodgy'.

As Opera hands out tea in bone china, we talk about the neighbours. She is quietly forceful and casually dressed. Historian defers to her on many matters and announces her achievements in the community, which she is too modest to claim for herself. Like Lady, they have experienced the temporary neighbours on short-term corporate postings, many of them attracted to 'Le sud de Kensington' – as Opera calls it – by its renowned international school, the French Lycée. But more disturbing still are the ghost neighbours, who are (almost) never there. I suddenly realize why their flat is so quiet. Only two flats on this floor have anyone living in them. Mansion blocks, which often have concierges, are easily left empty for long periods. Historian says that, increasingly, properties are bought by people who treat them as either pieds-à-terre, to be visited infrequently, or investments, where they have no intention of living. In this scenario, 'It doesn't really matter if they remain empty, because if you're buying something at several million pounds and you've got a 10 per cent growth rate, which is what's been happening over the last couple of years, then you're making enough money out of it just as an investment. You don't need to do anything with it. You don't need to let it or anything like that.' But, 'For those of us who live here and enjoy it as an area with social connections, it is very sad.' Flats like these rent for £2,000 to £2,500 a week. Opera says that their friends who live in a mansion block on Marloes Road tell them that only three out of fourteen flats there are occupied.

Serious money's eagerness to buy up residential space also undermines the viability of commercial enterprises. This is a problem in Kensington, as it is in Shoreditch. Corner shops, pubs and, sometimes, restaurants are driven out of the area as planning authorities agree to applications for change of use from commercial to residential. Opera says, 'It spoils things for people who do live their normal lives here.' Consolidation of smaller residential units into single occupancy homes also changes the character of the streets because only the wealthy can afford to live in them and prices continue to spiral. 'Smaller flats, smaller houses are under enormous pressure and disappear, so there's nothing cheap here but there are modestly priced places.' Modest to her means under £2 million.

The premiums commanded by residential space also reduce the social 'mix' so valued by the wealthy women of Notting Hill. Opera tells me the story of a developer who was required to construct social housing as a condition of getting planning permission in Kensington – but the council allowed him to build it in Peterborough, 90 miles away. Apart from the disruption to social tenants' support networks and jobs, she says: 'Most of us actually need a cleaner; blocks of flats need porters. We need other [kinds of] people.' A serving class. She recognizes that this 'sounds terrible'. High premiums threaten public space too. Opera says that even Holland Park is under siege. It is being used for closed, ticketed, corporate events for more and more of the year, including extending the Opera's run. There are now 'fringe tents' reserved for the wealthy, and corporate employees and clients, 'a fringe tent for dinners, and another fringe tent for this, that and the other'. Uber-wealthy neighbours bring all manner of changes and restrictions for everyone, but most notably for the poor, who are purged, so that neighbourhoods are reconfigured in their absence.

Historian and Opera wave me off at the lift, pointing out uninhabited flats on the way. It's time to move on and follow the basement stories further south. I cross Officer's territory on Victoria Road and Kynance Mews once more. As I reach Cromwell Road, the character of the area changes abruptly, becoming busier and more anonymous. I keep walking south, crossing the equally congested Old Brompton Road until I reach the subdued hum of drilling and building work on Tregunter Road. I am meeting someone who has researched this street and the surrounding area: a fellow sociologist, Roger Burrows.

As I arrive, Burrows is walking up and down the street with a microphone-wielding interviewer and a cameraperson, both from a German television documentary company, so I sit on the pavement and watch the street. Tregunter Road is a quiet, tree-lined residential street in Kensington, a short walk from Gloucester Road Underground Station, where the District, Circle and Piccadilly lines converge. Substantial, four-storey Victorian semi-detached houses that sell for between £8 million and £15 million are arranged on four floors, a few of them converted into flats. They are set back from the street behind black spiked metallic railings and entry-phone operated gates, leading to private carports. What I am now thinking of as familiar plutocratic planters are sprouting the usual foliage. Of the goings-on inside these houses, there are few clues. Opaque windows, expensive curtains and blinds conceal the lives inside. There are occasional hints though. An Ocado delivery van pulls up and the driver carts several crates of bottled water to the front gate of one of the houses. A disembodied voice, in beautifully modulated English tones, authorizes the delivery man to proceed to the front door and hand over the water.

Life inside these houses is invisible, while those who service its desires and directives come and go. A man balances on the windowsill polishing the glass until it sparkles. Middle-aged Eastern European women wash doors and polish knockers. An electrician wanders past me holding a length of cable and disappears into one of the houses. A man in a yellow high-visibility vest pulls up in van with *Jetform Swimming Pools* on the back and disappears into another of the houses. Several young Filipina women walk past, pushing pale, listless children reclining in strollers. Dog walkers speed past me, managing a tangle of leads restraining assortments of impeccably groomed pedigree pets. All this activity takes place to a soundtrack of drilling and building.

Skips and building debris are the only visible signs of the story that Burrows is busy telling the German documentary film-makers. He and his colleagues have done some digging of their own, on the planning portals of London boroughs, and discovered that Tregunter Road, along with nearby Harcourt Terrace and Cathcart Road, is the centre of a cluster of 'large' and 'mega' basement digs.[2] We are in London's luxury basement central.

Tregunter Road alone had twenty-one basement digs between 2008 and 2017. Most are classified as large, and three of them are mega. Large basements are two storeys deep, or a single storey that extends beyond the footprint of the house beneath the garden. Mega basements are either three storeys deep, or two storeys and extend beyond the footprint of the house. As Burrows speaks into the microphone, builders move in and out of building sites and deposit debris in skips. Tons of earth are moved to build a two-storey hole in the ground. As the cameraperson approaches the builders and asks permission to see the basement under construction, they shake their heads. Owners will not want their basements featured in a German television programme about the space-gobbling activities of London's plutocrats.

What will these basements be used for? A review of planning applications by Burrows and his colleagues reveals what Historian and Opera have observed among their neighbours: large and mega basements usually involve an indoor swimming pool, and are often also used for wine storage, games rooms, steam and sauna rooms, gyms, parking spaces with lift access, and staff accommodation. In 2015, the Royal Borough, which had the second highest number of basement planning applications in London, with just over a thousand, revised its policy. In future, basements will be restricted to a single storey and cannot take up more than 50 per cent of the garden. Such planning controls are an effective tool for limiting the underground ambitions of the uber-wealthy.

Struggles against the basement diggers have been based on the area's 'history', as I discovered. The Kensington Society was formed in 1953 to *ensure that our part of London retains its magnificent heritage of buildings, parks and gardens alongside the best of contemporary architecture and design*, and to *exert a real influence on the planning decisions in the Royal Borough of Kensington & Chelsea*,[3] following extensive rebuilding after the Second World War. In this stand-off between history and the digger, I am interested in what exactly this history consists of. After all, cities are constantly being built and rebuilt, so what makes the city building investments of one era better or more worthy than those of another? Both Officer and History referenced a 'before', a pure historical past they are seeking to preserve. But what do they mean?

Victorians, wielding earlier versions of the digger, created Kensington as it is today, constructing rows of terraced houses in the gardens and estates of the big country houses, which had themselves once sprung up around the court of William and Mary (*reg.* 1689–1702) at Kensington Palace.[4] Speculative builder-developers like Charles James Freake, who built Onslow Square (between 1845 and 1865), shaped the streets of Kensington. Much of this wealth was the result of industry and colonial expansion. Crystal Palace, the vast exhibition centre, once on the banks of the Serpentine in nearby Hyde Park, displayed the industrial arts and crafts of a confident imperial nation during the Great Exhibition of 1851, turning London into a spectacle of invention, scientific and industrial wonder, and modernity. Kensington was the fulcrum of this project, a living example of the arts, crafts and scientific discoveries – the all-round superiority – of the imperial capital. After the Great Exhibition, in 1857, the Victoria and Albert Museum opened to give a permanent home to the colonial plunder that had been displayed. Alongside it, the Natural History Museum and the Science Museum (1909) created South Kensington's museum quarter along Exhibition Road. At the north end, the Royal Geographical Society celebrated the great voyages of 'discovery' and plunder, which filled the capital's museums. Imperialism's industrial, artistic and cultural swagger are stamped into the streets of Kensington. This was always dirty money.

The histories invoked to halt the diggers are elite white histories built on racist thinking; the stories of old money, much of it stolen from colonies, are wielded in struggles against new money, skimmed through financial wizardry and laundered, this time by an international kleptocracy. These battles between different kinds of wealthy people are fought across the Royal Borough as the rich take on the super-rich for control of the streets, house by house, one basement at a time. It is a case where the 'Haves' take on the 'Have Yachts',[5] not just in battles against basements, but over what the Historical Society describe as the 'tidal wave of steel, glass and concrete' breaking over London. One local historian argues that Kensington is just part of the 'raw capitalism of the metropolis', that from Roman times London was 'invented to make money'.[6] He is right. Cities have always been manifestations of excess, monuments to more money than the rich can spend even when they try their hardest. But unless the brakes on excess and luxury are applied, they reshape cities uncontrollably, in line with the private desires of the wealthiest citizens. Patrolling to curb the excesses of money is a good idea, even if this, too, comes from a position of wealth and privilege.

The Kensington Society recently objected to the Kensington Forum Hotel's plans to build the borough's highest building. Already rejected by the Royal Borough's Planning Committee, plans were later approved by London's Labour Mayor Sadiq Khan, against the wishes of all local residents associations, the Royal Borough's Council and the local MP. The development is to include socially rented flats, and the Mayor has London's poorer residents to consider too. This is what luxury developments continually miss: that there should be a place in the city for everyone.

14

Dirty Window

When did you leave Moscow? Soviet is baffled: 'I didn't leave it.' It is my turn to be confused; their family home has been in Kensington since 1997. 'In a sense,' he qualifies, 'I left for two years for New York.' This was as the Soviet Union was collapsing. 'I returned and set up my own firm. It was like a start-up. I travelled all the time. But I never felt I left Russia. My business was there.' His family was by then in London, though his wife also travelled widely for work. But now? He has taken a step back from his business. 'I would say I'll never turn back. So now I am an immigrant: an immigrant in a good way.' His 86-year-old mother stayed behind in Moscow, Soviet says. 'She is old and strong and she doesn't want to live here in my house.' Soviet has Russian and UK citizenship. Sweating and red faced, he is dressed in a worn tracksuit, having been summoned for our appointment straight from his basement gym, deep in the bowels of his house, by his Russian housekeeper. She is a tall, stern woman with short grey hair, who answered the door to me and checked whether I speak Russian.

After wading through more streets of Victorian stucco to get here, I am surprised to see that Soviet's house is modern: straight white walls, sliding glass doors and contemporary furniture. I wonder what his stucco neighbours think of it? He tells me his wife refused to leave this neighbourhood, having come to love it while living in a smaller house nearby. So he decided to build 'something special', something that would accommodate a growing family and a growing art collection. This street was bombed during the Second World War, and afterwards new houses were built in the gaps. Being of little architectural or historical significance, they were not listed. He bought two next to each other and demolished them to build this house, guided by a famous modern architect. Constrained by the height of the surrounding Victorian buildings, Soviet's house has three storeys above ground and two below: underground there is a pool and a gym. Not quite an iceberg house, but large. The walls and three staircases are hung with Russian art.

I am surprised this house is so open to the street: no electronic front gates like Tregunter Road. When I started thinking about London's wealthy Russians in preparation for this meeting, I grazed on the popular media diet of oligarchs, panic rooms and close personal security. I got up to speed on the lengthening roll call of suspicious deaths – Dmitry Obretetsky, Alexander Litvinenko, Nikolai Glushkov, Boris Berezovsky, Sergei Skripal – which the UK media speculated might be the handiwork of the Russian state, or the mafias with which it sometimes appears to be interchangeable. Whether or not this is the case, the list of possible executions points to the trouble that some wealthy Russians bring to London along with their money.

Curious about how these situations are handled, I attended the inquest of Alexander Perepilichnyy at the Old Bailey.[1] Perepilichnyy was an apparently healthy 44-year-old commodities trader – his wealth estimated to be in the region of £55 million – who dropped dead after a run outside his Surrey mansion in St George's Hill near Weybridge in 2012. As I listened to the court attendants outside the public gallery waiting for the recess to end, speculation was rife. Could his wife have poisoned him? What was all this costing? A Russian mess, our courts: justice does not come cheap. Who was paying for it? The day before, several officials in dark suits from the Russian Embassy had attended the hearing: the Federal Security Service (FSB)?

Compelling arguments and counterarguments filtered through Court Number One. Perepilichnyy's family were occasionally sighted, listening, and whispering to their lawyers. Lawyers argued that Perepilichnyy was executed because he blew the whistle on money-laundering operations that extended to the highest level in the Russian state. Step forward Vladimir Putin. The Special Branch police officer refuted the money-laundering thesis as speculation. Surrey police were negligent in not treating the death as suspicious until it was too late to collect such crucial evidence as CCTV footage, now taped over. The Special Branch police officer said there was no bodily or forensic evidence of poisoning or any other method of execution. Special Branch is linked with the Intelligence Service, MI5; each has its own national security brief. Were members of Russian organized crime networks visiting London at the time of Perepilichnyy's death? The agencies that monitor these things said no. MI5's counterparts in the Russian secret state had been pressed for answers. They didn't kill him. The inquest went through his Credit Suisse bank account, his credit card data, the receipt for his last meal, surprisingly modest, from Tesco. Nothing suspicious. He was in London on an investor visa. But had he actually invested in a business in the United Kingdom? This seemed to extend the inquest's brief. And so it went on. In the end, the coroner ruled that he died of natural causes.

By contrast, Soviet's life is much more ordinary. I have walked straight up to the wide front door and rung the entryphone. Floor-to-ceiling windows at the front are covered by white blinds that filter light into the lounge. Soviet tells me he feels secure living in this neighbourhood: 'Our small street around the house is like an extension of the house itself. That's what I like mostly about Kensington. We never get any issues on the streets.' In New York, on the other hand, you 'might live in a very nice apartment, or a nice building, but one block from this building, if you are on the street, anything could happen.' I want to ask if he feels safe from the long arm of the Russian state. But I don't. I do not want to suggest that he ought to feel uneasy or repeat popular stereotypes of Russians in London. Only obliquely does he discuss his relationship with the Russian state, and he does not live as though it is trying to kill him: quite the contrary.

We sit in a vast lounge on low white-leather sofas, with white walls hung with abstract art and grey slate floors. Except for the sliding glass door that opens onto the garden at the back of the house, which is dirty and smudged, it is pristine. They have a daily cleaner, he says; his wife is fussy about cleaning. All the plutocrats' homes I have visited are groomed to perfection: a dirty window is unusual. He catches me looking. 'By the way, you must be surprised why this is not cleaned, this window. The reason is that my little one is a keen tennis player. He's six, but he's so keen on tennis. What he does, he uses that [window] for playing tennis all the time.' Soviet takes his son to their private tennis club each morning and trains him for an hour before school. After school, his son spends two hours hitting tennis balls against the window. There is no point cleaning it: 'Every day is the same. It's a hitting wall for him.' He speculates, 'He's definitely going to be as good, maybe even more than our oldest son, because he's quick, his reactions are right. He has a natural talent for tennis. He's really, really conscious about practice. He's in a tournament, even at the age of six.'

Energy and effort run through this house. Soviet moves and talks with the force and speed of a tornado; he says he doesn't have a personal assistant, because he is faster. Sporting, musical and academic attainment is prized by these two wealthy, successful parents. Soviet studied engineering, science and mathematics. Until recently his wife worked in the London branch of a top global bank connecting Western investors with lucrative Russian investments. It was her job that brought them to London in 1997. Their elder son, now 25, went to a top UK private boarding school and then to an American Ivy League university, and Soviet did his bit as a parent, attending lunches, galas and sports days. The youngest, the budding tennis prodigy, impresses his talent on the window. Soviet says he will go to Eton 'if he is good enough'. Entry, he says, is now based on 'merit only'. Exam success has superseded heritage, social connections and wealth in recent years, clarifying the key metric by which schools are judged – results. This is a high-achieving, aspirational family, accustomed to succeeding in whatever they do.

The household is run by the best staff. As well as the housekeeper there is a nanny, who has been with the family for twelve years, and is 'fantastic'. 'She's probably, professionally, a top nanny in a sense. She does all the schooling and all the logistics with the day schools.' Soviet and his wife are responsible for defining their 'strategy', and nanny takes care of 'execution'. Nanny and housekeeper both live in. It's a big house. Spoken like the joint-CEO of the family firm. I wonder if sometimes corporate life provides a model for running family life. Then again, this focus on hard work, and artistic, sporting and academic achievement, would not be out of place in the former Soviet Union.

If people are what they do and how they live, Soviet gets an early start. His day begins at 5 a.m. First, he says, 'I work only on the papers, on the reviews.' These are the reviews of the art exhibitions he co-curates. He loans artwork from his private collection for public display, rather than stashing it in vaults as an asset and avoiding tax. 'It's completely public, for scholars, on loan to museums. I encourage other art collectors to do the same, because otherwise if they don't, what [is it] for? To keep for yourself? It's very strange.' Sociologist Elisabeth Schimpfössl argues that in Russia patronage of the arts is a way of converting financial resources into cultural credentials.[2]

After Soviet has coached his son at tennis each morning, a two-hour gym session, which I interrupted, follows. Then he works on his investment portfolio – 'the financial management for my family' – a hands-on approach to the family's invested wealth. In the afternoons, there are meetings about art exhibitions or the family foundation, which supports various art and music projects with donations. Otherwise, he follows a broader range of pursuits. He extends his knowledge of art with reading and research. He updates his academic interests in science, engineering and mathematics. What about leisure? 'I'm also an adventure traveller in mountains, like high mountains. I climb top mountains.' He takes three-week trips twice a year to climb: 'The Himalayas, that sort of place. Not the highest. I climb 7,000 plus metres. I'm not at 8,000 yet, but I'm close to this. We'll see. This is how I live my life.' Physical effort and competition fill Soviet's leisure time. This is who he is. It is a glimpse of a very different life to that of his neighbours, Lady and Officer.

Soviet says, 'Actually I love this life more than when I used to run businesses.' He is reluctant to discuss the precise nature of these businesses. He tells me only that it was tough: 'It was fourteen hours a day working in the office. I had hundreds and hundreds [of people] in place working for me.' His businesses were in Moscow, which meant commuting weekly between Moscow – only a four-hour flight away – and London, the family's main home. There are few clues as to how he made his money originally. As far as I can tell, he worked in finance and was supported by well-established foreign banks. When he sold his finance company to a bank, he moved into private equity, a lucrative area of investment that allowed him to slot easily into London's money scene.

In addition to finance he was involved with IT companies, in fintech. At one point, he was caught up in a Moscow dispute about the origins of some of the shares in one of the companies he bought. But in the murky atmosphere in which Russian business operates, the legal provenance of companies is difficult to establish and easily leads to accusations of fraud or tax evasion: allegations that the Russian state sometimes levels against wealthy businessmen it wants to frighten into compliance. Soviet closed his businesses a decade ago.

Unlike other businessmen who became wealthy in the 1990s, Soviet did not benefit from the opportunities furnished by the post-Soviet state. These famously included the privatization of former state assets, especially oil and gas, alongside fresh opportunities in the new Russia. This was the heyday of the oligarch, a term used in Russia from the early 1990s to describe those who suddenly became very rich through these newly privatized assets and who were involved in political intrigue and power plays in defence of their wealth, notably under Boris Yeltsin's presidency (1991–9). Soviet says: 'The 1990s was fantastic, actually. It was the best period.' Elisabeth Schimpfössl notes that, while at this time the number of people living in poverty in Russia trebled to include a third of the population, others who were well positioned, by virtue of elite education and political contacts, prospered. Soviet social, cultural and intellectual assets were converted into new forms of personal enrichment. This best describes Soviet and the sources of his wealth. He is *not* one of the infamous oligarchs – but there are reportedly plenty of them living in London, using the complex financial instruments provided by London firms to hide their riches from the Russian state.[3] And, through these routes, the corruption of the post-Soviet state reaches deeply into London's financial and economic life,[4] just as assassins appear to operate with impunity. When current president Vladimir Putin came to power, he divested oligarchs of their political influence, but allowed them to retain their wealth.[5] A 2013 law required Russian government officials to relinquish foreign assets, forcing them to choose either political influence in Russia or their houses and bank accounts in London.

Soviet, as already indicated, is just a rich Russian, not a political player. Trading business for high culture has given him a new life in London as a wealthy bourgeois Russian philanthropist. The shift allows him to cultivate a disposition rooted in intellectual and artistic pursuits, admired as much in Russia and the old Soviet Union as in London and the circles in which he now moves. Art makes Soviet a model Russian, not a dodgy oligarch – 'immigrant in a good way', as he puts it, acknowledging that 'immigrant' is often a pejorative term in popular UK parlance. Good immigrants are also rich immigrants. This is baked into UK immigration rules, which favour 'investor migrants' able to leverage £2 million into a business; migrants defined as having 'exceptional talent' in arts and sport; and a handful of high earners on company transfers or with skills in short supply, who are eligible to apply for a limited number of visas.[6] Cut conveniently loose from the origins of his wealth – just like Blazer, the former dotcom tycoon in Mayfair – Soviet becomes a wealthy philanthropist, a model migrant patron of the arts. His reinvention obscures the extent of his wealth, as well as its provenance. I wonder if he is a billionaire or merely a multi-millionaire? His London house – one of three – is estimated at £10 million, and his art at £40 million.

Russian business is the hinge connecting the two halves of Soviet's life. At 50, he says, 'I walked away.' The happy prerogative of those who have made all the money they are ever going to want. Mischievously referencing the planning cycles of the Soviet economy under Stalin, he tells me that his departure was part of a 'five-year plan'. His wife calls it 'financial evacuation'. From her vantage point at the bank, she saw how things were moving in Russia and knew they had to 'get out'. As tensions increase between Russia and the Western world, with clashes ranging from the invasion of Crimea to accusations of electoral interference, international sanctions pile up and consolidate a decade of declining private investment. The business climate in Russia is increasingly difficult. In this situation, Soviet explains, 'You cannot sell the business. So you only run the business. You cannot expand it. Investors don't want to put money in, only take it out. The economy is down completely. It's an economic crisis over the last three years. It's going down, down, down.' Instability in exchange rates between the rouble and the US dollar, among other (political) factors he does not mention, have been creating difficulties for international and Russian investors since 2014. Volatile exchange rates complicate financial planning and bring uncertainty. It's a 'melt-down', he says. He has friends who failed to get out before this collapse and must live with the consequences. He still has a flat in Moscow, and travels there once a month for art exhibitions and family visits. His trips are 'event driven' not 'business driven' now. He says he still loves Moscow. 'It's a lovely city', but, 'I feel home here in London.'

His relationship with Moscow is complicated, as I discover when I ask about his early life. He lived in the city until he was 20. Born in 1962, he was a child of the Soviet Union. Expecting a rant on the privations of communism, I am surprised that he speaks with a quiet, affectionate nostalgia for a world that no longer exists. 'Moscow was a pretty safe place I would say.' He was allowed, aged six, to get the bus by himself from home to tennis training: 'Everyone did this.' He says, 'As kids, we didn't have much to play with, actually. There were no TV channels. Maybe there were one or two stations. There were some cartoons, but not international cartoons. There were no videos. There was nothing like this, only books, if you had time. I spent almost all the time reading. Except for sport.' He lived in a block of flats with a communal area where he and the other children played hockey. 'I enjoyed my childhood because it was safe, easy and all people lived the same way,' he says. His family had a very small two-roomed apartment, about seven square metres total.

His parents slept in the living room, and Soviet and his brother shared the other room. 'Most families lived like this,' he insists. 'I hosted my friends from my school for parties and for dancing, and we enjoyed it because that's the way it was. In school, we were more equal.' He sounds wistful, 'It's gone. It was different. Communism is a completely different civilization. Most people lived where they were born and died, completely in isolation from the rest of the world, because the country was closed. This is how the people lived. I cannot explain to my children what exactly it looked like; they wouldn't understand.' I had not expected to hear fond memories of simpler, more egalitarian time while sitting in the living room of a £10 million house. The surprises of Kensington. I head off, letting Soviet whisk me out through his front door, to return to his day and his reveries.

Time to walk. Lately, I have been feeling that Kensington deserves better shoes than mine, which are flat, serviceable, cheap ballerinas. If areas were shoes, Kensington would be something designed by Jimmy

Choo or Manolo Blahnik, a snakeskin slingback or a polka-dot mule. These elegant entitled streets were made to be trodden by the soles of beautiful handmade shoes. Crossing over Kensington High Street – in the right shoes I would shimmy rather than clump – I head along Wrights Lane and Marloes Road, past more oxblood-coloured mansion blocks. Past the nannies in jeans and trainers pushing oversized prams. On Marloes Road, I catch up with a woman in her thirties tripping daintily along in a flowing off-the-shoulder coat and the most expensive and impractical high-heeled shoes: Jimmy's, I think. As she walks, she relives last night's cocktail session on her mobile phone: 'I was soooo tharsty.' In *The Great Gatsby*, Scott Fitzgerald describes Daisy as having a voice 'full of money', and this line comes into my head listening to her. I follow her for a bit and then turn towards Abingdon Road and Café Nouvelle.

I want a broader take on Russian London. So, I am meeting with Journo, a commentator on Russians in London. I am hoping she will have the inside track. I suspect her Russian London will be younger than Soviet's, too. She arrives in a rush and plonks herself down next to me. She is small, redheaded, open, instantly friendly, gregarious, and all got up in cheap flash. Delicious. As we sip tea, she lifts the lid on Russian London.

Many of the young Russians in London specialize in IT or finance or both, since that works for fintech. Fintechs, as Cake described them in Chiltern Firehouse, fuse traditional financial products with sophisticated technologies. 'Technical education is very good in Russia, especially maths and physics; they have good technical specialists, but most of them try to leave Russia,' Journo tells me. 'Many already studied in Europe, especially those from rich families. Some of them just have this entrepreneurial mind, and probably the UK gives more opportunities for creative people and entrepreneurial-minded people.' She describes a brain drain of young tech-savvy Russians gravitating to London, where no one will 'tell them to share their profits with the government', which 'usually happens in Russia'. Journo confirms Soviet's earlier observation that there is no specific Russian community in London: Russians in their twenties are indistinguishable from a pan-European workforce. Young Russians 'don't consider themselves as Russian', she says. Soviet told me that 'community' is the wrong word to describe Russians in London: 'They don't want to live with each other anyway. There's just no way.'

This invisibility extends to Russian businesses. Andrey Andreev, in his mid-forties, whose wealth is estimated by *Forbes* at $1.8 billion, started the dating apps Badoo, Bumble and Lumen. The Chinese restaurant chain Ping Pong Dim Sum is owned by Russian-born Artem Sagiryan, and bankrolled by his high-profile investment banker father. Nikolay Storonsky and Vladyslav Yatsenko started the fintech Revolute, a global financial services platform valued at $5.5 billion. Storonsky is described by the *Financial Times* as 'the UK's youngest self-made billionaire'. He was born in Moscow in 1984, studied physics at the Moscow Institute of Physics and Technology, and is also a champion swimmer. He started his working life in London at Lehman as a derivatives and equities trader. Yevgeny Chichvarkin, the Russian billionaire who made his fortune in Russia by being a front runner in the mobile phone market of the 1990s, just as it was opening up, owns the luxury Mayfair wine merchants Hedonism, which I have passed many times on my walks, and a Michelin-starred restaurant called Hide. While these Russians and their enterprises are a significant part of plutocratic London, their Russian-ness melts indistinguishably into the landscape, so well does London suit their skills and their drive to make money. (Multiple money channels connect London with Moscow; the connections spread much further than oligarchs' ill-gotten gains.) Journo, in contrast, runs an enterprise that claims and celebrates the successes of London's invisible Russians.

I discover that she is a reluctant migrant. She moved to London to marry her classmate, leaving behind a flat, friends and a life she liked in Moscow. Now established in London, she says she will not return to Moscow, citing political and economic uncertainties – with the value of the rouble and a constitution that puts Putin in power for ever – as reasons to stay in London. Moscow, a 'great city', is also a 'difficult place to live'. She has family difficulties too, complicated by the rapid pace of social change. While Journo lived in Moscow for many years, she grew up in industrial Russia, where her parents still live. Her parents, both highly skilled professionals, are among those who have lost out in the new Russia. Neither is valued or well rewarded, and her parents feel anxious about the uncertainties of life in Russia today.

They are Putin supporters, a fact which Journo and her brother find 'incomprehensible'. The gap between generations is also a gap between the Soviet Union and the new Russia. They do not understand her careless attitude to consumption, to items like shoes and cake that they had to queue for, pull connections for and use coupons to buy. In London, she buys these luxuries as easily as she discards them. 'I really love my parents,' she says, 'but we are very different.' In times of rapid social, political and economic change, the lines separating generations are raw, jagged and painful to navigate.

There is no reliable estimate of how many Russians live in London. Generally, estimates range between 150,000 and 300,000. Ukrainians, Kazakhs, Georgians and others from the former Soviet Republics, many of them Russian speakers, are often misidentified as Russian. Russian millionaires and billionaires can easily move to London because their money makes them investor migrants under current immigration rules. Sometimes feuds and arguments with the Russian state follow them here. But these are the minority. Most Russians in London, Journo says, are 'just like everyone else': 'They take mortgages. They buy flats. They have dogs. [They are] professionals who live here, and are very well educated. They earn quite good money, but they are not millionaires.' I say goodbye to Journo and try a different path.

15
Waiting

I have been listening to the voices of serious money, coaxing rich people to speak. But now I want to mute them for a moment, and tune in to a different conversation: to the quiet whispers in the corners of rooms. I have visited the homes and workplaces – the public faces – of the rich. But to get behind closed doors, to see how the rich actually live, I am trying a different tack. This is where Butler comes in, telling me what he saw, letting me peep into some of the best addresses in Kensington and Knightsbridge. Legal contracts and draconian non-disclosure agreements with crippling penalties restrain butlers from speaking about their job and their employers, officially making them voiceless. Butler will only speak if I guarantee he cannot be identified from what I write. He is taking a big risk; discovery would destroy his career.

The right to speak and act freely while silencing others proves the power of money. But Butler has spent seventeen years working with demanding royal families from the Middle East, and he is ready to talk. His employers were those who were vastly enriched by the sale of fossil fuels and live in London for large parts of the year. While the Butler's experiences are undoubtedly specific, they are unlikely to be unique, nor do they only describe Middle Eastern royalty. Newspaper reports reveal that senior members of the House of Windsor are just as difficult.[1]

He is tapping into an increasingly lucrative market. The London-based Work Foundation reports that 2 million people now work in domestic service in the United Kingdom, the highest number since the Victorian era, and insists that the master–servant relationship has been updated for the twenty-first century.[2] There are no precise figures for the number of butlers in the United Kingdom or in London, where they are clustered along with the rich whom they serve. A butler placement agency, Greycoat Lumleys, reports having 5,000 butlers on its books. A 2013 estimate suggested the United Kingdom has 10,000 butlers.[3] There are more working overseas.[4] Butlers are a UK service-industry export, targeting the Middle East, Russia and China. It is no coincidence that globally these are also the hotspots generating new money, and, through butlers, looking to old money for guidance on how to be rich.

The Ditchley Park Butler Valet School and the Guild of Professional English Butlers suggest on their websites that strong demand signals the rise and rise of the 'super-super-rich'. Conceding that old-style butlers servicing old money are 'few and far between', the Butler Valet School's website targets new markets: 'Demand for the buttling arts is rising in London, where Russian oligarchs and hedge-fund billionaires are employing servants in displays of status unrivalled since Victorian times.' The Butler Valet School reworks the master–servant relationship, supposedly modernizing and democratizing it. In this version, butlers help the newly rich cultivate habits and dispositions befitting 'high society'. Because 'A mansion and a butler do not an aristocrat make', the new rich must be mentored – it's 'lavatory' not 'toilet', by the way.[5] In this surreal twist of contemporary servitude, the butler moulds a wannabe aristocracy, adding a caricature of a caricature – P. G. Wodehouse's Jeeves and Wooster – a fantasy exported around the world. This adds to the list of arcane UK exports of ideas about elite life, along with J. K. Rowling's Hogwarts, private school education and TV programmes like *Downton Abbey*. The butler is the embodiment of and guide to what is *proper*. And proper is evidently a significant UK cultural export.

Butler can offer me a glimpse of realities behind a lavish Kensington front door. As we wind our way through quiet Kensington backstreets, heading towards Knightsbridge and its grand department store, Harrods, he tells me a story about one family he worked with. They were rarely in the same place at the same time, but they were gathered together in London on this occasion. The daughters had returned from universities in the United States. Four butlers were on duty in the pantry, 'just sitting around waiting' to be summoned. When the family called for tea, the butlers sprang into action, pouring tea into six Meissen porcelain cups. Earlier that day one of the butlers had dropped two Meissen porcelain cups and so they had to find substitutes. Butler says: 'Don't get me wrong, they [the replacements] were very expensive cups as well. The mother, the Princess, happens to get one of the tea cups that wasn't Meissen porcelain, so five minutes later one of the daughters comes into the pantry banging that cup into the work surface.' He does an impersonation of her voice, haughty and indignant, '"What do you guys think you are doing? You are serving my mother tea in a cup that is not Meissen porcelain."' That was one in the morning. We had been working sixteen hours.'

Butler suspects this family was the result of an arranged marriage, a classic manoeuvre to protect dynastic wealth. He does not know if the family members love or even like each other. Could this explain why they spent so little time all together? 'The boys are all right, always hanging around together, giving trouble to the chauffeurs and to the security. The girls we didn't see that much, but whenever they were around it was just that sort of trouble.' Like the trouble of the Meissen porcelain. The Mother-Princess struggled to orchestrate family meals. 'She would spend forty-five minutes getting the nannies and the secretaries to summon everyone for dinner, but it felt like a forced thing. They didn't really want to be there ... It was embarrassing, actually, because she would get the chefs cooking millions of things and huge dinners, and no one would show up. So, she would get the secretaries or the underlings to sit with her for dinner. We felt, not sorry, because she was horrible to us, but almost embarrassed.' We are on St Albans Grove, just on the edge of Officer's territory, keeping to the backstreets, where, I suspect Butler feels less likely to be seen or overheard by anyone he knows.

Another door opens to reveal another peep show. A wealthy boss – butlers call them principals – lost his temper with a valet, because the valet didn't know how to wind up his £250,000 watch. Butler watched this scene unfold, incensed at the price of the watch and the expectation that staff should somehow know how to make it work. Behind a third front door, Butler's female principal ordered him to give the receipts from her shopping trip to her PA so that she could claim back the VAT when they left the country. The receipts showed she spent £160,000 on handbags in just an hour.

Behind the next door is the woman who stayed up until 5 a.m. watching television alone, while butlers waited at her pleasure: 'We were simply not allowed to leave the pantry.' So they had no idea what was going on in the rest of the house. Sometimes she would tell them when she was going to bed so that they could go off duty, but at other times, he remembers, 'She'd just go to bed and let us wait until morning. Just in case she called.' Butler says, 'It sometimes feels like they're bored and they want to play at something: you're their little pet.'

Butler is a tall, dark-haired and handsome Latino man with plenty of experience in private houses. From his home city of Buenos Aires, he moved into catering in the United States, where he was improving his English. He has a European passport via his parents, and this opened a route to London. He worked in hotels, freelancing at night as a butler at private events to earn extra money. He soon moved into being a butler full time because it paid well. Self-taught, he says he learned the job from a book. There are many 'how to' books for butlers: *A Butler's Guide to Table Manners*, *The Pocket Butler*, *A Butler's Guide to Gentlemen's Grooming* and *Modern Etiquette for a Better Life* are just some of the titles currently in circulation. A stint as a footman at Buckingham Palace provided a 'seal of approval' and a CV that indicated 'you've trained at the Palace'. In the world of elite service, it doesn't get better than the Queen.

Although there are some female butlers, in the main it is a man's job. Salaries are in the region of £35,000 to £45,000 a year, depending on whether the butler lives in or out – living out brings higher pay. Butler says salaries of up to £80,000 or more are not uncommon. These salaries are boosted in value when employers pay in cash or into offshore accounts. 'It depends on the principal,' he says. 'You can also get all sorts of extras. If you travel a lot, you tend to get extra money. Also, you get to travel and stay in fantastic places and eat the very best food. It's pretty hectic, but it can be a very interesting lifestyle if you work for the right people.' Despite the stories he has told me about his clients, Butler still thinks it is a pretty good job.

It is a role with imprecise duties. 'Sometimes in a big household you're going to be assigned just to look after the principal lady or gent.' Alternatively, the butler may run the entire household, or a section of it, in a management position. The largest and most elaborate households employ cleaners, waiters, maintenance staff, housekeepers, security staff, drivers, gardeners, chefs, nannies, tutors, PAs and, sometimes, multiple butlers. The twenty-first-century domestic service labour force is as complex and specialized in its own way as its nineteenth-century predecessor.

Butler's experience is managerial and mostly in very wealthy households. The 'classic butler', he says, looks after the silver, serves meals and liaises with the kitchen. But a butler might also do the packing and unpacking for journeys abroad and look after the principal's wardrobe. It all 'depends on the complexity and size of the household'. His can also be a menial job, in households with few staff, where he is expected to mop the kitchen floor, clean shoes, drive and wash the car or walk the dog. The term describes menial labour in family offices too, as I discovered. The butler's work is as varied as the demands of the household they serve.

Butlering involves long hours. Butler says, 'You never work less than fourteen hours a day. You don't have time for anything else. You basically sign away your life. You put them to bed and you get them breakfast.' Butler lived in at first, which put him on call twenty-four hours a day. Later, he learned it was better to live out, which still meant working from 8 a.m. until 10 p.m.: 'Before they wake up, you're already doing things, coordinating schedules.' Breakfast must be prepared, and the housekeeping taken care of. If it cannot be invisible, housekeeping must be unobtrusive and fast, so as not to impose on wealthy life. Nothing can be damaged or broken; everything must be 'impeccable'. The principals, he says, tend to be very 'picky' and 'possessive' about things. 'You have to make sure that the chauffeur is going to be right on time; the meal, the breakfast or whatever they're eating is going to be prepared correctly, when they want it.' Butlering demands finely tuned domestic coordination to achieve an impression of seamless perfection. The domestic life of money must resemble a high-functioning, well-maintained machine.

Sensitive management is vital, because 'There is a whole lot of politics and bitching. The first thing you do, you get on the right side of the Filipinos. All the houses have scores of Filipinos, mostly house-keepers and cleaners. They are very nice people. They're very hard-working. They have this spirit of cooperation, which is really, really strong, even if they hate each other.' According to Butler, they will both 'do anything to keep their jobs' and 'do anything to get rid of non-Filipinos'. It is important not to annoy anyone: 'If they go against you, they're going to make your life hell.' Butlers have more contact with rich bosses than other staff, and this can lead to jealousy: sometimes it puts them in impossible positions between upstairs and downstairs. While housekeepers and cleaners tend to be Filipino, 'Chauffeurs tend to be English. Security is mostly ex-army, ex-security forces. PAs will obviously be English females.' In the largest and wealthiest houses, experienced butlers are promoted to house managers, in charge of the entire complex domestic enterprise of wealthy life.

A butler must look good. 'I've been in a couple of jobs because they just like the way I look, because I look good in a suit and that's it,' Butler acknowledges. Attractive butlers are more likely to get day shifts, so that visitors will see them. 'It's extremely superficial,' Butler admits. It is important to be young and slender. Fat is unacceptable. As the butler opens the door to money's domestic world, he must look as flawless as the rest of it. First impressions begin at the entrance, and appearances are everything. Butlering is about 'playing a part' in the theatrics of plutocratic households. 'It's how you open the door and how you answer the phone and all that. Some people are employed just to be there, just to look good and to open the door as you should open the door.' He tells me the story of an older English butler, a Jeeves character, whose employers kept him by the door to strike an impression of old money, rather than to do anything very much in the house. The butler is an extension of the house and expected to function much like any household appliance.

In a world where there is a right and wrong way to open a door, Butler training can teach 'the technical side of it, how to fold a shirt, how to pack a bag, how to lay a table'. The British Butler Institute is one port of call. Henderson's Butler Training, in a two-week course, also teaches private household management, picnic preparation, classes on wine cellars, meal preparation and serving, setting up pantries, the care of silver and antiques and (my favourite) 'theory classes on cigars and how to store them'.[6] Mrs Beeton's Book of Household Management, first published in 1861, guides the wealthy on what is proper. The Butler Valet School also gives advice on how many staff to employ and how to treat them. It is not done, for example, their website notes, 'to invite servants to sit with you during a meal, offer them the use of your car or swimming pool when you are out of town, or say "thank you" for every task performed'.[7]

Yet, Butler says, experience and the ability to adapt and fit into the household are just as important as technical knowledge. 'You have to be years in the making, I suppose. You have to experience a lot of different situations. The more experienced the guy is, the more he's going to be able to adapt to a new situation. You cannot really teach that.'

What makes a butler but cannot be taught? The right disposition: knowing how to be in a wealthy household. Butler says that the 'number one' rule is discretion. 'You're invisible. You have to be invisible. You're there and you do your job. You serve, you prepare, you fetch, but that's it. You don't talk. You never start a conversation, never. You're supposed not to exist, really.' This doesn't bother him, because 'I actually don't want any personal contact with these people.' He learned not to talk to his employers, because 'The more you open your mouth, the more you could get into trouble. They can get offended very easily. The telling off and dressing down that they give you is just unbelievable, like a tantrum.' The good butler is invisible and mute. His existence manifests only in the smooth running of the household. Butler stops speaking as we cross Gloucester Road, the busy thoroughfare, but resumes his story as we slip into the quiet of Gore Street and then to Wells Way.

Meeting the demands of rich bosses, often with little notice, is the butler's mission. Bosses' demands can be reasonable and predictable, or unreasonable and unpredictable – or sometimes contradictory. 'It can be really full on, because you are in the middle of everything, so you're getting grief from the top and you're having to deal with lots of people, lots of different needs and demands and [you have to] give instructions to people and organize things.' One Middle Eastern royal Butler worked for would decide on a whim to go to Geneva for the weekend, and say to him: ' "Just bring your passport tomorrow." ' They would travel in a private jet, which waited in Geneva over the weekend before taking them to Paris. And then, 'From Paris, you go to Madrid and back to London, just because he wants to see a particular painting in the Prada. The jet is going to cost £30,000, £40,000. You're always, always going to be in the best hotel in town in the best room.' The room alone can cost £10,000 a night. Butler describes the expenses as 'massive'. Being a butler was exciting, luxurious, challenging and completely disruptive of Butler's own life with his family, which always had to take second place.

These unanticipated demands and sudden changes of plan have been the most challenging part of Butler's job. 'They don't understand how long it takes to prepare things,' he says, 'to have everything done, how the back of the house works.' For instance, some principals would ask for dinner for two, before changing their mind, inviting their friends over, and demanding dinner for fifteen, with no notice. As Butler says, with some understatement, 'It's difficult to organize a complicated dinner for fifteen people in an hour's time.' This is difficult in London; at sea on a yacht it is impossible. Butler's starts telling me about his work on yachts; he has accompanied his bosses to the Mediterranean in the summer. This is a detour from the streets of Kensington, but I cannot resist. I am curious about how rich people inhabit their yachts. He tells me, 'They don't even travel in those yachts.' They just stay in one place, or sometimes 'go from Italy to the south of France'. How do they spend their time, I wonder? 'They sleep,' he says. 'They visit other people on other yachts that are moored nearby or they go to restaurants. They like to go to famous restaurants around the world: "Oh, this is the best restaurant in the world, so we're going to go there to have a meal." It's almost like a box-ticking activity. It's, "Oh, I've been there, done that." ' Butler's bosses are driven by a desire for instant gratification, novel experiences that only they can afford, and personal whims.

In this context, trivial desires take on supreme significance. Once Butler told the yacht crew master that the principal wanted a chocolate biscuit. 'She goes to the pantry and there are fifteen different types of *white* chocolate biscuit. I said, "Wow, you're quite well stocked." She said, "Yes, because imagine we are out on the high sea and they want for something. If we don't have it, they don't care [that] we are out on the high sea. We don't have it." They're berated for not having that specific type of chocolate biscuit.' I try to imagine a person who expects to get exactly what they want, when they want it, and what it would do to them to always have these demands met.

Are there limits to the job? We are skirting around the back of Imperial College, another quiet spot. 'Whatever it is they want, no matter how stupid, I always say "yes". They simply are not used to [anyone] saying "no".' Even so, Butler says, for him, illegal activities like sourcing drugs are off limits. Are there other boundaries, desires or activities kept private from staff? It depends, he says. Some things in the house are kept private. Butler would sometimes walk into the bedroom of one of his principals and 'He would be stark naked in bed.' That's the prerogative of 'people with a lot of money'. Moments like this, he says, are uncomfortably intimate. 'I know of butlers that do the nails,' he says. 'They do the pedicure for the principal. I tend to try to keep professional, but some butlers, I think they cross the boundary of what they should be doing.' Old money, he says, tends to 'know how to behave', but new money can be unpredictable and doesn't always observe what he considers 'proper' standards and limits.

Personal boundaries are about culture and habits. These are enormously varied in a global city like London. Navigating unknown and shifting boundaries takes Butler's knowledge, flexibility and skill; it takes knowing how to *be* inside someone else's private domestic space, without causing offence or being offended. 'There is a lot of abuse,' he says. 'If any little thing goes wrong, it's just the end of the world. You wouldn't believe the size of the reactions.' He describes them as tantrums. Butlers must be able to navigate these emotional outbursts in private settings and unguarded moments.

Above all else, butlering is about *waiting*. Waiting, to do or fetch something, perfectly encapsulates the vast divide in power and authority between money and its serving class. One waits to serve the other at their convenience. 'You just wait. You just read', though, 'You have to be careful because you're there to wait. They want you to wait and stand by.' Reading must be discreet – best on a mobile phone – a book is too obvious. Before he became a butler, Butler was a valet for another Middle Eastern royal family. His job was to sit outside the principal's bedroom. 'There was a little bench in there and I spent hours and hours just waiting for him to call. I was travelling around with him, just packing, unpacking, running errands, doing anything that he possibly could need and want.' Alongside him was a private secretary, both 'just standing by the whole day'. In case. Waiting – in line, for jobs, for a pay rise, for the end of the working day, for housing, for meals – is a way of being in the modern world that shapes the time of supplicants and servers. African security guards, whom I have seen regularly on my walks, guarding the treasures of the plutocratic city, also wait, like butlers and the crews that run yachts. Some months after my walk with Butler, I will visit Monaco and watch the yachts lying idle in the harbour, their crews slowly polishing bits of chrome on the hull, waiting to set to sea. I will remark on the beauty of the $30 million super-yacht *Lady Beatrice*, owned by David and Frederick Barclay, identical billionaire twins and former owners of The Ritz hotel. The captain will reply, 'Thanks. We just clean it.' Time is not just time. Rich-time has more control and matters more; this confers importance and entitlement. Butler-time, serving time, is about waiting to do things. Finding ways to fill the time that waiting empties of any meaningful activity.

Butlers are disposable. Staff can be fired for nothing. The best way to avoid this is to do whatever the boss wants immediately and look good doing it. Butler tells the story of a man who worked for a wealthy Greek family for twenty years. 'One day he was just summoned into the living room' and fired because 'The wife perceived that he was a bit too old.' She thanked the butler, and told him, '"You've been amazing, but we're going to let you go."' Her husband demurred, but told him, '"The wife wants you to go, unfortunately."' He then went to his office and gave the butler £15,000 in cash. Butler says, 'He's really fickle. "Oh, you don't fit the bill any more, so we're going to get someone younger and better looking."'

I ask Butler what this kind of behaviour signals to him about how wealthy people think about themselves and their staff. 'They actually believe that they are better than everyone else just because they have lots of money,' he argues. This changes how they relate to people; anyone who serves them is automatically 'stupid': 'You're serving me, so therefore you're not intelligent enough.' Butler summarizes the wealthy world view as '"I possess all this, I command all this, so therefore I'm special." You start to believe that you are something different than everyone else.'

'From the servant point of view, you just need a little bit of respect. That establishes a good relationship,' Butler says. This is, evidently, not always the case. 'Some of these people, they just treat you as another thing that they own. They don't care if you need to sleep, you have to rest, you have to have some sort of mental space for yourself. You are something that they currently have, they currently possess.' If you don't function efficiently, you're fired. 'They don't care why.' He thinks, 'They don't see you as a person, necessarily, no. Some of them, of course they do. Some of them don't.' Respect restores humanity to servants who otherwise are treated as objects – machines – there to do the master's or mistress's bidding.

In addition to being expected to function *like* a machine, household objects shape master–servant relationships in other ways: 'Principals are constantly on the lookout for items going missing.' Butler says, 'It's more a psychological thing', a concern that 'people are taking advantage or stealing or something'. Wealth brings just this kind of paranoia. Rich employers are often 'quite worried, preoccupied with possessions'. He gives the example of a man with 150 suits, who will one day notice when a suit that he hasn't worn for three years has gone missing, and turn it into a 'whole big saga'. Butler has an explanation: 'They sometimes get really bored and just pick on little things just to make their days a bit more fulfilled.' Equally, he argues, the 'shouting' and 'being difficult' is part of a 'play'. 'It's not necessarily that they are super pissed off or their blood pressure is going up. Being difficult is part of the image.' Being rich confers a leading part in the drama and expensive objects become the focus of intimidating performances that serve to alleviate boredom. Objects are also a physical emblem of trust. Missing objects spell danger for servants. For the rich, who have too many things, keeping track of them is both impossible and a source of stress.

How can people with so much money be bored? Because 'They spend so much time just idling around.' The rich and their serving class seem to share a sense of futility and boredom, although each experience it quite differently. Just as they control time, the rich control boredom, and the conditions in which a poorer serving class can operate.

Butler's peep show introduces a species not yet encountered on these walks – the idle rich. So far, I have met only the overworked, overachieving rich, who don't know how to stop working. Even when they don't need the money, men like Legacy and Sturgeon need the stress to feel alive and important. The rich who substitute this wealth-amassing work with equally relentless philanthropy, like Blazer and Soviet, do so because they must be busy; they do not know how else to be. The idle rich, on the other hand, are an ancient species, with aristocratic and royal pedigrees, like Butler's bosses. They have no need to work. They may never have worked. They may have little idea what work is, beyond the exertions they observe in those who serve them. They have everything they could ever want, and more besides, and therein lies the problem. We stop and sit on a bench in the peace of Oratory Gardens for a while, before setting off again along a quiet mews called Cottage Place. As we walk past the garage doors and first-floor terrace gardens that run along an old brick wall, Butler finishes his stories in this most secluded backstreet: the front door is about to swing shut again.

As our conversation draws to a close, Butler emphasizes the unhappiness that money brings. He believes, 'The more money you have', the more 'bored and unhappy' you are. His wealthy employers are not necessarily 'super-happy' or 'super-fulfilled'. 'They all seem to be always chasing something more expensive and more complex just to give them a little bit of a thrill, to relieve the boredom that comes with having everything on a plate.' While there's no need to worry about anything, there's also no motivation to do anything, the drive most people have to get on in their lives: 'Everything that you want or you can possibly wish for, you have.'

What Butler saw is a private world of money usually obscured by confidentiality agreements. In this world, money attempts to cultivate perfect domestic lives through the work of legions of servants with specialized functions, covering all possible requirements. These servants are invisible, mute, machine-people, serving, while at the same time adorning, elaborate homes, alongside paintings, furniture and other objects. They look good and are easily disposable. As they wait to serve, they cede control of their own lives and labours. Butler himself needs to get back to work. Leaving the quiet seclusion of Cottage Place, we turn onto busy Brompton Road, and walk to Harrods, where I say goodbye to Butler and wander past its glittering seductions for a while.

The world of serious money is a world in a sense without limits, organized by the often trivial demands of the rich; in this narrow focus, they also make this world small. Their miniature kingdom is governed by their rule, and it is absolute. They command it through temper tantrums and emotional outbursts. In this world, instant gratification is the norm, as money gets exactly what it wants, when it wants it. And having made the world of money this way – into a small place run by despots – money is bored, and so must generate new dramas and experiences, and buy bigger toys to keep entertained.

Chelsea

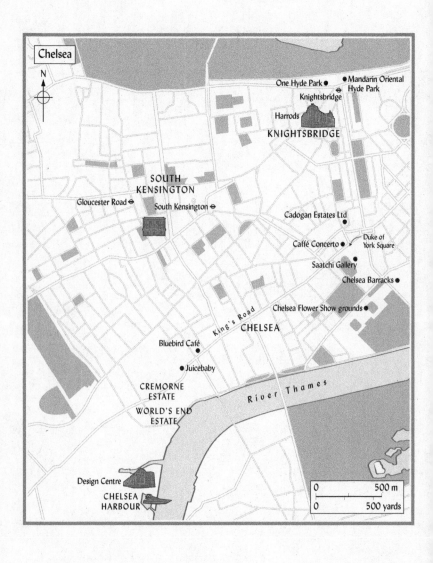

Chelsea

N

One Hyde Park ● ● Mandarin Oriental
Hyde Park
Knightsbridge ⊖
Harrods
KNIGHTSBRIDGE

**SOUTH
KENSINGTON**

Gloucester Road ⊖
South Kensington ⊖

Cadogan Estates Ltd
●

Caffé Concerto ● ↗ Duke of
York Square

Saatchi Gallery
●

Chelsea Barracks ●

Chelsea Flower Show grounds ●

King's Road

CHELSEA

Bluebird Café ●

● Juicebaby

**CREMORNE
ESTATE**

**WORLD'S END
ESTATE**

River Thames

Design Centre
**CHELSEA
HARBOUR**

| 0 | 500 m |
| 0 | 500 yards |

16

Made in Chelsea

'So, so sorry I'm late. I had to take one of my handbags to the shop.' As she hugs me effusively, Bags explains breathlessly that trading in her bags for the latest models is a sensible, cost-effective way of staying bang up to date in the handbag department. She's chosen to meet me in Juicebaby because it sells 'kale salads and cleansing juices'. Well groomed and manicured, with long blonde hair, she is slender and beautiful. In her tight skinny jeans and a shaggy fur jacket, she looks like a celebrity. Heads turn as she enters the café. Her boyfriend, Barbour, moves in behind her, dressed in a country-boy-in-the-city look I am willing to believe is ironic. In his green, waxed, Barbour jacket with its brown corduroy collar, he looks as though he should have dogs and a gun like the faceless hunting mannequins in the Mayfair shop window. They are both 20 and Chelsea is their place.

Chelsea sits between Mayfair and Kensington to the south of Hyde Park. Approaching Chelsea from Knightsbridge and walking along Sloane Street is the best way to get the measure of it. Sloane Street is a mix of designer handbag and clothes shops, as well as the stuccoed garden squares of the Cadogan Estate. I have walked past Louis Vuitton, Miu Miu, Bulgari, Hermes, and at the stucco end of the street, the Danish Embassy. On past the Cadogan Hotel is Tiffany's the jewellers, and Smythson, the upmarket stationers. I then turned into Sloane Square, and from there headed into Chelsea's iconic King's Road, the playground of the young and wealthy.

Chelsea is all about luxury shopping and King's Road is its main commercial artery. As I walked along it, I reached the Saatchi Gallery, set back into a large green at Duke of York Square. Charles Saatchi, who made his money in advertising before turning to art, donated this once private gallery to the public in 2010. Soviet sometimes exhibits his collection here. South-east of the gallery are Chelsea Barracks, a 12-acre £3 billion housing and retail redevelopment, sold by the Ministry of Defence in 2007 to the Qatari royal family. The barracks extend all the way to the Thames at Chelsea Embankment, where cranes mark another giant housing development under construction along the river. In the square outside the Saatchi Gallery, I mooched around the food stalls and cafés, and listened to the buskers. I spotted the Maldon seafood stall and watched the Saturday crowd queue for oysters: their version of fast food, perhaps. Thirty-something couples pushed well-upholstered buggies with small fretful children aboard. Almost everyone was carrying multiple carrier bags. Young men strode about in orange trainers and red jeans; fancy cars – Ferraris and Lamborghinis – were parked along the street. Chelsea is young, casual, chic, well-shod and has good wheels. Once known for the artists and craftspeople who lived here, it was *the* iconic London Street in the 1960s and 1970s, centre of the 'It crowd' and a place to be seen. Now it feels just a little cloned, the shops the same as upmarket high streets everywhere, a bit sterile and very expensive. Still, it has a certain wealthy buzz.

We order cold pressed kale and carrot juice, because it is healthy. Bags and Barbour tell me they are both from the country. Bags's family home is near the Cotswolds. Her parents are property developers. She shows me photographs of a fabulous 30,000-square-foot modern house with an indoor swimming pool that they built: building homes for plutocrats is how her parents make money. Bags and her elder sister were boarders at Cheltenham Ladies' College, and, with classmates, spent their weekends in Chelsea. Bags struggled with the discipline of this famous school, and finished her education in London with private tutors. She describes herself as 'feisty' and 'going against the grain'. At school, she announced to her teachers, 'I can do whatever the hell I want.' Cheltenham Ladies' thought otherwise and they parted company.

Barbour's family live on the Wentworth Estate in Virginia Water, in Surrey. He describes it as a 'very prestigious golfing resort' with 'beautiful houses'. 'It's really lovely,' he says. 'It's very secure, but still you're very much in the country; you've got your own space. It's a good address.' It is indeed. Houses are gated; the streets are private. I'll return to Wentworth later, on my last walk. Their other house is in Florida, and they also have an apartment in the prestigious One Hyde Park block developed by sibling celebrity property tycoons the Candy Brothers, known for paying as little tax as legally possible. Barbour was reading History at one of the colleges of the University of London, but dropped out when it didn't provide the 'university experience', by which he means the social life which his friends enjoy on the provincial campuses of Exeter and Durham. He says it 'was just a few hours a day and you do your own reading'. It's sometimes hard for wealthy students from private schools to adapt to independent learning. When I taught at the University of Southampton, I was once asked by one of my few wealthy tutees, whether he should think of me as 'nanny or matron'. I suggested he get on with some reading. Barbour explains the other reason he dropped out of university: 'My family is in property, so I've always known what I'm going to do. I realized that at the end of three years I wouldn't have gained anything to help with the business I wanted to go into.' Or, even worse, had any fun. Property speculation is a familiar route to riches for him, and his view of education is entirely instrumental. Bags, for her part, decided against going to university.

Bags and Barbour's London is Chelsea, with Knightsbridge and High St Kensington at its edges. This is where they socialize and shop; it is where their friends live. He says: 'I feel it's like a bubble here. If you're in this area, no one really leaves it; they've got everything they want here, and you just make friends, and you stick to what you're comfortable with.' They live together in a flat on the fourth and fifth floors of an older apartment block in a quiet cul-de-sac. Her family pay the rent while the couple search for 'the perfect place' to buy in Chelsea. As I mentally unfold their map of the area, I discover that it revolves around food. Bags tells me their groceries come from the local Waitrose, Wholefoods in Kensington High Street and Harrods Food Halls. But they rarely eat at home, listing between them the sushi restaurants they like best. Pizza Express is mentioned as somewhere Bags does not eat. Instead she prefers Jak's and Zefi, because they offer 'really healthy juices throughout the day'. Bags thinks about herself through the prism of health and diet; her sense of wellness is thinness. These preferred hangouts then turn into a bar at night: 'It's packed pretty much every single night, because it's a chilled-out vibe and they do really nice cocktails.' Young people from Russia and the Middle East also go there, 'everyone dressed up', with their cars waiting outside. Whereas Historian and Officer were hostile to the international super-rich, she finds these youthful displays of wealth seductive.

Her Chelsea is beautifully groomed; the young woman and the street are as one. 'I love the glamour,' she tells me. 'Even if I'm [just] going to Harrods, I'll put my make-up on, put on a nice jacket, and have my nice bag and whatever. And I like that. I like having my nails done, I have my nails done all the time.' Her hairdresser and manicurist is Paul Edmonds, where a manicure costs £200. She shops for clothes at Harrods too. 'I'm obsessed with shopping; I have a problem, don't I?' Barbour rolls his eyes in agreement. Her 'main problem' is bags. 'There's always a new bag. I have a few Chanel classics, Dior, the Lady Dior.' The bag she bought at the bag exchange, on her way to meet me, was a black Saint Laurent, since it's 'more modern now' than Dior. Her Chelsea life revolves around shopping, grooming and looking good. Barbour's version of luxury consumption revolves around expensive watches, Tom Ford suits – he has fifteen – and cars: his is a limited edition McLaren and cost around £170,000: a Chelsea car. Their lives revolve around gendered displays of wealth, supported by the luxury shops that line the streets.

Their Chelsea begins no earlier than the afternoon. They go to sleep most nights at three or four in the morning, 'even if we're not out', Bags says. 'We go out for a drink maybe every night, or we'll go for dinner . . . go for another drink, get back at 11 p.m., and then watch films and stuff.' They wake up late, around one or two in the afternoon. 'Then we go to lunch, go for a walk. We'll both see our friends.' Sometimes they drop into estate agents to talk property and the development (money-making) potential of local flats. But otherwise there is 'nothing that's productive' in their days, because 'Obviously, I don't have a job,' says Bags, and Barbour is 'doing his own thing'. And yet, she finds, 'In London I get so exhausted, so we eat out a lot.' At the family home in the country, on the other hand, she cooks and doesn't dress up. I glimpse the ingredients that make young wealthy women.

The gym is an important part of her Chelsea wellness crusade and a counterbalance to all the eating and drinking. Bags tells me, 'Hopefully next year we're going to join KX ... a private members' gym which is absolutely stunning; it's amazing.' But for now they are making do with LA Fitness in South Kensington. KX costs £2,000 to join and £6,000 a year for membership. Celebrities use it. That's its draw. The gym provides structure in an otherwise aimless day and 'gives you more energy'. Bags says, as she is, 'Everyone around here is obsessed with looking good and being fit.' Looking beautiful is *the* imperative in her life, a source of pleasure and unease. Wealthy men have high standards and plenty of options in intimate relationships. With their money comes bargaining power; and women are trophies to be won and lost. Other women are competition. Bags should know: she is the younger daughter of her dad's much younger second wife.

The popular television programme *Made in Chelsea*, a 'structured reality' soap opera that blurs the line between fiction and life,[1] is my other window onto Bags and Barbour's lives. It explores the dramas of wealthy young people: a stream of treacheries and rivalries against a backdrop of seemingly continuous social activity. Though most of the action happens in this corner of south-west London, it is often shot at the Boy's bar in Shoreditch. I was keen to speak to Bags because she had a walk-on part in one or two episodes of the show and I wondered how it compared with real life. She tells me the show's producers recruit participants by stalking them on Facebook, and then asking them to be on the show and bring their friends. Her friend was approached and Bags went along. Since the producers liked her better, she, and not her friend, got a part. This point is emphasized. Competition with other women provides a measure of self-worth.

She says it wasn't much fun. 'I found it very exciting at the beginning, being asked to do it, and having been interviewed and signing a contract,' she recalls. 'They made me feel like I was going to be the next big star. But there was no room for me to go further without some romantic thing' – a love affair with one of the male stars. She was not willing to do that, because she was already going out with Barbour. 'I think a lot of young girls would have split up with their boyfriends to do it,' she says. Instead, although the producers thought her really 'interesting' and 'confident', Bags only did 'one or two episodes', before girls who were more willing, but less interesting and beautiful, replaced her. Behind this highly staged version of youthful plutocratic life lies a darker sexual economy, one in which she refuses to be complicit, having decided not to cash in her boyfriend for temporary TV fame. A friend of Barbour's was in the show for longer, and saw the artifice up close. He told Barbour that some of the actor-participants are actually rather 'normal', as in, not rich at all. The whole thing is a 'real fake': it both reflects and conflicts with Bags's real Chelsea life at the same time.

In their 'real' lives, Bags and Barbour are poised on the edge of the adult world, waiting for the future to begin. She says, 'We're both driven to earn our own money.' He feels he will get more pleasure from spending money he has actually earned. 'People might not think it, but you do get bored of having nice things' when they are simply given to you. 'I'd quite like to walk past somewhere and be like, "I built that, I did that,"' Barbour says. 'I think that would be a nicer achievement than actually just buying things and wasting time.' The future begins with work and earning money, rather than dependence on the family firm. This next move, as wealthy children become wealthy adults, will involve a 'proper' use of their time. What is proper concerns them.

Bags tried working. She got a job in the City, because 'I'm driven.' She repeats, 'I want to make money for myself.' Viable adulthood means earning money. The City job was in recruitment – often a women's niche – for technology platforms and hedge funds. 'It just wasn't me,' she says. This was followed by a bit of nannying, because 'I love children.' But nannying didn't work out either, and, since then, Bags has been 'a lady of leisure' for a few months, because 'I didn't know what I wanted to do.' She is considering an offer to work as a sales and lettings negotiator with a European estate agency that usually trades in large villas and is hoping to set up nearby. She thinks this might be 'cool' since she's 'always been more interested in property' – the family business.

Barbour meanwhile wants to extend his family's property portfolio to London and buy small, high-value flats in Chelsea and Knightsbridge. At the moment, they operate in Surrey, developing big houses. 'My dad said that he will back me buying a flat around here.' His dad will buy the property, but Barbour will be, 'doing it up myself, so that I can learn on my own a bit with guidance'. He sees this as 'building my way up' before joining the family business. 'So, if I can do my own thing for maybe five, ten years, get good at what I do, then I can bring something to the business' – a new London angle. 'It's a lot less work,' he thinks, compared to Surrey, 'especially around this area: it's a bubble. The money is the same for a much smaller area; people pay much more.' He thinks he sees a gap in the market, as he wanders Chelsea and Knightsbridge. Rich young Chinese and Middle Eastern investors, whom he meets socially anyway, want a London bolthole they will use infrequently. His father will let him keep the profits he makes, and he will spend them on another car. This is his way to build his wealth and leave his mark on these streets.

The life the young couple anticipate replicates what they know: making lots of money through buying and selling property, and living a good life in a large house in Chelsea, Kensington or on the Surrey fringes – they are still deciding where. Bags says once again, 'I want to work, and I want to prove to everybody and myself I can be successful. Why are you laughing?' Her question is to Barbour. 'But I don't want to work for ever. He's fully aware we probably want to get married in three years.' Bags plans to stop work when she has her first child, since she has always imagined herself as 'a very motherly and caring person': 'So I think I'll really enjoy looking after children. I love to cook for everybody, so I think being a mum at home is my dream.' Alongside this, she wants to do charity work, rather than being a mother who 'literally just goes shopping every day to Waitrose'. She wants to do the school run, all the shopping and all the cooking. 'Hopefully I'll have a nanny.' Barbour laughed when she mentioned being successful at work, but he does not demur on the marriage and family plan. I sense the same retro atmosphere, set somewhere in the 1950s, with the stay-at-home mother and working father, as I experienced in Notting Hill. Bags is a rich Notting Hill wife in training, right down to her aspiration for a charity portfolio.

I ask if she had a nanny. She did. Did Barbour? 'My nanny is still with me,' he says. He is the eldest and the family still employ the same nanny. Bags is certain she will want help, since 'I want to be able to spend time with the children, and not have to do the cooking and clearing up while I have a baby in my hand, or whatever.' Paid 'help' will also leave her more time for higher callings: 'charity work and keeping productive'. She is particularly interested in mental health charities, 'for people that are depressed in their teens': 'That's a really difficult time; it's things that I have been through myself, and I'd love to help. I've always felt from my experience I've got a lot to tell people and help people with.' Her self-confidence conceals a troubled adolescence. Whatever else it does, the fun-time Chelsea playground cultivates ultra-conventional versions of wealthy adult life in the young. Their money provides them with so many opportunities, and yet they seem incapable of imagining different ways of being.

I am surprised their lives are so tame. But maybe they are editing for my benefit. I know, from our previous research of London's 'alpha spaces', that the nightclubs where Bags and Barbour play have a dark predatory side they don't discuss. Clubs are patrolled by 'door girls' in high heels and fur coats brandishing clipboards and lists of names, ushering VIP guests inside. Tables start at £600 and cost as much as £10,000, the most expensive prominently displayed in the centre of the room or on a raised platform. While there are many places where wealth is stealthy, as I discovered in Mayfair, in these venues it is a spectator sport. Pretty, slim girls in shorts, cropped tops and high heels bring drinks to rich men's tables, and the men compete to buy the most expensive champagne. When champagne arrives, it comes with a fanfare of sound and light creating a spectacle, a 'champagne train', to draw the most attractive women to the wealthiest men. Sociologist Ashley Mears describes similar excessive displays of conspicuous consumption in the United States, as ritualized waste, signs of extreme wealth. In Chelsea, as in New York, champagne is drunk straight from the bottle, given away or sprayed around. For such clubs, separating rich men from their money is the underlying business model, but other transactions are at play too. Women are selected for their youth and beauty; often they are models or students. They get to party for free, and bait rich men for their own reasons, as they urge them into competitions to outspend each other. 'Promoters' working through Facebook encourage 'girls' to bring their prettiest friends to clubs. They must – as Bags and Barbour know too well – have a *Made in Chelsea* look: not too revealing, just jeans, heels or boots, minimal make-up and natural hair; wealthy boho. Women who are overweight, badly dressed or who do not meet high standards of conventional beauty are denied entry by doormen who rapidly scan assets.

Young women live on the ambiguous, slippery edge of the night, part guests and part offering. They must navigate the sliding scale between, at one end, accepting expensive drinks and providing conversation, and, at the other, escort services, casual sex or even upmarket prostitution duties for rich men.[2] Mears suggests that wealthy men do not see the women they pick up in clubs as potential marriage partners, and this constrains how women decide to spend what she calls their 'bodily capital': do they want to be rich wives and girlfriends or good-time girls? 'All girls exist on the thin edge of a moral boundary [socially understood as] separating them from sex workers,' Mears says. This might account for Bags's emphatic identification of herself as a wife in the making and not a playgirl.

We have long since finished our detoxifying cold-pressed juice, and it is time for Bags and Barbour to do whatever they do in the late afternoon – check estate agents' windows and get some lunch, perhaps – before the evening's social rounds begin again. I want to probe the reality gap between their Chelsea and *Made in Chelsea* a bit further. I walk south-west along King's Road to one of the filming locations for the series, the Bluebird Café. Here, in the late evenings, young and beautiful people congregate to gossip.

The upstairs bar at the Bluebird Café is vast. At one side, there is a bar running along the wall; at the other side are windows onto King's Road, with carefully arranged intimate seating areas between them. It's empty, this late afternoon. The barmaid, dressed in black with tattooed arms and legs, tells me it gets busier around 8 p.m., when a young crowd arrives. I order a drink and sit at a table near two white men in their fifties and a younger woman who may be of Asian descent, in a black sleeveless dress and flat red suede shoes, who seems to know one of the men. One of the men wears a linen jacket, jeans and battered leather loafers; the other is in an open-necked short-sleeved shirt and jeans. While the first man is quiet, the other has a loud, commanding – read rich – voice. They are all drinking espresso martinis, and the men are reminiscing about their time working on the

Hong Kong stockbroker scene for Morgan Grenfell, while the woman listens. At least she is not required to smile. 'Remember Pilkington-Smyth?' the loud man says. 'I knew his brother in Hong Kong. Now lives in Sydney. Has one son.' They order more espresso martinis and talk about 'the Chinese', life in Sydney, Hong Kong and its house prices, until the quiet man says, 'Let's go for an Indian.' 'I don't know where,' the loud one replies. And, as they move towards the exit, 'You know common people.'

I'm waiting for Student. She lives in suburban north London but goes to the Bluebird with friends from university – she won a scholarship to one of London's private universities. They charge higher tuition fees than regular universities, and attract the children of the rich through smaller class sizes and – shall we say – a less socially diverse student body. The same age as Bags and Barbour, Student is in her final year. Her hair is scraped back in a ponytail, and she is thin and intense, in skinny black trousers and high platform shoes. I want another take on rich Chelsea youth and thought she would have something to add.

Who are her fellow students? She tells me their parents are a mix of new money millionaire or billionaire Europeans, who are in business, especially tech, and English old money types, who are less wealthy but still educated at expensive private schools. Their fathers seem to be CEOs, or work in investment banks. These students are often bought flats and even houses in Kensington, Chelsea, Marylebone and Islington. They navigate London in cabs. She, on the other hand, lives at home with her mum in a single-parent family that struggles financially. She works part-time while she studies.

Her daily exposure to wealthy students over two years makes Student acutely aware of what she calls their 'sense of entitlement'. By this she means a taken-for-granted ease. While it rarely enters the consciousness of those, like Bags and Barbour, who live it, it stands out to those who do not. 'You can see the entitlement a mile off,' she says, citing the way they interact in social gatherings: 'They talk over each other in a mass.' Their conversations are not dialogues. Instead, they perform self-aggrandizing sound bites in competition with each other. In class, they 'intellectually peacock', without making a relevant point and often express illiberal views on issues like poverty. It's the poor's fault, apparently. 'No one's ever challenged them or told them "No", [so] they think they're entitled to say whatever they want.'

Entitlement, Student reflects, means not having to consider other people's circumstances and sensibilities. They might pretend to have bought their designer clothes in charity shops – implicitly acknowledging that it's not cool to be rich – and yet post Instagram pictures of themselves on super-yachts. When Student and her friends are deciding where to go for dinner, they will 'casually' suggest somewhere that costs £200 each. Or, 'They'll order a bottle of wine when they're in a group that costs £300 and expect everyone to split the bill.' Expecting others to pay: also entitlement. Student remembers going to a birthday party where 'Three girls, who all have enormous wealth, kept ordering bottles of Prosecco and got very drunk, and left before the bill came.' She is certain 'It wasn't even a malicious thing. They literally assumed that everyone else would be able to afford to pay for them.' She tells me about another small group of students who spent £3,000 on a single night out in Chelsea.

These young socialites live without boundaries and consequences: further marks of entitlement, as Student describes it. 'There's no sense of accountability or responsibility,' Student says. 'They don't really care.' This translates into doing 'as many drugs as they want': 'They'll get very messed up.' They also cheat on their girlfriends and boyfriends; they skip class and fail to hand in assignments. 'It's because they have this background radiation, which is telling them that no matter what you do, it's going to be okay,' Student thinks. 'You don't have to work hard or be a good person because someone is always going to give you a job or open a door for you.' 'Background radiation' is an interesting description: toxic and unavoidable at one and the same time. No matter what, the family safety net will catch them. 'Some of them have family lawyers on retainer to get them out of whatever trouble they get into,' Student explains. 'They tell hilarious stories of themselves wreaking havoc while on holiday, and being busted out of prisons by family lawyers who fly over to wherever they are. It's insane.' She says, 'They see it as a badge of pride to see what they can get away with. If you live a life where there aren't any consequences, and no matter what you do it's always going to be okay, then you're going to do some pretty destructive things.' Student has spent holidays with university friends flying on private planes to private islands, and has seen the emotional damage in self-harming behaviour first-hand.

The family safety net also ensures that the future is already laid out for rich young people, as Student uncovers still further vistas of entitlement. She knows friends who are guaranteed a job at a bank when they graduate. She was initially confused, asking, 'What do you mean you've got a job at a bank? You haven't applied.' It invariably turns out that their father is the CEO or knows the CEO. As a result, she says, 'They don't really understand what it's like to actually have to work for anything. If they want to start a business, they can just get a £10 million loan from one of their parents.' While this may be an exaggeration, Student expects to struggle in her own future. Her debt when she finishes university will be the student average – £50,000 to £60,000 – despite her scholarship. She hopes she will get a job, although competition is fierce, and earn enough to rent a flat, some day.

Securely mapped-out futures are not very exciting. Some of her fellow students have 'dreams and visions of the world that are far greater than . . . what their path is limited to': 'A lot of them are like, "I'd love to go and be a painter or do this and do that", but, instead, they're going to be an investment banker because that's the path laid out for them.' Money seems to produce insularity. Some of them are 'genuinely very nice people', Student says. 'It's just because of the way they've been raised, they don't ever think outside themselves.' They are certain that whichever path they take will be the right one, because as one of them said to her, '"I'm going to be very rich and have everything I want."' Perhaps the price of security is boredom. And, as I found with Bags and Barbour, there is little room for imagination and manoeuvre: 'Even the richest girls always talk about marrying rich. They see themselves as having ambition and drive, and working hard at university, but when they talk about the future, they talk about husbands rather than jobs.' Male students talk about becoming a CEO or starting their own company. Her observations suggest a limited grasp of the world, in which wealthy young adults mimic their parents' lives and ways of making money, their options heavily prescribed by gender and tradition.

Entitlement also encourages instrumental relationships. Student says, 'They literally see each other as means to an end.' She finds that her mega-rich classmates, the millionaires and billionaires, are very distrusting of others, because of the 'vulturistic culture' in which they are reared. 'They don't actually have real friendships. They don't accept that someone could just want to be their friend. It's always like, "What do you want from me?"' She says this extends to their most intimate family relationships, seen in equally instrumental terms. Rich children learn to value their parents because of their money, the doors money can open, and the lifestyle it brings. 'It's all in relation to material wealth,' Student thinks. 'I very rarely hear them talk about their parents like, "I really love my mum; I really miss her." It's always in terms of the instrumental value of another human.' It is an emotionally limited world, if connections are always just that.

At the same time, it is a world of extravagant display, where the spectacle of wealth is constantly performed. This is exacerbated by Instagram, which intensifies 'these amazing, crazy, wild parties and trying to outdo each other'. The attitude, Student says, is '"Oh, you had a chocolate fountain at your party, so I'm going to have a swimming pool full of jelly at mine."' Displays of crazy excess also manifest in drug use: 'There's obviously a lot of drugs and cocaine that gets floated around.' She knows many rich young people who are addicted to cocaine, simply because 'They can afford it whenever they want, and it's the culture.' Of course, the pressure to party works against the imperative of looking beautiful, which Bags describes. 'They all look immaculate from their hair to their nails to their skin to their make-up because, if you can afford the best, you're going to look good,' Student says. Some have hair and make-up artists visit every morning before they go to university, which is 'ridiculous'. Student is irritated by their vacuous, competitive, performative lifestyle: going to spin classes early in the morning, having juice cleanses and so on. 'They just look perfect and it's really annoying.'

With this disturbing vision of Chelsea's entitled young plutocrats in my mind, I say goodbye to Student, who is meeting friends, and walk south-westwards along King's Road to where it becomes the district known as World's End. I am hoping there are better stories out there somewhere: perhaps there are other, more exciting, and original, versions of rich life in these streets. Student has revealed an assumption in my own thinking I was unaware of. I imagined that wealth and security would free people to be more creative and experiment with living in different ways. This, of course, is the prejudice of people like me, whose lives are shaped by the imperatives of earning a living. Instead of creativity, I am finding rigid conformity and the precarious mental health that Student has described as emotionally 'stunted' and 'neurotic'.

17

Stuff

A walk-in wardrobe the size of an average house has space for 600 pairs of designer shoes. A unique dining table is made from the skins of forty stingrays. LED crystals embedded in wallpaper make a room glow; a wall hanging is crafted from 2,000-year-old petrified moss injected with silicone; an occasional table has been hewn from a 400-year-old olive tree dug out of the gardens of the Palace of Versailles, redolent of the gravitas of its royal provenance. Exquisite is good, rare is better, being on the point of extinction is better still. I am on the sofa watching *Millionaires' Mansions*, pretending I'm doing research. The British television programme reveals what goes into making the 'palaces of our time', as one of their featured designers put it, inviting viewers to graze on a mesmerizing spectacle of excess. Interior design embeds the substance of wealth, as it turns money into stuff.

London is internationally recognized as an interior design hub, and Chelsea is design central. I tear myself away from *Millionaires' Mansions* and venture out to explore Chelsea some more. To reach the Design Centre at Chelsea Harbour, I walk along King's Road heading south-west, and turn left into Flood Street, where former prime minister Margaret Thatcher once lived at number 19. Cheyne Walk, parts of it built in the eighteenth century, once numbered Rolling Stones – Jagger, Richards and Wood – among its famous residents. I find the Design Centre, part of Imperial Wharf on the north bank of the Thames. It is a building site. Cranes predominate, and giant hoardings announce the arrival of a *stunning collection of 89 luxury apartments*, illustrated with photo mock-ups. River views, and the Thames especially, are real-estate gold. Rising out of the building chaos and the sound of drilling is the Design Centre, in soft red London brick, topped with three glass domes, originally built in 1987, and since extended.

The daily work of maintaining the Centre it is in full swing as I mount its marble steps. Windows are being cleaned, floors vacuumed, furniture is being wrapped ready for transit, and well-dressed men and women sit at small tables in their tiny shops staring at Mac laptops. I chat to the Nepalese concierge at the front desk, as UPS workers come in and go out with deliveries. The components of luxury interiors are passing in large boxes right by me; this is a good place for me to think about what luxury is and learn about how it is assembled.

The Design Centre is an emporium of 120 small shops brimming with top quality materials and design ideas, between them showcasing 600 of the world's luxury brands. Its atrium construction reveals tiers of tiny shops, each specializing in an element of interior design. Swathes of coloured fabrics hang from the ceiling below the glass-domed roof, as a gleaming white tiled floor reflects the colours above. Various decorative accessories are displayed here, including urns, and outsized china leopards and giraffes. The shopfronts open to the domed atrium are stuffed with rugs, throws, cushions, fabrics, wallpaper, furniture and lighting; the entire building is a cabinet of stuff waiting to be incorporated into seriously wealthy homes.

I climb all the way to the top of the building and look down from the top tier of the atrium into the café on the ground floor, where I can see the man I am here to meet working at a table. I descend towards him in the lift. 'Is that Miyake darling?' He means the Japanese fashion designer Issey Miyake. Colour greets me, touching my jacket, casting his professional eye over my clothes. 'No,' I say, 'it's a good fake though.' I like a good fake. I spend too much time in Beijing, where the fakes are excellent. In fact, they often improve on the original. Colour is instantly friendly and effusive; although we have just met, I feel I've known him for years. This is his skill. He shows no sign of urgency or impatience, though I am his third meeting of the day and it's only 11 a.m. He looks twenty years younger than his almost 60 years: tall, slender, shaved head, designer stubble beard, big expressive gestures, designer jeans and orange Vivienne Westwood T-shirt. (He knows her. He's a fan.) A self-described 'gay boy', he is flamboyant, creative, charming; it is himself, his ability to make people feel good about themselves, as well as the interior visions in his head, that he sells to the world's wealthiest people. As clients often want further designs and many have several properties, he tells me he's never looking for work. One of his wealthiest clients has no fewer than five Gulfstream private planes: what an excellent way to measure wealth. He tells me 'Skinny is the new black', and so I order two skinny lattes.

I want to understand the alchemy of interior design. How is it all put together? Colour tells me he starts with the outside and collaborates with architects, if he is working on a rebuilding project. Exteriors and interiors must be integrated. No detail is too small: even the hair dryer socket must be in the right position in the bedroom. 'It's all about the visual. Everything I do is about aesthetics. It's about how it looks; it's never about spend, because I work with billionaires.' One Zurich client is spending £144 million redesigning his 30,000-square-foot interior.

His style? 'I give you colour,' he declares expansively. 'I give you texture, I give you an eclectic mix of things, and I pull everything together – travel the world to find objects and things.' He does not do minimalist Scandi bland. He begins with the living areas. 'I create colour palettes. I might do an autumnal pattern – there has to be what I call a thread that links each room. Because you don't want to do an autumnal room and then you walk into a silver room. It needs to be this infusion of autumnal colours that runs through the home.' Palettes are assembled on 'mood boards', which create the tones. Then the bedrooms, 'which I always call cocoons', follow. He tells clients: 'It's *your* bedroom; we need to have this beautiful space. We need to have this seating area. And I think your derrière must only sit on cashmere. We must do cashmere and we must do silk, and we must do raw silk and we must do solid silver. And we must do bespoke, pearls and whatever. It's their space; we are going to make it super-luxurious.'

Colour builds and shapes his clients' literacy in materials. 'Every fabric is going to be the best. Why? Because *you* are the best. *You* are fabulous and this is *your* bedroom. You want your bedroom to be sensational, so luxurious that whatever you touch and stroke, it is just beautiful.' He tells me how he created a bedroom seating area with sofa and chairs covered in 'soft pale duck-egg grey cashmere sitting on wild silk'. 'Wild,' he reiterates, emphasizing the difference by rapping on the table. Wild silk is gathered in the Chinese countryside, not cultivated. It is better, rarer and more natural in not being mass-produced – the free-range eggs of the silk world. Equally superior, I learn, are solid elm doors, hand-carved basins, fine merino wool mounted on walls, £30,000 hand-made beds, and mattresses made from horse-hair, cashmere and more wild silk. Each room tells a story that complements the taste and cultivated refinement of its owners, newly tutored by Colour in what rare and expensive materials can do for them. 'It's about proportion,' he says, 'it's about shape, it's about form.' The aesthetics of wealth. Materials have provenance and character, stories traced in their grain, like the table made from the olive tree at the Palace of Versailles – another monument to luxury – and the opposite of mass production. Colour's job is to spin narratives like these, offering something that is 'enchanting' and 'magic'. My first lesson in luxury: luxury is seduction! It's certainly working on me.

With the design, the palette and the price settled, Colour commissions the job, ordering its components, sometimes from the Design Centre, and appoints the right craftspeople: carpenters, lighting designers, tilers, and the rest. London, he says, has the best of the best. He orders lamps made to specific designs, not off the shelf. He finds rare veneers, timbers and woods. He visits the rug shop on the top floor of the Design Centre: 'They'll do standard rugs, they'll do silk, they're beautiful. A rug from there is only going to cost maybe £50,000.' He shows me a photograph of a rug that costs a quarter of a million pounds. Why? Because, of course – it's wild silk. After all, Colour explains, 'The whole point of what I do is to bring to them something that will not be everywhere, that will be unique to them.' He says, 'If you pay what you want, you can have what you want. Whatever the texture, whatever the colour, whatever the fabric, whatever the timber, it just needs to be a little bit more precious, a little bit more special.' His wealthy clients deserve the best because they are special. Their money proves it. And their homes are assembled to reflect their value.

Colour's relationships with clients are convivial and intimate. Some – he cannot be specific without breaking client confidentiality – become friends and invite him to social occasions. Others are more businesslike. He is part of the high-end plutocrat serving class, respected and well rewarded for a job at which he excels and loves doing. When it comes to the bill he says: 'I want to be impeccable to the last penny. Most billionaires think people are after them for their money.' This makes it vital to order and charge correctly across thousands of items, showing transparency, but prioritizing a love of design above the money that it costs. It's not about the money. That would be grubby. The commercial reality of the client–designer relationship is obscured beneath a luxurious pile of cashmere. We talk more about his job, about his clients, about his life, until it is time for him to visit the architect he is working with in Kensington. I walk with him to the Overground station nearby at Imperial Wharf and we say goodbye.

I wind my way inland from the river and along the southern end of King's Road, around World's End. Here is a cluster of shops that also service interior designers, perhaps a little more avant-garde than the Chelsea Design Centre, still a short walk away. In an unpretentious café, I meet Atmosphere, to hear about another world of upscale design. She works with a famous studio designing domestic and commercial interiors for hotels and restaurants, as well as individuals. In her thirties and dressed in jeans and T-shirt, she juggles cycling helmet and backpack as we sit down to talk. There is an empty child's seat on the back of her bike reserved for her three-year-old daughter, who is at nursery. She is also a part-time design lecturer at a university, skilled at teaching design as well as practising it.

She tells me about a job on the house of a 'Russian oligarch' in Kensington. He has eight houses and he and his girlfriend use this particular house infrequently. Unable to meet with the design team in person, the couple relayed their brief through intermediaries, which is not unusual with rich clients. Not having met them, she says, 'We had to invent them.' The brief was no bling, just low key: 'They just wanted to be normal.' It sounds like Colour's worst nightmare. In one of Kensington's most prestigious streets, normal translates into Scandi bland but in expensive and 'authentic' materials, not Ikea. The design team created enormous bookcases and then, realizing too late that they had no books to fill them with, employed a curator to assemble a collection of art, design and rare books, compiling a library for two people they had never met. The oligarch's kitchen was kept out of sight in the basement and fully staffed, but on the main floor they installed an adult-sized 'play kitchen' because his girlfriend liked to make cupcakes. The house had an entire wing dedicated to security, and three or four security people in that office at all times. A panic button had to be built into the custom-made bed. Atmosphere says the design team reviewed the merits of different kinds of panic buttons and checked which side of the bed it should be installed on, baking security into design.

Atmosphere says interior design must reflect people's ideas and fantasies about who they are. She builds 'theatre sets', stages on which clients will live the lives they imagine and desire. They want interiors to express, in objects, fabrics and colours, the lives and selves they aspire to be. Design is about aspiration, a step beyond what is, a step towards something better: better selves, who will bake cupcakes and read classic literature. And the interior designer is a translator. Atmosphere translates aspirations into arrangements of objects – a pot here, a cushion there, bookshelves oozing erudition in the corner. Successful translation means these arrangements convincingly reflect their owners' sense of who they are.

Atmosphere creates atmospheres: this is her genius. She has an instinctive sense for the feelings and imaginings that objects and decor convey. She unlocks the stories embedded in artefacts with long histories: like people, objects have biographies. Old furniture, she says, has soul, like 'an art collection' of 'beautiful, rare and original pieces'. The messages that are ingrained in objects and furniture, or in combinations of materials, are released when artfully combined. Of course, these intangible qualities are not immediately obvious, and Atmosphere must explain them to rich clients in the same way as Colour educates them in rare materials. Composition is everything: 'You are working with beauty, and you are working with history, and you are combining things in a way that starts to tell a story.' Interior design is a carefully composed stage set on which rich people play out the storylines of lives they imagine for themselves. On this note, Atmosphere cycles off to pick up her little daughter from nursery.

I am left wondering about the craftspeople who realize these ideas. Colour and Atmosphere assemble luxury. But who makes it? I do not have to look far for an example. One of my neighbours in Hackney,

Light, tells me how he got into making the lighting for luxury interiors. We talk in his flat, in a modern block overlooking a tangle of main roads, which, like my own, is a far cry from luxury. Sitting among the toys abandoned by his children, who have finally gone to bed, we talk about how he started out. He graduated from art school, with spectacularly bad timing in 2008, and struggled to find work. Scanning the city for opportunities, he set up a company making light sculptures with his last £50. He says these are not chandeliers, but feats of art and engineering, costly and time consuming to design and create. Light sculptures adorn the homes of the rich and illuminate the entrances of corporate buildings. While I am wondering if I could afford one, if he gave me mates' rates, he tells me they start at £50,000 and that half a million is not an uncommon price.

While London was tightening its collective belt as austerity bit, Light was surprised to get his first commission. It was at One Hyde Park in Knightsbridge, the apartment block designed by architect Richard Rogers and developed by Nick and Christian Candy. The Candy brothers bought the site for a reported £150 million originally; the biggest of its eighty-nine apartments was thought to have been sold for £160 million when it opened in 2007. Sixty-four of the apartments are registered as owned by companies, rather than people.[1] At night, the apartments are ominously dark, suggesting there are few permanent residents. The apartments overlook Hyde Park and are linked to the room and concierge services of the Mandarin Oriental Hotel next door. It is hard to imagine why the developers needed to cut costs by employing young, aspiring makers, like Light, but he says they are good at this. While his clients must not pay him particularly generously, or he wouldn't live in the same neighbourhood as me, Light travels on private planes all over the world to install his creations. He tells me how he was whisked off on an oligarch's private plane, at short notice, to install one of his sculptures on the oligarch's yacht. On yachts, 'luxury is non-negotiable'.[2] Alongside Light's fabulous creations, they feature such items as backlit onyx staircases, fully kitted-out en-suite bathrooms, spas and, even, leather seats for the submersible. Yachts are simply another stage set for luxury. Yet, Light does a job he loves, using his creativity and imagination. He makes me think of all the other craftspeople, tilers, curtain-makers, decorators, cabinetmakers and the rest: people whose skills make the luxurious interiors of the plutocratic city, but are not especially well rewarded.

What is luxury, then? Apart from being the stuff that only serious money can buy? Colour's notion of luxury is tactile: the finest, softest, most unique materials, delicately wrapped around the most valuable bodies and lives. Atmosphere's luxury is the 'authenticity' very rich people crave, perhaps because they feel its absence. It is difficult, she says, to 'manufacture that sense of realness and authenticity and culture'. I think of the women in Notting Hill, who admire their poorer neighbours for bringing authenticity to the neighbourhood. New stuff, Atmosphere thinks, is a little like Disneyland – 'fake'. Old money prides itself on generations of slowly accumulated stuff, but for the newly wealthy it must be created instantly, and it must match. Luxury interiors then are real fakes, just like my Miyake lookalike jacket. On this, both designers agree. Luxury in interior design is custom-built, carefully coordinated and curated.

As she prepares to go, Atmosphere tells me that she leaves these illusions of luxury at work. When she sees a rug or a chair that she can afford at cost price, she says, she reminds herself of the realities of her life: 'Oh the cat's going to be sick on that rug and my children are going to smear peanut butter on that sofa.' The luxury interiors of the rich on the other hand are untroubled, or so they must believe, by the inconvenience of children, cats and peanut butter. Theirs is a life cleared of mess. Above all, luxury is pristine and seemingly effortless: maintained through the efforts of others, the specialist life-smoothers.

These visions of stuff as embodying ease and abundance convey important social messages about what it means to be rich. American sociologist Thorstein Veblen, who wrote *The Theory of the Leisure Class* at the end of the nineteenth century, coined the term 'conspicuous consumption', to describe how the rich mark their privilege and distinguish themselves from the masses. Much later, in 1979, French sociologist Pierre Bourdieu developed the idea of distinction.[3] He argues that the stuff people buy sends powerful signals about their social standing, in the process defining 'good taste' for the rest of us. Buying objects that are distinct from the stuff that most people can afford – like wild silk – is what *makes* the rich and the lives they lead.

They are rich because their money allows them to live among fine things in fine homes.

Do the rich define luxury for the rest of us? Sociolinguists Crispin Thurlow and Adam Jaworski build on Bourdieu's argument to suggest that the luxuries enjoyed by the rich provide a model of the good life for us all, that ideas about luxury trickle down to the masses.[4] Who doesn't like a bit of luxury? Even in tiny instalments – a hotel room, a scented bath, a silk scarf, chocolates. Equally, though luxury is a popular aspiration, Thurlow and Jaworski acknowledge that small, occasional luxuries like chocolate are not the same as the dense concentrations of luxuries that only the rich can afford. And I like to think that ideas about luxury do not just trickle down, but get reworked along the way; we see it, adapt and recreate it, as luxury is popularized and massified, like high tea at the Savoy Hotel. Last time I visited, the restaurant staff were juggling coach parties from various parts of the United Kingdom, who, like me, were sampling a little luxury, rolled out factory-style for the masses. Most of us are seduced by luxury. It would be dishonest to pretend otherwise, and I am as taken in as everyone else by its many seductions.

It is difficult to resist the lure of luxury. Magazines relay it for popular consumption in the glossy pages of *Vogue*, *Tatler*, *Prestige*, *Haute Living*, *Elite Traveler* and the rest. *How to Spend It*, published with the UK *Financial Times Weekend* magazine, has modelled luxury for its readers over decades. Its content is a glossy string of advertisements for luxury brands of jewellery, clothes, travel goods, food and wine, leavened with glimpses of the lifestyles of the rich and famous. There is nothing in it I can actually afford to eat, wear or do. And yet it fascinates me. Qing Wang, an expert on consumption quoted by *Guardian* journalist Andy Beckett, describes it as an 'Argos catalogue' for the rich. Supposedly, a well-thumbed copy was found in Muammar Gaddafi's compound when he was captured in 2011.[5] Aimed at the global elite – it is estimated that less than a third of its million readers live in the United Kingdom – *How to Spend It* guides the global new rich on what to want and do.

I set up a meeting with an insider at the *Financial Times* in Caffé Concerto on King's Road some days later as I retrace my steps around Chelsea. She tells me the conceptions of luxury in *How to Spend It* are 'vulgar' and entirely commercially driven, as we tuck into coffee and cake. 'Look,' she says, leafing through it, 'this looks like something from the court of Louis XIV.' Primarily made up of cheap, stock advertising photographs with little actual journalism, it rakes in the advertising revenue that keeps the newspaper afloat, and extols the virtues of the luxury goods its journalists are supposedly testing. *How to Spend It* is one of the most enthusiastic champions of a certain kind of commercial luxury, which it helps to define. But the magazine has come under new management. Its new editor, Jo Ellison, is a top fashion journalist and brings a modernizing agenda and an inclination towards philanthropy and environmentalism. While luxury consumption and environmentalism are radically opposed objectives – it is hard to imagine that the materials and resources that go into making a stingray table represent a benefit to the planet – Ellison is responding to the public mood for sustainability. Journalist Lucia van der Post, reflecting on what has changed in her twenty-five years of writing about luxury, says that previously, 'Intrinsic to the idea of what constituted luxury was the premise that it had to consist of objects or experiences that only the very wealthy could afford.'[6] As some luxuries, like tea at The Ritz, become affordable in small quantities, the search for expensive novelties moves ever onwards. 'What they want are things rarer still: pure air, silence, starry skies.' 'The appeal of "stuff",' van der Post says, has lessened, and 'Special experiences matter more.' Like money itself, luxury is an ever-shifting concept, always with an eye to new exclusivities. From an environmental perspective, this endless search for new frontiers of luxury is a disaster. Luxury and sustainability cannot inhabit the same planet: one destroys the other.

Like many wealthy adventurers before them in a quest for new frontiers, plutocrats have taken to the high seas. Private planes aside, there is no more expensive and environmentally damaging item in the realm of stuff than a yacht. There is no more emphatic a statement of being seriously rich. Yachts stand poised between the world of physical and intangible luxuries, like acquiring new experiences through travel. I visited Antibes and Monaco, the top yacht spots in the Mediterranean, last summer, and, as I was standing looking out over super-yacht harbours, it dawned on me that yacht size is a visible proxy for degrees of wealth, as much a ranking tool as the *Sunday Times* Rich List. The starting price for a small one is $100,000; the average yacht price is over $8 million. Roman Abramovich's yacht, *Eclipse*, is thought to have cost £1 billion to buy – much of it in extras like the missile defence system and luxury fittings – and £40 million a year in upkeep, and is reputedly the world's *second*-largest yacht, even though it was the largest when he ordered it. This is not his only yacht, and Abramovich regularly upgrades them, so he has the fastest, the longest, the most expensive. Currently, the world's biggest yacht is *Azzam*, 57 feet longer than *Eclipse* and owned by Sheikh Khalifa bin Zayed Al-Nahyan, president of the United Arab Emirates.

Yachts announce, in their own language of length, metal, speed and toys, the size of the fortune on which they depend: they are a floating global hierarchy of serious money. Before me the gleaming white metal hulls of trillions of pounds sat bobbing up and down in the searing sun. But what surprised me most, as I toured these Mediterranean harbours at the height of the summer season, was that most of the biggest yachts were sitting silent, empty, unused. I saw an occasional sunbather; someone with an iPad piping out a little music; maybe there were people inside, sleeping or watching television, or using the spa or pool; but the overriding atmosphere in Antibes and Monaco was a deathly stillness.[7] One of the world's largest concentrations of money is sitting idly in harbours, providing little pleasure to anyone. What, then, could be the point of a yacht, except to signal extreme wealth? Serious money? This is seriously dead money.

Still thinking about open seas, pure air and starry skies, the experiences that eclipse stuff, I have arranged to meet the owner of a bespoke luxury travel service. It is easily identifiable, so I cannot say where it is without breaching my guarantees of anonymity. As I arrive at his offices, Traveller and his team are finishing watching a slide show of photographs taken on a recent trip to Ethiopia, while they eat Ethiopian food. This group of dedicated and enthusiastic young travellers are reliving the trip's highlights. 'If you want what's inside your head,' Traveller tells me, 'we are going to charge you for that.' He says they organize standard luxury safaris, but also take parties to visit Somalia, Northern Sudan and the Central African Republic: countries the UK Foreign and Commonwealth Office (FCO) strictly advise against visiting because they are regarded as dangerous. This comes at a price; the average trip is $80,000. These kinds of trips involve 'unlocking complicated logistics'. Traveller's father once ran supplies for the Red Cross to Nigeria during the Biafran war, so he has plenty of experience to draw on. Logistics and the African landscape are in his DNA. He describes a recent helicopter tour of Kenya, which entailed sending ahead a truck with 'probably ten drums of fuel' from one of their bases in Addis Ababa. They spent a week driving ahead to various points on the tour, 'dropping the drums off at strategic locations'. At the same time, they were working to secure flying permission from civil aviation and the Kenyan Ministry of Defence. Next, he says, they set up a private mobile camp, which took two days to mobilize from Addis: 'It is the only mobile camp in Ethiopia that has an en-suite bathroom with a flushing toilet.' Only then did they confirm the helicopter's itinerary, 'so it all stacks up and keeps our Russian oligarchs smiling'. Bear in mind that most Ethiopians and Kenyans don't have a flushing toilet or running water. The new luxury, Traveller says, is space – the solitude and quiet of the wilderness. 'You can buy a seven-star hotel but you can't buy this. To them it is original, authentic, inspiring.' Pure luxury. And, of course, travelling to unusual and potentially dangerous places comes with 'bragging rights', fuelling the endless competitions of the rich. Space travel, of course, is the new plutocrat frontier, as Elon Musk and Richard Branson vie to break new boundaries. Meanwhile, London's most expensive neighbourhoods await their return.

At its most fundamental level, money translates into stuff: more money means more stuff. Wealthy people, and the makers and assemblers that serve them, bring to the streets of London its glitzy over-lit curio cabinets, its shop windows with extravagant displays and its streets of houses with beautifully curated interiors. Less immediately visible is the multi-million-pound industry that has sprung up in the city to advise the rich what stuff to buy and how to live with it. Wine experts, fashion experts, art experts, interior design experts, property experts, food, nutrition and exercise experts all specialize in showing plutocrats how to spend their money in ways that show they are sophisticated and discerning, as well as rich. Living with stuff is no simple matter.

Regent's Park

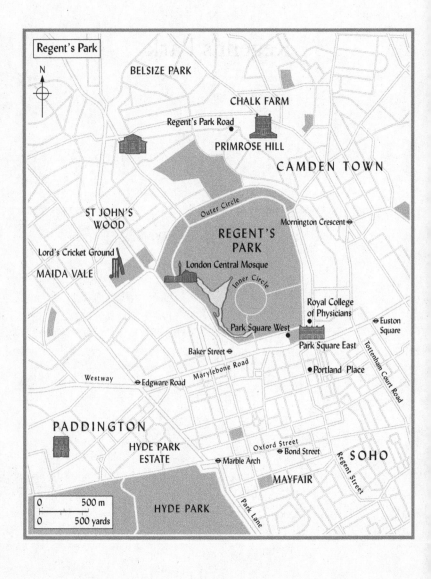

Regent's Park

N

BELSIZE PARK

CHALK FARM

Regent's Park Road

PRIMROSE HILL

CAMDEN TOWN

ST JOHN'S WOOD

Outer Circle

REGENT'S PARK

Mornington Crescent ⊖

Lord's Cricket Ground

London Central Mosque

MAIDA VALE

Inner Circle

Royal College of Physicians

⊖ Euston Square

Park Square West

Park Square East

Baker Street ⊖

Westway

⊖ Edgware Road

Marylebone Road

● Portland Place

Tottenham Court Road

PADDINGTON

HYDE PARK ESTATE

Oxford Street
● Bond Street

SOHO

⊖ Marble Arch

MAYFAIR

Regent Street

0   500 m
0   500 yards

HYDE PARK

Park Lane

18

Gobbled by an Octopus

The southern end of Regent's Park is fringed by a gentle arc of the stucco terraces at Park Crescent. Completed in 1822, the crescent is one of the finest examples of the work of John Nash, the star architect of elite Regency London. Now, as then, these properties are leased to some of the city's wealthiest people, making it a small but important slice of plutocratic London. I have wanted to visit it ever since meeting Banker, who lives on the north side of the park in Primrose Hill. Park Square is branded by black lamp posts and railings with telltale golden crowns and 'ER' lettering: I am back on Crown Estates land. The roads are brushed with the same pink pigment as the Mall, which sweeps up to Buckingham Palace. The magnolia, Ionic-columned landscape of the Crown Estates and its Paving Commission – which attends its pavements and gardens – is among the most uniform, groomed and gracious in the city.

Park Square and Park Crescent lie next to Portland Place, which is to the north of Oxford Street, the northern boundary of Mayfair. This patch of wealth and privilege extends northwards through the royal park to Primrose Hill, and west to the gleaming, golden Central London Mosque in St John's Wood: all of it plutocratic London. The mosque was built with a large donation from King Faisal bin Abdul Aziz Al-Saud of Saudi Arabia: another pile of oil money. Fittingly, the architecture in this area embeds and celebrates royalty and wealth in the most spectacular style. The giant golden mosque, next to the uniform, muted elegance of the terraces, once more reveals the displays and concealments of money – old and new, local and international. The inhabitants of the southern fringes of Regent's Park have perfected the art of living among elegant historic architectural displays.

Party, who lives in a £6 million flat in the Nash terraces, is a master of plutocratic spectacle and hedonism. Enter the idle rich. He is the son of a billionaire. Party runs some of his dad's money, creating an offshoot of his empire. Rather than walking with Party or his father – who are unlikely to agree to it anyway – I am meeting someone in their close social circle, another insider-outsider: Assistant. Assistant is part of the professional serving class, though I am unable to say exactly what he does without giving away his identity. Assistant got to know Party and his domestic life in surprisingly intimate ways. At the same time, he was able to observe his circle of prominent politicians and celebrities. It is late afternoon when we begin walking the streets around the Park. We pass the Royal College of Physicians and, later, trace a cacophony of sound to the back gate of the Royal Academy of Music. Music and medicine also make these very wealthy streets. We note the warnings about surveillance and spot banks of cameras at every corner, as well as a small glass security booth, with rows of monitors and switches, not far from the Royal Academy of Music.

Assistant's relationship with his boss was complicated and poorly defined, merging the obligations of employee and confidant. 'When you work for these people, if you become close to them, they want you to be part of their inner sanctum and domestic life, as well as wanting you to deliver for them professionally,' he says. This requires 'total commitment' and 'value for money', but at the same time, 'You've got to be a good friend, which is something that they pay for, and you've got to be constant company.' Assistant found this 'very, very, very, very emotionally demanding'. In this strange, unbounded world, personal and professional relationships overlapped and dominated Assistant's life. Throughout our conversation he refers to 'these people', to mean Party and his entourage. I want his take on their world and this way of living with money, by blowing it on excessive parties and social activities.

Assistant observes that 'these people' live in the city in ways that are distanced from it. Party entered the London elite 'establishment' as the host of parties attended by A-list celebrity film stars, musicians and politicians. A 'socialite' on the London scene, he creates glamorous social events where important people meet each other. Social importance demands constant affirmation and parties are a means of acknowledging and sustaining status. Who is and isn't invited? Who gets to be *somebody*? Moving in selective circles sets people apart, as fluid hierarchies of importance are constructed and dismantled from one party to the next. These displays of wealth also distinguish the players from their audience: the spectacle of wealth demands both. Glossy magazines celebrate the way Party lives his money. The rest of us gaze on.

They are distanced from the city in other ways, too. Close personal security creates a bubble around them. As Assistant puts it, 'There is a protective shield that insulates them from having to talk to normal people.' There is an element of spectacle to this, too. The security personnel employed by the rich are drawn from the ranks of ex-combatants, sometimes the Special Air Service (SAS), repurposed from Iraq, Afghanistan and other theatres of war. They work as drivers: Assistant says they are not really needed for security purposes – London is no war zone – but for the aura of importance they provide. If you have security, you must be somebody and you must be special. 'Security,' Assistant asserts, 'is a way of sending a signal to other people, to say, you know, "I am really rich and I really matter."' Spectacle is, by definition, not a routine part of everyday life, but an eye-catching display of money that few can afford to stage.

Party and his friends drive around in cars with 'blacked-out windows, so they don't have to see people's faces that they don't want to see', according to Assistant. He argues that they are 'very, very profoundly disconnected from the lives of normal Londoners'. Plutocrats 'don't take public transport' – with the possible exception of the Lebanese multi-millionaire with a Freedom Pass. 'They don't cycle along the same streets, they don't even drive their own cars.' This creates a 'comfortable distance between them and the ... quotidian realities of working in London'. Their life, as Assistant sees it, is about endlessly being driven to appointments, 'from an expensive hair appointment, to an expensive doctor appointment, to expensive fashion appointments'. He considers this 'such a vacuous existence', without any contact with 'normal people' or 'poor people'. 'Even when they see poor people occasionally,' he says, 'those poor people are like objects at a distance – a bit like being in a zoo, really, a bit like looking at a tiger in a sanctuary.' Serious money buys separation from city life. The uber-rich navigate the city enclosed and privately, and this reduces the possibility of chance encounters with others: some of the city's greatest pleasures.

The enclosed world of socialites is not confined to a single city but lives on the move. 'Travelling itself allows you to display your trophy assets,' Assistant suggests. As well as the yachts of Monaco and Antibes, there is the private jet, which allows you 'to host people and be generous'. Assistant thinks that in the world of the rich, travel is an 'escape from the tyranny of the world, in which you feel so empty and vacuous: a kind of permanent flight from reality'. Keeping Party company, he has spent a huge amount of time in foreign homes. 'You'd be sitting round a dinner table where there's a leading politician, a bunch of A-listers, some nightclub owner, and, basically, it's the most completely bizarre collection of people.' Then the private jet takes you home, and you find yourself returning to the office and normality. For Assistant, his proximity to the spectacle of wealthy life has an *Alice in Wonderland* feel, dropping him into a parallel reality and then back again into everyday life.

He was part of a wider supporting cast, an entourage. 'The entourage comes in layers,' he tells me. The immediate entourage is security people, whom he considers 'just travelling companions who are pretending to be security people, who actually just fold up your pants and pack your bags, because you can't be arsed to do that yourself'. The next layer is close friends, who do not pack the bags, but are effectively on retainer as permanent travelling companions. The third layer he describes as 'hardy perennials who you often see on these trips, who are returning heroes and heroines, who can always be relied upon to turn up in Portugal, or Spain, or France, or Germany, or Italy for a mad weekend'. Beyond this are people to impress and, perhaps, influence, 'the kinds of friends who are shipped in to have a really good time, and to drink really nice wine, and eat really good food'. Good times in new places provide distraction and entertainment. The same parties with the same people but in different places; the interplay of variety and sameness that wealth creates.

As in Hollywood movies, the best spectacles need the best and most famous actors. And professional help is available in casting the show.

Well-connected public relations experts supply the right contacts – at a price. 'This advice industry is a fraud, basically, a conspiracy against the rich,' Assistant thinks. '[PR people] sell a bit of advice, they comfort and offer a kind of therapy to people, and they open doors.' From their 'black book' listing influential people, they provide access to government officials, business leaders and the media. As well as extending plutocrats' connections with the right introductions, they make sure these connections get noticed. Most significantly, these PR experts with access to the most important and influential people have special skills in reputation shaping, in managing the ways in which the rest of us view their clients. Like all spectacles, these are contrived, since experts manage and manipulate their clients as well as the audience.

Assistant is referring to experts like Roland Rudd, chairman of the public relations and communications company Finsbury, and former *Financial Times* journalist. Rudd is a multi-millionaire thanks to his black book. His clients include luxury retailers who want to finesse their brands, and corporations who need reputation management following crises and scandals that damage their standing and, most importantly, their value. Finsbury have worked on political campaigns too, like the 2018 People's Vote campaign for a second referendum on the United Kingdom's EU membership, exerting their influence to shape public opinion. As the company's website indicates, 'Reputation is our Business'. And when they work with the rich and famous, public relations experts create brands for people. Assistant says: 'These guys run huge, huge public relations operations that make rich people feel very good about themselves.' In its 'Family Office Personal Risk and Reputation Management' pamphlet the accountancy firm Deloitte describes the reputation of wealthy families as among their 'most important assets to establish', as well as 'the easiest to lose and the most difficult to restore'.[1] 'Perception', it says, is 'everything'. Though they have advantages in informally broadcasting the glamour of wealthy life, social media – unlike traditional media – are also especially leaky and hard to control, as people can jump in and have their say. Even so, public perceptions of plutocrats are highly mediated. Professionals manage the wealthy's reputations and performances. All part of the spectacle.

As PR firms well understand, there are good looks and better looks. Philanthropy and charity are a good look. The British royal family have long understood that this distracts public attention from their extensive landholdings, privileges and the other benefits of hereditary wealth. Dodgy sources of wealth are not a good look, but public relations experts can disinfect these and their online traces. This is reputation laundering, staples of dictators and human rights violators the world over. Wealthy lives are amplified by publicity, so that they are heard above the cacophony of sound composing the music of the city. In the process, they drown out other voices, other lives, other causes, other ways of living in the city. With the help of their PR shape-shifters, the rich have a high degree of control over how people see them. They and their spectacular displays of wealth are manipulated to suggest they are a natural, integral and even beneficial part of the social and cultural life of the city.

As we walk past shrubberies and flower beds, Assistant admits he senses a purposelessness that lurks behind spectacles of wealth. The super-rich Londoners he knows, who are like the people in the pages of *Tatler*, lead wholly empty lives: 'They literally spend all of their time socializing with each other.' A typical day is built around lunch, followed by a cultural outing in the afternoon – 'an exhibition or some new fashion thing' – and a social function in the evening. The evening's activities are 'the driver of what they do', because they don't have to work during the day. 'They have a good time; they stay up pretty late, and will often spend the [next] day recovering.' This sounds familiar from my conversation with Bags and Barbour. Socializing is the 'centrifugal force', Assistant says. 'Social functions aren't a sort of addition or addendum to work life. They are work.' Yet they rarely provide the purpose that engaging work can. 'A lot of people who have a lot of money and who are materially wealthy are morally poor, and don't really have much that gives them a sense of fulfilment or satisfaction in their lives,' he believes. This lack of purpose is amplified in those who inherit, rather than make, money, not least because others do not take them as seriously, since they are not money-makers, only money spenders. This seems not to bother old money. He says, 'You've got to prove yourself. That can seem a burden.'

Assistant sees this as an attempt to counterbalance Party's inheritance:

that he lacks the substance, adrenalin, ambition, drive and sheer testosterone that money-making implies. But Party does not run the daily operations of these enterprises. Employees like Assistant run them for him. Having to make work, and make social occasions last and shape the day, leads to the 'suffocating vacuity' and 'emptiness' that Assistant detects in places like Sloane Square and Kensington. Can it be that all confections and spectacles of wealth are ultimately empty and unfulfilling, for participants and audiences alike?

On this beautiful, bright and sunny day, the paths, trees, shrubs and water – the park's unmoving green features – are glittering and immaculate. We sit on a wooden bench for a while and take in the world (literally) running and walking by: so many different outfits, conversations both intense and casual, in many languages. I watch an elderly couple, propping each other up, arm in arm, moving slowly. At lightning speed, young men and women in shorts and T-shirts fly past, panting and sweating. Children on skateboards, scooters and bikes race beyond their parents. The human texture of the park, in contrast to the houses on its borders, is in constant motion, shooting by at different speeds, a tangle of uncoordinated missions and mindsets on the go.

What is the true nature of the personal and social relationships at the heart of the spectacle? Surely drinking Party's fine wine and travelling on his private plane bring loyalty from his friends? Assistant suggests otherwise. 'These people', he says, do not squander time. 'They're not there for you when the chips are down. They're there for you at the fun parties, giving you the air kisses, eating your food, drinking your wine. That shallowness, that genuine lack of depth and affection is one of the defining qualities of that world.' Friendships are empty spectacles too, then. But how do rich people like Party establish close personal relationships? Does their money cut them off from others instead of bringing them closer? As Student also said, the wealthy struggle to believe that others are interested in them as people and not just their money, and this is one of their biggest difficulties. Assistant finds it 'curious': 'These people seem so, so far away because they're in this intergalactic different social sphere. Yet, if you get close to them, they *gobble you up like an octopus*, because they really need you to be close to them.' I try to imagine the tentacles and suction pads that entangle him in the spectacle of the ever-moving rich show.

All relationships rely on trust, so how does this work for the rich? 'Once you're in the inner circle, you're really in the inner circle, and then you're very much trusted.' But trust, it seems, is not a one-off and must be constantly stress-tested and renewed. Being brought into the inner circle means 'you've passed a kind of test of trust', Assistant says. 'So, you might be at a house in Europe, and the fact that you're there means that you're someone that can be trusted.' Insiders are expected to follow a code of conduct: 'There's an unspoken rule that what goes on tour stays on tour, that conversations won't be misrepresented, and that people won't take pictures where they ought not to, and that kind of thing.' He says friends of the rich are constantly tested: are they telling the truth? Will they leak privileged information? 'It's like living in an exam the whole time.' He gives an example of a financial adviser who tells him something in confidence about his client, 'worth £500 million', to see whether Assistant relays it to the client. The trust bar is set high and regularly checked for security breaches: serious money's constant testing of loyalty and confidence potentially corrodes relationships.

Beyond the fair-weather friendships of the good times and the trusted inner circle that must be regularly tested, wealthy people's closest relationships are with their domestic servants. Wig's divorce cases revealed large numbers of staff. Assistant says this leads to a 'bizarre' lack of privacy: 'They often live with total strangers.' If someone is worth £300 million, their live-in staff might number seven or eight people: 'Your house is a kind of rumbling milieu of different people doing different things . . . [Staff] become your surrogate family, because they're the people that you spend all your time with.' But knowing that they are paid to be there and the relationship is fundamentally transactional 'can leave you feeling somewhat imprisoned'. He describes these relationships as 'misaligned', since rich people are rarely explicit about what they want from staff. They want services: '"Sort my ironing out", "Make my lunch", "Build me a beautiful garden."' But they are also buying companionship to fill 'an intense loneliness'. Close relationships are secured through wages, contracts and non-disclosure agreements. What strange intimacies money buys.

From talking to Butler about the other side of the transaction, I know that these transactional domestic intimacies are emotional minefields. Assistant takes this further. He thinks the rich suffer 'total paranoia about people stealing stuff': 'If you've got loads of art, and amazing cutlery, and incredibly valuable stuff in your house, you want every single thing listed. You want to be able to say, "What was item 2289?" I know of houses where everything is indexed, absolutely everything is indexed.' This often falls to security staff, who have time on their hands. 'So these former Marines are wandering round saying, "Silver fork with embossed Royal Doulton, item 1742. Next."' Even then, wealthy employers may demand to see the ledger and the item in question. Even in its inner sanctum, money's spoils must be safe-guarded from the supposedly predatory intentions of others. Paranoia and stress are the dark, emotional underside of wealth.

Most taxing of all in the emotional life of money, Assistant thinks, is the intense energy that it takes to maintain the spectacle. 'The thing about mixing in a world of glamour and wealth is you have to keep it up, you know? You have to maintain it.' These performances demand constant vigilance and attention to the most mundane of details: 'When people come round, if there's going to be mayonnaise, it can't come out of a Hellmann's bottle. It's got to be made by the finest chef.' This is a lifelong endeavour. Assistant says, 'You've got to give the appearance of always being super-rich. So, while your actual material fortunes might fluctuate because of the price of gas in Singapore or because of the oil markets, you can't be seen to be vulnerable to those fluctuations. You're meant to rise above it.' Beyond merely maintain-ing wealth, Assistant argues, 'If anything, you're meant to edge ever so slightly upwards. So, you're meant to get slightly better cutlery, and slightly nicer candles, and a slightly more expensive chef, and serve four courses rather than three, and provide a slightly better wine. I think a lot of headspace is taken up by that feeling of furiously peddling to maintain the artifice.'

We leave the bench and walk northwards, past flower beds, trees and playing fields. Why this pressure to display ever-rising opulence in what is already a spectacular world of extreme wealth? For Assistant, it comes down to reputation management again: 'It's a form of adver-tising and it's a way of promoting the brand.' It is also about belonging, 'a way of acquiring membership within a bullshit club', consisting of other rich people – membership that would be lost if the money were lost. Still, he thinks, it is ultimately hollow: 'Eventually you go home, and you're in your empty house, and you don't feel like life has got much purpose to it. The kind of exhaustion of having to pretend you're interested in people's lives, when you're really not, gets to you.' The rich suffer performance fatigue as well as the pressure to be – or at least to look – ever richer, borne ever upwards on a tide of rising fortunes. It seems that just being very rich is not enough. Wealthy life has – in the cases Assistant refers to – inner mechanisms that drive it onwards, stacking ever-greater piles of money and displays of excess, until they reach the biggest yachts and private planes. It would not be surprising if this left invisible scars on the psychic life of the rich.

Living in what Assistant calls the 'gap' between the artifice of the spectacle and a far grimmer reality, the rich suffer unease and anxiety. I am not suggesting they deserve sympathy – as Assistant himself notes drily, 'It's not the worst burden in the world' – but I am trying to understand their inner lives. Assistant says: 'I think quite a lot of these people are absolutely terrified about being found out. They build up a false picture for the world of what they really are.' Everything must be amplified and exaggerated: their wealth, but also their interests, and their 'moral virtue or valour'. 'They want the world to think they're actually X, when the reality is a slightly grubbier Y.' He points to the 'huge gap' between the image wealthy people want to project to the world and the reality they live, which is as deeply flawed as it is for the rest of us, if in quite different ways. This must be especially acute for a socialite like Party. If the reality were exposed, this logic goes, 'They'd lose control, and people would know, actually, they're not that smart, or they're not that rich; or they're not that interested in culture, or that kind of painting that they're pretending to care about, or that exhibition that they patronize by giving lots of money to, or that awards ceremony that they're involved in, or that film production that they invested in.' Imposter syndrome? Perhaps they are trapped in their own illusions, spun for public consumption and for other rich folk.

The reality of wealthy life, Assistant says, is this: the rich do not have any friends to spend time with. They have no privacy at home, and no relationships that are non-contractual or last after the party. Trust must be constantly tested, and they worry about protecting their expensive stuff against the depredations of predators. Assistant describes this as a 'toxic combination' and suspects that it creates depression as well as paranoia. While no one I have spoken to would admit to this, apart perhaps from Bags, as testified by studies, wealth and power may be linked to depression and other mental illnesses. Suffice it to say that the conditions in which the rich live, which Assistant describes as lonely, destructive and fraught with anxieties, are hardly conducive to their mental health and well-being. Quite the contrary.

We have arrived at the north end of Regent's Park, towards Primrose Hill, where a more playful smugness in pastel pink, blue and yellow stucco, replaces the regal grandeur of the Nash terraces. The vast green space of the park sits between these two areas. Assistant leaves to collect his daughter from school. I walk around the edge of Primrose Hill until I reach its little commercial strip of upscale cafés, restaurants and small shops selling flowers, clothes, shoes and books on Regent's Park Road, to browse a while.

Richmond

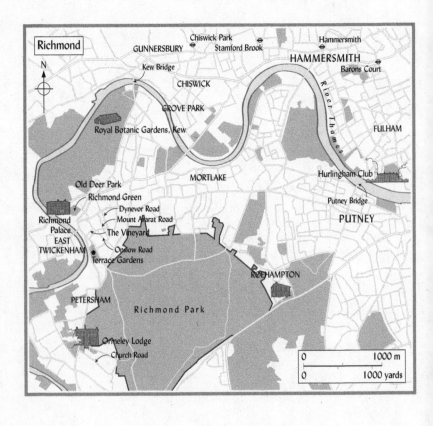

19

Riches and Risk

Just to the east of Putney Bridge, in Fulham – the new Chelsea – the Hurlingham Club sits complacently on the Thames, as if it has always been a natural feature of the river. 'One of Britain's greatest private members' clubs,' its website claims, boasting 'quintessentially English traditions and heritage' in 42 acres of 'magnificent grounds'. The membership waiting list is so long they have closed it. Dress code for tennis and croquet is 'at least 80 per cent white'. I expect it is. But the exclusive club is not my destination. I am walking to Richmond, where the county of Surrey extends to London, touching the city's richest neighbourhoods. Serious money stretches from the City, through Mayfair, Kensington, Chelsea, Regent's Park, and into Surrey, through Richmond, forming a corridor, a vortex of extreme wealth. And wealth, as I have learned, brings its own anxieties and demands for security, so I am visiting a security expert who lives here.

To get there, I am walking west along the Thames, as it loops northwards at Hammersmith and then heads abruptly south again to Barnes. Around Dukes Meadows, the setting looks decidedly pastoral, but it switches back to urban at Chiswick, with the tangle of main roads around the M4 motorway. Crossing south over the Thames at Kew Bridge near the Royal Botanic Gardens, I skirt around the Old Deer Park, created in the early seventeenth century as a royal hunting ground, avoiding the Duke of Northumberland's rather run-down estate on the north bank, heading for Richmond Green. This is the scenic, walkers' route from West London. Regular fast trains connect Richmond to London's Waterloo Station in eighteen minutes: this is commuter country, combining pastoral and city life more seamlessly than almost anywhere else.

Before meeting the security expert, Sailor, I'm walking with Author to get the lie of the land. A Richmond resident for forty years, she has watched its shifting landscape as her own life changed. She is a retired historian turned novelist, and she tells great stories, circling what is, with an eye on what was. Dressed in walking gear, we stride out from the Green into the streets of Richmond at a pace I hope I can maintain. Author moved to this area in 1981. Her grandparents had lived in a very different London, working in Bermondsey and Walworth river businesses like rope-making – London labour aristocracy. Author arrived in Richmond just in time to witness the last remnants of multi-occupancy housing of the 1960s and 1970s, whereby any number of tenants rented rooms in large rambling houses. Then came the first waves of gentrification, as in Notting Hill, in which professional classes with arty and literary inclinations moved in and renovated. She points to the house of former neighbours: 'She taught French and he was a British Airways pilot.' Our walk takes us along the various streets Author has lived in over the years, moving as her housing needs changed.

As we walk up Church Road, there are large Victorian double-fronted houses, carefully restored in place of the much shabbier exteriors she remembers; far wealthier people live here now, as plutocratic London has expanded, reaching ever deeper into new areas of the city. Where will it end? Looping off Church Road, a main artery through the area, we walk along Dynevor Road. Substantial Victorian villas with well-kept gardens in this neighbourhood change hands for sums north of £5 million. We walk along The Vineyard, which has Victorian and Georgian houses, as well as Elizabethan almshouses, and onto Mount Ararat Road, which runs parallel to Church Road, and is lined with three-storey residences with their own driveways at the front.

As we walk, Author tells me a story about the local Italian restaurant, owned by two Portuguese brothers who were once waiters there. A popular restaurant – the food isn't great, but that doesn't seem to matter – it was recently caught up in raids searching for illegal restaurant workers. The raids were a part of the UK 'hostile environment' policy intended to discourage migration, introduced by the Conservative then home secretary Theresa May in 2012. A waiter of thirty years' standing, who paid taxes and National Insurance contributions, was deemed 'technically illegal' in the raid. The police and licensing authorities 'descended like a ton of bricks'. But locals rallied round, they wrote letters to the council, packed the council chamber and fought back, alongside the owner. In the end the owner was fined, but kept his licence and the restaurant remained open. While Richmond is indisputably rich, its plutocrats tend towards liberal values.

In the 1980s, Author lived in Onslow Road, in a nineteenth-century four-storey and six-bedroomed honey-coloured brick house with white window frames. Her neighbours were journalists, photographers, editors at publishing houses, BBC news presenters, a smattering of lawyers, civil servants at the Foreign Office: outward-looking people who took an interest in the world and in their own ways influenced how others thought about it. Nearby is Friars Stile Road – 'Richmond Village' to estate agents – with large, majestic houses in the £8 million to £10 million range. Naturalist and broadcaster David Attenborough lives near here. Author's daughters went to local state primary schools, but these days private prep schools, sometimes squeezed into the bigger houses, pepper the landscape: private education and determinedly old-fashioned uniforms dominate the streets at certain times of day. We stop and gaze at the sweep of the Thames below and the steep slopes of Terrace Gardens that lead down to its banks. Trees, fields and the shiny silver snake of river stretch away into the distance. This vista was made famous by Turner's landscape painting and Wordsworth's poetry. When model Jerry Hall and Rolling Stone Mick Jagger split, she kept the house here – and the view.

Turning away reluctantly from the view, we head to Richmond's 2,500-acre royal park, complete with deer herds. As we stride through the park, with Author still setting a brisk pace, we pass Ormeley Lodge, a vast eighteenth-century red-brick mansion, positioned in extensive green acres on the edge of the park. The Lodge's current owner is Lady Annabel Goldsmith, whose first husband, Mark Birley, named his 1960s Mayfair nightclub Annabel's after her. Her son by her second marriage, to James Goldsmith – a billionaire with a finance empire – is Zac; or, more properly, Baron Goldsmith of Richmond Park, who inherited a fortune from his father. Zac Goldsmith was the local Conservative MP from 2010 to 2016, and from 2017 to 2019, representing the seat in which (or perhaps *to* which) he was born. Author thought he was a terrible MP. After resigning (2016, reselected 2017) over the third runway at Heathrow, which he opposed – the deafening noise of aircraft is Richmond's soundtrack – he lost his seat in 2019 to the Liberal Democrats. Fortunately for him, he had the kind of friends able to ensure his elevation to the House of Lords, where he sits as Minister of State for the Pacific and the International Environment. Author dislikes the entitled former MP, whose anti-Islamic 2016 campaign to become Mayor of London unravelled, when the Muslim son of a bus driver, Sadiq Khan, was elected instead.

We quicken our pace, putting this unseemly tale of money and politics behind us, skirting the western end of the park and walking along Petersham Road to its northern end, where it hugs the Thames not far from the Green. Around this Thames-side stretch is the ancient part of Richmond. We circle the ruins of medieval Richmond Palace, and, in winding, narrow streets, pause to look at the grace and favour houses. Palace courtiers are still rewarded with elegant historic places in which to live. Royalty is never far away in wealthy London – Hampton Court Palace is only a few miles west along the Thames. Finally, we get back to where we started at Richmond Green.

Author has shown me what she and Richmond have lived through: a seemingly inexorable plutocratification of the city, and how liberal values can survive and provide an impetus for change, nonetheless. The fact that the Goldsmiths share the area with Jerry Hall, David Attenborough and palace courtiers shows that the rich in Richmond as elsewhere in London are a diverse group, and some are more open to progressive causes than others. Author needs to get home to put the finishing touches to her latest novel, but first she walks me to the house of her neighbour, Sailor, an expert on maritime security who safeguards super-yachts, perhaps, as I suggested earlier, *the* most iconic manifestation of excessive wealth.

Sailor lives on a quiet, tree-lined residential street of modest and beautifully restored Victorian houses. A second-wave gentrifier, riding the surge that brought financiers and rock stars to the grander parts of Richmond, he works from home. His house is shiny, newly refurbished. A stylish custom-made jeep, roughly the size and weight of a small tank, sits outside. His large open-plan kitchen, where we talk, is high spec: clearly Farrow & Ball, painted in tones that reproduce the elegant colour-schemes of the Victorian era. I see that Farrow & Ball have a 'grace and favour' wallpaper range too. Very Richmond. The kitchen segues into a small back garden, which is tiled to extend the inside to the outside. I perch on a high stool at the kitchen island and listen to Sailor's security stories.

In his late thirties, wearing long navy shorts and a light green T-shirt featuring pink flamingos, and with bare feet, he looks as if he has just stepped off a yacht in the south of France. He once poured himself into the suit of an investment banker, 'for my sins', he says. But when the financial crisis hit in 2008 and bankers' reputations were in ruins, he took a job at sea. Nautical life is transient, physically demanding, exciting. But his priorities have recently shifted again. Now, he says, 'I have three dogs and I am about to get married.'

His search for a viable way to earn money on land, now that he is settling with his partner, led Sailor to a new job in maritime security. It appealed to him as a land life that looks towards the sea. He describes his new job: 'If you are taking your super-yacht to the Seychelles and you have to go through the Gulf of Suez, we supply ex-British Special Forces (SAS) providing armed support.' His company has a firearms import licence, and Sailor knows where the private floating armouries and armies are moored around the Gulf of Aden waiting for commissions. They protect valuable cargoes, like oil, from piracy, but this nautical military machine also guards the super-yachts of the super-wealthy. Like most security companies, Sailor's predominantly employs ex-military personnel, and Sailor says this brings 'a certain mindset'. He means a diligence and obedience to a chain of command, which is appropriate in security, but less suited to expanding lucrative security markets around super-yachts. Sailor brings new perspectives from his finance background to the Technical Security Department he heads. What he describes as his commercial, elite service-based approach, chimes with the shiny kit rich people want on their yachts. They want smart and sexy as well as secure. He calls his company's clients 'high-net-worths', but means ultra-high-net-worths, as the cost of yachting is generally too high for people with less than £20 million in assets – excluding their main residence – to afford.

Either way, Sailor's clients are wealthy people who chose to live in a London protected by the security barriers the company offers. Sailor says they are new money: Silicon Valley types flush with tech money, entrepreneurs of various stripes, finance moguls and celebrities, including sports celebrities like footballers. Old money, he tells me, does not do security. Apart from royalty, I guess. What are his clients like? 'They are guarded. They are unlisted. Travel plans are usually quite guarded. The sources of their wealth are initially quite guarded. That's probably the way they want it to remain.' Confirming Assistant's suspicions, he tells me: 'The UK high-net-worth market is mainly based on privacy protection rather than an actual real (physical) threat to individuals.' They are, after all, physically removed from most danger. He says: 'What we've found is that actually high-net-worth individuals have no interaction with the man on the street at all.' Security in London protects the rich from the life of the streets, keeping the social lives and money-making activities of wealthy Londoners opaque, unlisted and inaccessible. I had been wondering whether Assistant was generalizing from the idiosyncratic behaviour of a handful of neurotic billionaires. But Sailor meets a broader range of newly rich Londoners, and agrees that they chose to live in the isolation provided by security.

I am not quite sure what is actually involved in securitizing lives. Sailor runs me through the company's offer. First are human shields, old-fashioned 'manpower' offering 'physical means' of protection, which he calls 'close protection'. Close personal protection – bodyguards – often live-in, working shifts on 'residential security teams'. Other parts of the human shield include security-approved drivers who do 'pre-location sweeps': 'If you are going to a restaurant, or event or things like that, you may have a team that travel in advance.' This extends to private jets, or what Sailor calls 'non-standard channels of private aviation': security will travel ahead and check the route.

Although these former soldiers may genuinely need to protect the bodies and stuff of the rich occasionally, Sailor describes them as essentially path-smoothers. Assistant described them as pant-folders. They clear obstacles and inconveniences in the way of the wealthy, so that they can navigate their own peculiar, trouble-free version of everyday city life.

Assessments of 'risk' – in which security companies have a vested interest – determine the kinds and intensity of close protection wealthy clients 'need'. Sailor says that for 'a medium-level residential security team in London for a couple with no children, you'd probably be looking at around £300,000 a year, just for the physical team.' If you add children into the mix, depending on their age, 'You might be potentially looking up to £100,000 per child.' This would mean being present on the school run and, for older children, keeping tabs on their whereabouts. Sailor says, 'In close protection, spontaneous travel is an issue. If your 22-year-old son leaves the property and goes to work in an investment bank every day, it's fine. He gets driven there and driven back.' Problems arise 'when he isn't where he is supposed to be. Or he goes out spontaneously. Spontaneous travel causes severe security concerns. It requires multiple people in multiple teams, which are difficult to mobilize quickly.' He concludes, 'Routine is everybody's friend. As soon as you don't have routine then it becomes complicated. It becomes expensive very, very quickly.'

At £300,000 a year, security is a luxury available only to the wealthiest Londoners, who either choose to avoid the nuisances and inconveniences of city life and let professionals navigate them on their behalf, or are anxious to protect themselves from whatever they perceive to be the city's dangers. Individual anxiety, fear and perceptions of danger are crucial in these calculations. Risk is a richly suggestive idea; all areas of city life involve risk, but this is a dance between freedom and danger on the streets. Risk is defined and quantified by security companies – through assessments and the metrics underpinning them – and monetized. Security is a highly profitable industry, that both compromises and enhances the pleasures of wealthy life. Sailor talks about the 'risk–security matrix', where risks are compared to the restrictions security imposes on freedom and pleasure.

A well-known security company called Intelligent Protective Services posts a case study on its website, to show what close personal security means in personnel terms. The family is American. They are staying in London and Paris for six months. Their security needs – following a 'risk assessment' by the company – include close protection for the husband and wife, protective surveillance for the children and nanny, and a counter-surveillance and counter-espionage package to protect the husband's business operations. This requires a security manager; two close protection officers' team leaders; four close protection officers; two counter-surveillance officers; and a security-trained driver. The team of ten security staff outnumber those they protect – the costs are not listed. Significantly, the security team are elite ex-military trained specialist units. Intelligent Protection boasts that it can summon a team of Gurkhas, if necessary. It is difficult to imagine the circumstances in London or Paris that would justify deployment of army Special Forces, or a Nepalese warrior regiment of a British colonial army.

These are merely the human elements of security. Sailor talks me through the technological and barrier defences his company supplies to wealthy homes and workplaces. These include 'access control, front and rear doors, intercoms, use of remote access systems, CCTV, perimeter CCTV, security lighting, intruder alarms, doors and windows, procedures relating to evacuation, fire alarms, confidential data storage, IT security concerns, standard procedures in emergencies, tactical landscaping, which is everything like fencing'. They scope out properties and make recommendations – for instance, if a celebrity has privacy concerns, they recommend cutting down any trees near the property's perimeter, or 'removing the branches for the first 8 metres, which means people can't climb trees and look into your property'. The company also advises on: 'Hardening of properties, that's everything from reinforcement of garages, ground-floor windows, access grilles. Right through to advisory on artwork storage, valuables, installation of safes, and panic rooms.' Technological security includes blocking paparazzi drones. Then there is 'tactical security'. This involves sweeping for electronic devices, recording devices, blocking mobile phones, and blocking electronic communications in business meetings. This armoury would come under the counter-espionage package Intelligent Protective Services put in place to protect the American businessman's professional operations. In combination, these technological devices throw impenetrable digital cordons around the homes and workplaces of serious money, separating them, their homes and their assets still further from public life on the streets.

Such extreme measures of domestic and workplace security are beyond anything necessary to deter break-ins and stave off physical attack. The tactical security Sailor describes is similar to the secret-service operations and tactics of nation states, usually wielded in defence of national security. Just how anxious and secretive must money be to deploy this armoury of technological devices to protect its personal and business affairs? What in the personal and business lives of the rich must be kept so closely guarded? Why *is* money so secretive? What is it hiding? Journalist Robert Frank suggests that many of the business operations amassing great wealth are extremely mundane,[1] and Assistant and Butler, too, found the private lives of money to be dull and empty. Ways of amassing wealth that carry more intellectual interest and challenge, like those I came across in the City and Mayfair, are hard to justify and so shielded from public view.

Still thinking about these parallels between the deep state and the super-wealthy, I watch the dogs, while Sailor makes the coffee. Because it is Take Your Dog to Work Day, only two remain at home, the third having accompanied CEO to the City. The stay-at-home dogs are a thin, shivering whippet and a short, stout Scottie. While Sailor talks, the whippet scours the house collecting objects – a plastic detergent holder, a lump of wood and various dog toys – and stores them in his basket by the window. When he isn't paying attention, the Scottie steals his treasure and hides it. The whippet searches and retrieves it again and puts it all back in his basket. And so they spend the day.

The 'reputation advisory' service is the final element in the company's security operation. At first, I thought this must resemble the public relations operations Assistant described that shape public perceptions of the rich. Later, I realized there is a crucial difference in the way Sailor explains reputation advisory services, which are part of the company's military and counter-espionage operation. His reputation advisory service includes the 'management of social media feeds'; the 'management of photographs'; press appearances that might warrant 'discussion with journalists and newspapers about publication of individuals arriving at public events, such as Royal Ascot'. He pronounces 'discussion' in a way that makes me think he means something more threatening. My suspicions grow as he says 'leverage is applied in the right places to remove people, or manage people's profiles. That also extends to nightclubs and restaurants where teams of lawyers are used to protect reputations.' Tough talk. A militarized operation employing former soldiers from theatres of war brings an implied force to 'leverage' and a potentially menacing tone to discussions with journalists and newspaper editors. Of course, soldiers are not deployed on these particular missions, but they are the muscle standing in the background, defending the reputations and yachts of the rich.

Another security company, Schillings and Partners, suggests that it can 'shorten the time it takes to solve a reputation problem or a privacy threat' by using a combination of experts: intelligence specialists, investigators, cyber specialists, risk consultants, lawyers, and top people from the military, banking and government. Professionals, drawn from the most influential institutions of public – and not so public – life are available to solve the difficulties of wealthy clients. Schillings names some of these difficulties as fake news, hostile campaigns, bad leavers, inside threats and regulatory inquiries.[2] While this list of 'threats' is open to interpretation, I wonder if 'bad leavers' and 'inside threats' include whistle-blowers and those who attempt to challenge company policies, practices and the overall interests of the wealthy. In this case, security's role is to stifle dissent, and foil attempts to regulate the more egregious habits of the money-makers. Help batting away 'regulatory inquiries' is particularly useful in clearing a path to amassing large amounts of money without interference. It pays – literally – to have the government, the military and banking on side, as well as cyber specialists, lawyers and intelligence experts on call to protect the wealth and privileges of the rich. The rich, it seems, have access to the very same expertise as the official machinery that attempts, often ineffectively, to rein in their excesses. Professional help in avoiding regulation and dissent are among the many privileges money enjoys, making it especially difficult to manage and regulate.

Sailor's specialism is security on the high seas. He works with the yacht-building and design industry to securitize the piles of floating money I described earlier. He tells me that the security level of yachts can be set to change automatically under daylight hours and nighttime hours. 'Access can be granted and removed, revoked, audited, all from a centralized system. Gone are the days of keys, you might find fob access, card access, biometric, the use of fingerprints.' He suggests there are various ways to block drones from taking photographs, although he says, 'Electronic interference with drones is a grey area, because you are messing with broadcast signals. There is the option to create electronic interference around vessels to stop drone over-flight.' The use of smart glass and privacy glass stops people looking in and taking photographs. I discovered this myself in Antibes and Monaco: aiming my camera at yacht windows, I only succeeded in photographing my own reflection. Sailor restricts views into the private lives of the wealthy and celebrities at sea, allowing the only window to be through a perfectly curated Instagram post or glossy magazine feature.

Before I leave, he gives me some glossy yacht magazines, and shows me a little metal button a friend of his invented. Small and elegant, it alerts yacht staff when yachters need something – the channel on the TV changed, more champagne, sunscreen. At £1,000 each, he says this is the future, a highly profitable fusion of service, elegance and technology for the leisure classes. I get the point. Security is like a designer watch, something that the rich buy because they can and because it makes their lives easier or more luxurious. But security is a luxury that also changes the way rich people live. In activating their urban anxieties, deepening their habits of secrecy and restricting their movements, while simultaneously smoothing their pathways through the city, security 'makes people's lives very insular'. Security is part of the moving rich show. Celebrities, he says, want it for the status: 'If you would like four black Range Rovers to follow you around London, which they do, it's very easy. It will cost you £2,500 a day per black Range Rover, so there you go; of course, we can provide that.' London is a lucrative security market, he says, because of its lack of actual risks – no serious security measures are needed – and high concentrations of plutocrats.

As we stand in Sailor's hallway saying goodbye, the dogs circling at our feet, I wish him good luck with the wedding. He checks again that I won't identify him when I write this, and I repeat my assurances of anonymity. He jokes about having had to remind someone in other circumstances that it would be inadvisable to cross him, as his network of ex-military colleagues put him in a good position to cause serious harm. I say, 'I consider myself duly warned.' He laughs and says he does not mean me.

Virginia Water:
The Surrey Fringe

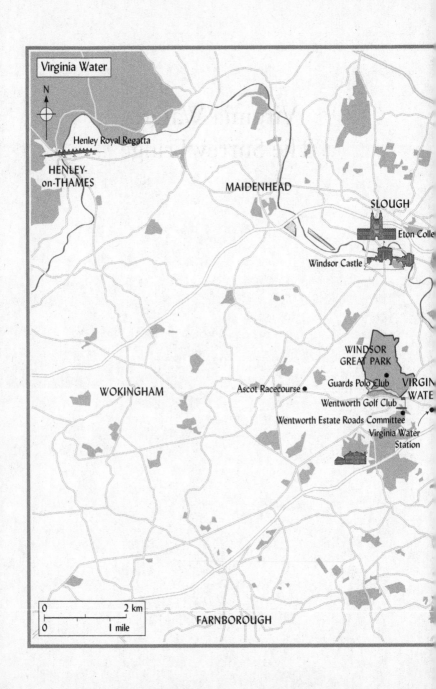

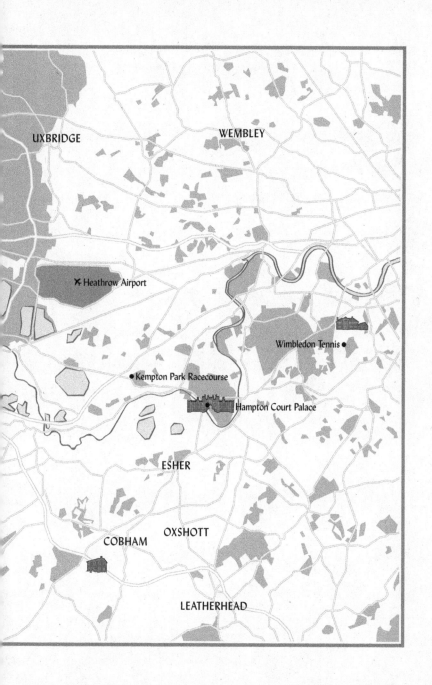

20

Dead Streets

From Richmond, I walk along the Thames as it dips southwards to Kingston before levelling out westwards to Hampton Court, just south-east of Kempton Park Racecourse. Heathrow Airport is just to the north-west, and to the east are a series of gravel-pit reservoirs. Moving further westwards beyond the M25 London Orbital road I am for the first time out of the city. I walk past Windsor Castle, one of the royal residences, and not far from Eton College, the feeling of city-ness gradually fading into the languid green of the countryside. This is the end of the *Serious Money* trail, the corridor of wealth and privilege, the vortex of riches that I have followed across the city from its eastern manufacturing sites. I am heading for my last stop, in London's most affluent commuter town, Virginia Water.

Walking through Windsor Great Park's 5,000 acres on the Berkshire–Surrey border, I pass the vast green fields of Guards Polo Club, where the royal princes used to play. I watch a woman searching for her bulldog, calling 'Tarquin, Tarquin', and pass afternoon strollers in country casuals with picnic baskets. Small quiet lakes create a seam between the park and town-suburb, giving way to the car park and the main road into Virginia Water. It is a place described by a young man with a distinctive spiky, sticking up haircut in the local estate agents as the 'most expensive village in Britain'; it is part of the 'golden triangle' of extraordinary wealth between Esher, Cobham, and Oxshott. Very serious money indeed.

The small cluster of shops by the train station is the closest thing to a town centre in a place that doesn't really have one, only low-density dispersed houses in quiet, leafy lanes. The two parades of shops around the station are rather ordinary. There is a bookie; a post office; the

Wine Circle café and restaurant, where the more convivial locals sometimes gather on a Friday night; a wine merchant, the Louis Roederer
Champagne providing the only hint of decadence; a newsagent; a
beauty parlour; a deli, infused with Mediterranean aspirations in its
combinations of goat cheese and olives; and a patisserie, offering a cup
of tea that is just a cut above ordinary, with gauze instead of bleached
paper teabags. I drop into the newsagent to ask directions to the town's
famous Wentworth Golf Course, and a small, elderly, beady-eyed man
with traces of elsewhere in his voice, buying a newspaper, instructs me
to take the long route, on which I cannot possibly get lost. He says it's
a long walk, and I say, that's all right – I like walking.

As I trudge off in steady rain, I slowly realize that it is not the long
walk or the rain that is the problem – there is nowhere to walk, no
pavements, only roads intended for cars. Not any old cars, either: big
four-wheelers, Ferraris and Lamborghinis swish past me at unnerving
speed. As I meet no one else on foot, I suspect that no one walks here,
at least not along main roads. A little Mini Cooper pulls up beside me:
the old man from the newsagent is at the wheel, offering to drive me
to the Golf Course. I gratefully accept his rescue from the dangers of
the road. On the short drive, I learn that he works at and lives in one
of the big houses nearby, tending to the grounds and doing routine
maintenance – someone from the local serving class. When he drops
me off at the bottom of the Wentworth Golf Club drive, he wishes me
luck.

Walking along the Golf Club driveway, I pass a small picturesque
pond with swans gliding across it. It is a quintessentially English village view, complete with what looks like a nineteenth-century stately
home in the distance. I discover that is exactly what it once was,
though now it is the Golf Club's clubhouse, repurposed for luxury
dining and drinking. The stately home cum clubhouse is the classic
architectural expression of elite life, complete with castle battlements
on its upper walls. I also notice a large, derelict, tumbling-down house
on the other side of the drive, which looks from the hoardings as if it
is being redeveloped. I learn later that older, more modest-sized houses
on the Wentworth Estate are bought for their land and replaced with
mega houses equipped with the latest amenities. Sometimes the plots
are subdivided, depending on whether this is permitted by local land

covenants, which might stipulate the required size of the plots on which houses stand. The value of the land encourages this, and tempts house owners to subdivide their vast gardens, and, if their planning application succeeds, grow money instead of roses.

A little way back I passed a sign: *Wentworth Estate. Private. Residents and Wentworth Club Only.* There is a reference to the Highways Act 1980 and Wentworth Estate Act 1964, which established the Wentworth Estate Roads Committee to oversee the common areas of the Estate. *This is a private road*, it repeats for emphasis, and then, *Members of the public use it only with the consent of Wentworth Estate Roads Committee.* I have no such consent, but I am not minded to turn back. As I get close to the clubhouse, I see two security guards standing at the main entrance and decide against trying to walk straight in. Two middle-aged men are wheeling golfing kit from the clubhouse to four-wheelers in the car park. The smooth glittering green of this famous eighteen-hole golf course, where the Ryder Cup is sometimes played, surrounds the clubhouse like a tranquil sea.

I survey the grounds and spot the outdoor pool and the tennis courts. A woman wearing a navy trouser suit and a name tag, who looks as if she works in the Club's administrative team, glances over at me quizzically, but does not challenge me. Having been refused entry by phone and email, the only other route inside is with a member, and I have not been able to arrange that; those with whom I raised this as a possibility were too nervous to agree. Like having two security guards on the door, this seemed an overreaction to me, and I wonder what unspoken anxieties justify such caution.

The atmosphere is quiet, almost eerily so, and I see no signs of the recent changes that prompted a furore at the Golf Club. The controversy began when the Club – one of the most prestigious in the country – was sold for £130 million in 2014 to the Chinese-born billionaire Chanchai Ruayrungruang, also known as Yan Bin. The new owner wanted to make the Club more exclusive. Members were required to deposit a £100,000 debenture in addition to the annual family membership fee, which was raised from £8,388 to £16,000 in 2017. By reducing the number of debentures, the Club's new owners aimed to decrease membership from 4,000 to 2,000. A stand-off followed between the Club's existing wealthy members and the plans to replace them with much wealthier new members. Another case of the 'Haves and Have Yachts'. Members, including one-time TV-show hosts Sir Michael Parkinson and Sir Bruce Forsyth, weighed into the struggle to preserve the status quo. A legal battle against these changes on behalf of the 'Wentworth community' – a self-selected body of locals constituted only for campaigns like this – was eventually lost and the former stately home underwent a £20 million refurbishment to its ballroom, bars, restaurants and other facilities. The new restaurant manager, Devid Isabella, hails from The Ritz and became focused on 'giving people whatever they want' as a new kind of elite service culture took hold of the Club.[1]

Those who live around it consider the Golf Club to be at the heart of the Wentworth Estate. The estate consists of approximately 1,100 large houses, originally built in the 1920s by master builder W. G. Tarrant, influenced by the arts and craft architecture of the late nineteenth century. Most of Tarrant's comparatively modest-sized detached houses have gradually been torn down and replaced by much bigger ones, like those on the drive. The estate, which now has its own private security force, is home to the most expensive houses in an already expensive area. A five-bedroomed house with three garages and servants' quarters sells for around £11 million. The new Tarrant is an exclusive luxury bespoke building company, Octagon. Who lives in these houses? In addition to elderly chat- and game-show hosts, the Chilean dictator Augusto Pinochet lived here in 1998, under house arrest while awaiting a decision on his extradition to Spain to stand trial for genocide and torture, his money pilfered from the people of Chile. Ron Dennis, who owned the McLaren car company, has a £30 million house on the estate. In our study of 2012 to 2015 (see Prelude), we spoke with women who lived on the estate and treated the Golf Club as an extension of their family home: their children drove around in golf carts, used the sports facilities, and put their meals and drinks on the family tab – all practices presumably discouraged by the Club's new owners in their bid for exclusivity. International billionaires who want the privacy and security that extensive grounds provide, footballers (the Chelsea training ground is nearby) and celebrities all live around here: a distinctive, suburban subset of plutocrats, quite different from those who live in Richmond.

Giving up on the Golf Club, I walk back down the drive, turn left on the main road and set off towards the town centre again, intending to turn down promising-looking lanes. It occurs to me that this landscape, created to serve suburban serious money, imposes a respectful distance on passers-by. It discourages proximity and scrutiny. Vast houses are set back from the roads at the end of long gravel driveways, dashing my hopes of getting up close. In fact, many houses are only just visible in the distance, behind screens of trees and shrubs. The closest I get is peering in from the wrong side of 25-foot-high wrought iron electronic gates and fences, while being monitored by security cameras displaying the logos of the private security firms patrolling them. Extreme kinds of privacy are built into the architecture and street plans of Virginia Water.

The architecture – from what I can see of it – is varied. Hints of individual whimsy are tempered by a more consistent sense of what a plutocrat's home ought to look like. Spanish-styled villas sit next to more traditional buildings in pink brick with dazzling white plaster finishes. Older houses built in the 1920s, much smaller than the new ones, show just how far the wealthy's expectations for their lifestyle and living space have expanded. 'Mansions' probably best describes the new builds; many are the size of country hotels. As I stand looking through front gates, I see what might be Indonesian or Filipina women flit in and out of doors intent on various domestic duties: a fleetingly visible serving class, essential in maintaining houses on this scale. New builds mostly try to echo the past, passing up the opportunity for imaginative modern domestic architecture, opting instead for neo-Georgian, neo-Victorian, neo-Tudor and the faux Greek and Roman columns of the Anglo-Palladian style. These reinterpretations of Roman architecture gained popularity in the design of English country houses of the seventeenth and eighteenth centuries. Arches and pillars add a sense of grandeur, importing the gravitas of elite histories into the contemporary palaces of the suburban uber-wealthy.

The designer Atmosphere, who has devised some of Wentworth's interiors, describes them as 'pastiche, old-fashioned houses that pretend to be eighteenth century'. Since the 1990s, Julian Bicknell has become a key architect of such contemporary mansions, along with a dramatic rise in the number of super-rich. According to Atmosphere,

Bicknell is, 'the king of that type of architecture ... all of these pastiche houses for the rich. Like a Disney world'. Bicknell – who now collaborates with the Prince of Wales's Institute for Architecture – would doubtless insist that, on the contrary, he has brought the lessons of history to contemporary building. Atmosphere describes the difficulties of finding the right bricks for Wentworth building projects and then 'tumbling' them to age them, so they don't look new and shiny, or too bling. Even so, compared to the solemn Victorian stucco of Belgravia or Regent's Park, this landscape, full of flashy ostentations and flourishes, is all about bling. New money.

Despite my best efforts through different routes and contacts, I am unable to get inside any of these houses. Defended with the full array of the security features Sailor described, their owners are unwilling to open their doors to inquisitive eyes. Some are occasionally featured in glossy magazines. Russian billionaire Petr Aven, for example, let the *Financial Times* into his Virginia Water mansion to see his art collection and tasteful interiors.[2] Aerial shots on estate agents' websites reveal vast gardens and swimming pools behind some of the houses, hidden from sight. Denied the chance to get closer than the streets or the pages of the press, I must rely on those who have been inside these fortresses to reveal what goes on.

Atmosphere told me about one of her Wentworth Estate commissions. She summed up the inhabitants of the estate – which she had not heard of until she was commissioned to work there, and imagined to be an upmarket municipal development of some kind – as 'the men doing the golfing, and the women in the Club and they've all got Botox lips'. As part of a design team discussing an interior makeover with a young Russian family, she noticed their eight-year-old daughter was busy making herself business cards and checking her stocks on Bloomberg. Atmosphere has her own eight-year-old, who shows no such inclination. Sadly, she said, the design got entangled in a last-ditch attempt to maintain the couple's marriage. Translating the couple's split into the design of the house, the master bedroom was adapted at the last minute, Atmosphere said, to add a dividing wall. Divorce followed while the design was still in the making. The wife got the house and the husband – who made his money in finance – moved to a flat in the city with his new girlfriend. 'I just felt so sad for her,' Atmosphere told me, 'because I think she pinned all her hopes on this project and what the project meant for her, you know, a house and a future and building this thing. I think she was very lonely and the kind of friends she had in the Wentworth Club, they all had their houses and their husbands, and I think she just felt trapped.'

Atmosphere has already given me a peep inside the Wentworth Estate, but I manage to go one better. I finally find someone with sustained insider access, who agrees to meet me: Babysitter, who has always lived in Virginia Water. Until, that is, she moved to Chelsea, which is where I meet her sometime later. Like other young men and women who grew up in Virginia Water and its prestigious estate – Barbour among them – she chose Chelsea. The youth of Virginia Water, the slow and steady suburb, find their way towards livelier city areas. As I sit with Babysitter in her local, her friends drift by: the young man who went to Eton; some of the young women she is close to, back from provincial universities; and others following family connections into the world of finance or property development, like Barbour.

Babysitter tells me that her mum and dad split up and each took new partners. The two families reconfigured their living arrangements around a new romance. In her late twenties, she is thin, with dark blonde hair and intense dark green eyes, delicate and pretty. She wears a little short skirt, flat shoes and an expensive gauze-like blouse. We are meeting on her way home from work. She works at a bank. 'We control the announcements that come out,' she says. She likes her job and spends weekends with her boyfriend, who runs his family's surgical support business in Birmingham. He has a flat in Kensington, and his parents own an apartment at the exclusive One Hyde Park development next to the Mandarin Oriental Hotel. Surgical supports are clearly a profitable, if not a very glamorous, way of becoming very rich.

Babysitter's mother is one of the few women I have come across who are wealthy in their own right. Moreover, she is self-made: rich through her property development business. Babysitter's mum saved and invested her money in property. She bought cheap properties in the midlands city where she had grown up in a working-class family, and rented them on the burgeoning market for student accommodation.

Now with her third husband, who has a small business of his own, she is a successful developer. With her property gains, she shifted to the local student accommodation market and, fortuitously, Virginia Water. Her intimate grasp of the Virginia Water property market and the demand for high spec housing, enabled her to accumulate a substantial fortune from buying, refurbishing and selling houses to other rich people.

Babysitter's mum took advantage of the rental market in Virginia Water too – where large houses rent for £10,000 a week and much more during golf tournaments – by letting some of the properties she developed. Babysitter says the family moved constantly. 'I've moved twenty-four times around Virginia Water because my parents do property. They didn't go far.' Once she refused to unpack, assuming it wasn't worth it. Her mother believes her two daughters should earn their own money, not expect to be gifted it. Babysitter's first job as a teenager was, as her pseudonym suggests, babysitting for a neighbour's children. Babysitter says she and her sister had the importance of earning money 'drilled into us'. She gives the example of another woman 'who owns one of the biggest property companies on Wentworth, some of the biggest £25 million houses', as another model. 'My mum's close friendship group are all workers.' Successful women grafters, they see themselves as different from their non-working women neighbours, the women who, as Babysitter puts it, would 'go and have their hair blow-dried just to go to school to pick the kids up'. In contrast, these self-made businesswomen think of themselves as more principled and down to earth, rather than entitled.

I ask Babysitter to tell me more about the neighbours. She talks about one of her school friends who lived nearby, who she 'always felt very sorry for'. The girl 'never saw her dad', because he was working in America, and she had 'a very strange relationship with her mum'. Babysitter says, 'I get the impression the mum used to just wake up, drink a couple of bottles of Laurent-Perrier rosé and go back to bed. That was kind of it. Their driver used to take them to school. She used to say to me, "I hate it, I don't like going with the driver." She just wanted to be normal, I felt. So, I used to take her in my little car to school.' Sometimes, when Babysitter was picking the girl up or dropping her off, she would invite her in: 'She'd just show me things.'

Another school and neighbourhood friend with fragile mental health came from what Babysitter judged to be a really good family situation. Nevertheless, Babysitter describes her as being 'in a really bad place', though she doesn't elaborate. This surprises her, because, 'Honestly, she's got a doting dad.' Doting means 'He's not away on business all the time.' Babysitter remembers, 'I used to go around and they'd have a family dinner every night; the four of them would sit down. My family never did, because, when I was very young, my mum and dad were unhappy. My dad came in late and it just never worked.' When her mum remarried, she would cook her children dinner, but then eat separately with her new husband: 'Because she was so madly in love, they'd have a little dinner together.' She compares this to her friend's family, where 'No one has had an affair, no one has been messed around. Yet you still have problems.' Babysitter provides snapshots of some of the fragilities of this seemingly solid suburban life.

Back in Virginia Water, I swerve off the main road and follow some of the smaller roads instead. Many of these roads are private, adopted and maintained by their residents. It requires collective action from residents to privatize a road – the aim is to raise the value of their property. Road ownership has spread through the area like a rash. Now it is a must-have: a way of maximizing accumulated housing equity. Private roads provide the protection of security cameras; they are no longer public rights of way – *Only Residents and Guests*, read the signs. These signs make me feel anxious about transgressing, as they are designed to. Once more, I am the only walker, and I sense the CCTV cameras of the residents and their security companies following me. I walk on, anticipating being stopped in my tracks at any moment. This place reminds me of somewhere I cannot quite put my finger on.

I wonder if driving is any easier. I discovered that the Wentworth Estate uses car number plate recognition software to identify vehicles with no business there. Estate management boasts a direct line – privileged access – to Surrey Police and to Cannon Security, the private security firm that guards the estate. It claims there are 24/7 patrols by liveried vehicles and guards, some of whom are ex-military. It also operates random checkpoints at the main entrances, where guards stop any vehicle not displaying the R that validates a registered resident. Last time I passed through a checkpoint with a uniformed security patrol, I was visiting Nairobi; I wasn't expecting to be faced with one in Surrey.

Some private roads have taken a step beyond security cameras and installed unmanned security barriers activated by codes and fobs instead. These restrict even those who live nearby, making circulation around Virginia Water a peculiarly syncopated affair. Disrupting road connections through shifting boundaries between public and private roads creates a complex patchwork of rights of way and permitted routes, which drivers and walkers must know how to navigate. As neighbours reroute their other wealthy neighbours, forcing them to drive around road barriers, I wonder how this shapes their relationships. How are permissions negotiated, fobs and barrier codes shared or withheld? How does this actually work at the everyday street level of neighbourhood life?

And why the private securitized streets? Virginia Water has low crime rates, according to the Office of National Statistics and Surrey police data, which hardly warrant its intense levels of security and surveillance. The crime rate is actually falling, in line with national trends across all types of crimes.[3] The largest categories of crime reported in the area are anti-social behaviour and public disorder, which mostly occur around its few picnic and public green spaces. I imagine residents are quick to report any misbehaviour from those who come from elsewhere to enjoy Virginia Water's beauty. This puts me in mind of the butlering manuals and their insistence on what is proper. These barriers are not erected against the usual urban anxieties of robbery and physical assault. Instead they seem to defend privileged people from each other and from random members of the visiting public.

This is not the solid and staid suburban landscape I initially imagined it to be either. It is instead a pop-up landscape. Old houses vanish to be replaced by new, bigger and shinier ones, also ways of growing money. The Golf Club is reinvented as ever more exclusive and expensive. Roads are cut off from the commons and new blockades disrupt circulation in the area. New relationships replace old ones: marriage, divorce, remarriage provides the base rhythm of this place. Young people suffer parental attentions and neglect as they learn to be rich and leave for the excitement of adult life in the city on their parents' money. This suburb, it seems, is anything but settled.

Stopping in my tracks, I decide to turn back. I think of myself as a moderately intrepid researcher: I have done research on rubbish sites in Addis Ababa, after all. But this eerie, unpeopled landscape of monster homes, hidden from view on streets where I am liable to be apprehended by private security guards at any moment, is getting to me. I am unlikely to be the first visitor to Virginia Water to feel this rebuff, which is deliberately built into its streets and domestic architecture. These streets are not even friendly towards those who live here; not intended to connect the neighbourhood and allow people to freely circulate; not intended to serve the usual functions of roads, to expedite movement. Instead, roads become barriers, protecting the property values, anxieties and seemingly unwarranted excessive privacies of money.

Johannesburg! I was searching my memory for the city suburb that Virginia Water most resembles. In post-apartheid, deeply unequal Johannesburg, rich white folk fortify themselves in suburban idylls against the imagined depredations of the impoverished black masses. Virginia Water is Johannesburg in Surrey – except that I am not sure what it is fortified against exactly. Yet, the visual resemblance between the two suburbs is striking. Both have vast detached houses in lush securitized grounds; the notices at the gate warning would-be trespassers that private security companies are watching, that they are on patrol; and the deathly quiet of private streets, with no signs of life, only signs telling people they should not be there. Unliveable, impossible landscapes both. Why would the rich choose to live this way? Does the gap between their wealth and the rest of the population make them uneasy? Do they even notice it? Or are they so immersed in privacy and social exclusion that they've forgotten there are other ways to live?

Epilogue

The zebra and the hunters in the Mayfair shop window have spoken. I have walked a long way since I first stood in South Audley Street, and wondered about the people who shopped there. I have walked further into the lives of the super-rich than I expected to, stumbling into the underbelly of the plutocratic city. Probing the public and private lives of the rich, I found a strange half-hidden world. I have seen how the plutocratic city circulates, expands and skims money; how it condenses it into ever-larger piles reserved for ever fewer hands; and how it embellishes wealthy lives with limitless luxuries. Meanwhile, local authority budgets for housing, social care, public health and welfare have been drastically reduced, and the city is diminished by neglect, homelessness and dispossession.

In the spring of 2020, the Covid-19 pandemic aggravated an already untenable situation. As London plunged into lockdown, as shops, bars, restaurants and hotels closed, and the city darkened, a skeleton bus service winged essential workers, and those too poor to stay away from work, through deserted streets. And Londoners absorbed the dangers of airborne contagion as they stood in straggling queues for groceries and medicines. Those who could afford to, holed up, pulled their children out of school and worked from home. The streets of Kensington, Mayfair, Knightsbridge and Chelsea were unusually quiet, as people stayed inside, or made for their country home, yacht, or international retreat, leaving the streets to dog walkers and walking researchers. I continued my walks, cycling from my home in the East End, but there was little to see and no one to meet. As public life drained from the city, plutocratic London's opacities deepened.

Until the news began to leak out. While the pandemic was still gathering momentum in the early months of winter, Zurich-based UBS, the world's biggest private bank, reported its best quarterly earnings for a decade. Credit Suisse was anticipating similar results. A UBS spokesman described these gains as a reward for courage: their clients did not panic, they built their 'positions', investing in equity markets instead. Whether or not you think having an eye for the financial main chance is equivalent to the kind of courage shown by frontline workers who braved exposure to the virus, praising those who did not panic as stock prices fell reveals a very different world and sense of values. The pandemic has made millionaires and billionaires wealthier still. And technology has led the surge in profits because it had the infrastructure to deliver online social connection and shopping. The net worth of Jeff Bezos, executive chairman at Amazon, rose by $73 billion between March and September 2020.

According to the *Financial Times*, 'Some bankers believe the last time the super-rich had it this good was in 2009, after the great financial crash.'[1] One journalist reported, for the rich, 'The pandemic is more of an inconvenience than an existential threat to wealth.' In June 2021, the Johnson government announced that business executives who were bringing 'significant economic benefit' to the country would be exempt from the quarantine restrictions that the rest of us were required to observe. Except for high-end travel and restaurants, the rich were still buying luxuries while millions were thrown out of work. Meanwhile, the IMF reported that the global economy had shrunk by 4.4 per cent in 2020 alone, throwing millions, worldwide, into poverty.[2] How can these diametrically opposed realities share the same streets without remedy?

The pandemic forced the government to intervene in ways that Conservatives normally consider unthinkable. In the early days of the spring lockdown, I cycled past groups of homeless men gathered in the entrances to grand London buildings, like the National Gallery and St Paul's Cathedral, as well as in the doorways of shuttered shops. Although deprived of their usual sources of money – begging, busking and the *Big Issue* – they had the city to themselves and some sounded a note of optimism when they spoke to reporters from the *New York Times*. 'To tell you the truth, Corona has been the best thing that has happened to the homeless,' a homeless man in London suggested.[3] In its Everyone In initiative, the UK government was shamed into sheltering rough sleepers in hotels on public health and humanitarian grounds, which had apparently not troubled it before. The homeless, especially rough sleepers, became the targets of a new sanitary politics, unleashed by fears of contagion. Between 1,000 and 1,400 of London's rough sleepers, out of a total of 8,555,[4] were sheltered in hotels, as the government allocated £517 million in emergency relief to local councils.

Always intended as a temporary solution, these arrangements quickly came to an end. The government still does not have a solution to the capital's most pressing long-term problem: acute shortages of affordable housing and homelessness. As I write, a new, and so far undocumented, group of rough sleepers are bedding down in the streets and doorways of the capital. Despite former housing minister Robert Jenrick's so-called 'landmark commitment' to provide 6,000 new supported homes in the capital,[5] this is still to materialize and in any case falls short of what is needed.

Should there be any confusion about how public finances, expanding wealth and deepening poverty are connected, an incident involving Jenrick himself reveals this. A wealthy property developer and Conservative donor, Richard Desmond, arranged to get a seat beside the housing minister at a fund-raising dinner, conveniently at the same time as he was lobbying for his 1,500-home development in the London Borough of Tower Hamlets to get planning approval. Desmond was trying to get the development approved before Tower Hamlets Council's introduction of a new Community Infrastructure Levy to pay for local services, in the process saving himself £40 million or more. This move would also deprive the citizens of Tower Hamlets, a borough with some of the United Kingdom's worst concentrations of poverty, of much-needed cash for local services like housing and social welfare.[6]

London in the Covid-19-era is poorer and richer at the same time. The gap between wealth and want has widened into a chasm. Serious money and the city it shapes is in an unsustainable relationship. The plutocratic city and its monster creation – the city of poverty and dispossession – has reached a tipping point.

The plutocratic city might appear entrenched, confident, with its fancy cars, its basement swimming pools and its many other wasteful excesses. My walks have shown that it is not so solid at all. Money's swagger serves to conceal the fact that it is actually perpetually fragile: in certain circumstances, it could collapse. Covid-19 has taught us that cities can change suddenly and dramatically – as can accepted ideas of what is politically possible. As the plutocratic city was made, so it can be unmade. Luxury industries could turn to more socially useful purposes. The yacht polishers and other plutocrat servants could find alternative occupations to waiting for the next order. What would London be like if the city's talent was no longer drawn into making the rich richer still? What collective benefits might this bring? Even the sturdy-looking money machine, once I took a close look, is cobbled together day by day: by poorly paid women in back offices, by algorithms written by maths geeks, by researchers who may or may not get it right, by investment portfolio managers who go for a pint and gossip after work, by speculators who win and lose their bets, by those who clean the offices and the streets, by men who cannot do without the adrenalin rush that making money gives them, and by those who remember the uncertainties of 2008, and understand that the machine can suddenly collapse. All that seems solid can melt into air; something else can take shape in its place. Political complicity with wealth and consequent neglect of the poor, of the majority, whose wages have stagnated and whose living conditions have plummeted, *can* be recast.

The biggest clue that serious money is seriously fragile lies in its overwhelming secrecy, concealment and separation of wealthy life: private streets, private clubs, security cordons, the proprietary secrets of the algorithm, private meeting rooms, private hideaways. Why this secrecy? What exactly is hidden and why? Why are Banker and Quant so reluctant to speak about what they do? Why is Buffer so defensive? My walks show that often nothing so very secret actually happens in these spaces. On the contrary, the secret lives of the super-rich largely consist of mundane, banal, activities, along with their bad behaviour, greed, multiple excesses, and their ways of expanding and skimming money: all hidden from public scrutiny. The rich cordon themselves off from city life because their money-piling activities and wasteful, unsustainable lives are publicly indefensible. Those who realize this – the philanthropists Blazer and Soviet, the women I met in Notting Hill and the Richmond liberals among them – are uneasy. The fragilities of the plutocratic city are implicitly acknowledged in their concealment as the rich conceal their own fear and uneasiness at the same time.

I can only conclude that being rich, as Jean-Paul Sartre put it in a radically different context, is an inherently nervous condition. The stories I uncovered along my walk are haunted by anxiety. Serious money doesn't appear to be a source of pleasure or happiness, even for the rich, as Student and Assistant suggest. Hoarding money is itself a nervous activity. Wealth is a profoundly uneasy condition, and yet the rest of us have been persuaded to aspire to its benefits.

A new, fairer politics of the city, that closes the chasm between the rich and the rest, is inescapable. And there are encouraging signs that, in the right political circumstances, things could change. The deeply ingrained popular aspiration towards money and privilege is slowly being countered by a growing chorus of influential voices ready to rein in these impulses and, instead, to redistribute the benefits of wealth more widely. Wealth taxes – acknowledging that income is not the only or best measure – are finally on the political agenda, even if the details of how they might work remain unresolved. Lord O'Donnell, cabinet secretary under recent Labour and Conservative governments, speaking from no less distinguished a place than the Institute for Fiscal Studies, said that Covid-19 created 'a clear burning platform for tax reform' targeting wealth.[7] Following the revelations of the 2016 Panama Papers (and the 2021 Pandora Papers), HMRC are doubling down on those who hide their assets to protect them from taxation. In 2019–20 HMRC launched 430 investigations into sophisticated tax evasion among wealthy people and companies, a significant rise on previous efforts, and has also created a Family Investment team so that it can 'follow the money' through family investment companies, and so bear down on inheritance tax evasion.[8] If only HMRC can marshal the funding and expert staff to deliver on these initiatives, and not be outspent by the rich, who can afford top accountants, the public finances could be greatly enhanced. The United Kingdom has committed to a register of beneficial owners of offshore assets in attempts to end some of the opacities of the rich.

Unexplained Wealth Orders, which require wealthy individuals and companies to explain how an asset over £50,000 was acquired, were introduced in 2018, as part of an effort to seize the proceeds of crime washed through London. Russians associated with the opposition leader, lawyer and critic of corruption Alexei Navalny hired a bus and gave guided klepto-tours of London in 2016.

Global trends are moving in a similar direction. The Common Reporting Standard, a 2014 agreement between the members of the Organization for Economic Cooperation and Development (OECD), helps to facilitate offshore tax probes, share information between nations and make hiding money more difficult.[9] The introduction of a global wealth tax on big tech and other multinational corporations, which would tax their profits in the countries in which they are made, was discussed at the 2021 G7 summit and subsequently, though no agreement was reached. Even Jim Chanos, the Wall Street trader dubbed a 'catastrophe capitalist' because he benefits from all manner of disasters through his short-selling hedge fund, recently criticized the way that banks' quantitative easing – pushing digital money into circulation – has made the rich richer still. His solution? Tax wealth – unearned income – and use the money to support low-waged workers' living standards with pay increases. The plutocratic city is on notice: change is coming, we have the instruments necessary to make it happen, but this is stalled by political reluctance to challenge the fortunes of the rich.

The movement to fight the impending disaster of climate change presents a different challenge to the plutocratic world. This chasm between the needs of ecology and the activities of finance was laid bare in June 2019, when protestors disrupted the British Chancellor of the Exchequer's Mansion House speech – in the inner sanctum of London's finance capital – and minister at the Foreign Office Mark Field was filmed roughly bundling a female protestor out, prompting an angry backlash. This tableau captures a shift in the public mood with potentially far-reaching implications for London's plutocrats, whose wasteful habits are an affront to sustainability. Frequent air travel, private planes, yachts lying idle in Mediterranean and Caribbean harbours, owning multiple homes, art and wine collections, interiors regularly gutted and redesigned around rare materials, expensive, rarely worn clothes: these are all potentially targets for censure. For all its greenwashing, finance has shown itself unwilling to implement meaningful reform. And, for the avoidance of doubt, the spoils of excessive wealth actively endanger the world we live in: a 2020 Oxfam study found that, between 1990 and 2015, the planet's wealthiest 1 per cent were responsible for more than twice as much carbon dioxide as the poorest 50 per cent.[10] The luxuries of plutocrats' lives are on a collision course with public sensitivities and urgently needed new environmental policies and targets.

A new, more socially just politics of the city would tackle wasteful consumption; it would address the unequal tax system and use the money gained to enhance city life with additional green spaces, libraries, arts and cultural programmes and facilities; and it would improve social welfare, provision for the homeless, rent controls and the building of affordable housing. London could be a very different city – a city organized for everyone's well-being instead of the privileges of the rich. A new politics of the city would reshape the skewed financial structures that support excessive wealth accumulation for the already rich. The vast infrastructures that serve the rich – accountants, lawyers, wealth and other advisers – and the serving class of butlers, cleaners and drivers that comes with it would be reduced, releasing money and talent back into the city, making it a better place for everyone to live.

Despite these glimmerings of hope, there are enormous obstacles to change. The seductions of wealth retain a strong hold on people's minds, imaginations and unconscious desires. The rich live inside us as well as on the city's best streets. It is unclear how recent moves to rein in tax evasion, for instance, will change the city without the resources and political traction to drive them through. The rich are formidable opponents: unlike HM government, they can afford to have the best lawyers and PR professionals join their resistance.

The wealthy's most common tactic is the threat to leave the city, and take their money with them, implying that this would have devastating consequences for collective prosperity. Economist Brett Christophers points out this has long been an empty threat: serious money left for its offshore boltholes some time ago. And where would the super-rich go?

In *The Sovereign Individual*, private investor James Dale Davidson and journalist Lord William Rees-Mogg, father of Jacob, take these arguments a step further. Davidson and Rees-Mogg set out a fantasy future world of wealthy omnipotence and retreat: a future that, though depicted over a quarter century ago, remains one to which some super-rich aspire. In this world, 'Individuals capable of creating significant economic value will be able to retain most of the value they create for themselves', and 'The lower classes will be walled out.' States will decompose along with their welfare systems, creating a destitute underclass, and the rich, unencumbered by government or social obligations, will repair to offshore venues in 'secure physical spaces'.[11] A version of these secure physical spaces is with us now, already, in the streets of West London.

Yet the vision of *The Sovereign Individual* remains a dystopian fantasy: one in which law and order, education, health provision, roads, transport, divorce, and, indeed, the social reproduction of the serving class on which the rich depend, all revert to individuals instead of the public authorities and infrastructures sustaining city life. A city without reciprocity, collective life and neighbourhood interaction, in which everything is bought and paid for, is a bleak prospect – and an unsustainable one. Indeed, the conviction that money provides escape – running like a seam through my encounters in this book – is one of the most disturbing, most entrenched myths of the plutocratic city. However secure the walls they build, we all breathe the same air, with all its particle pollution and zoonotic viruses. In the end, the rich must be forced to agree to a new deal in which they will share both the city and their wealth.

Acknowledgements

My deepest thanks to those who trusted me with their stories. Guarantees of anonymity prevent me from naming you, but, without you, this book could not have been written. I appreciate your openness and your willingness to talk. The Leverhulme Trust generously supported the research on which this book is based with the award of a Major Research Scholarship (MRF-2016-001) for which I am immensely grateful. Special thanks are also due to Anne Beech for her expert editing, many suggestions and good humour. Crispin Thurlow and Tim Tutton argued with my manuscript, making it better in the process. My partner, Bill Schwarz, sometimes walked along with me. His generous support, guidance and edits are much appreciated. Luke Ingram at Wylie provided fresh eyes on this project at a critical moment. And my deepest thanks go to Thomas Penn, Eva Hodgkin and Anna Wilson, editors at Penguin, for their patience and skill in bringing this project to press.

Heartfelt thanks are also due to the many people who helped me along the road in different ways: Judith Farquhar, Thomas Erikson, Sally Alexander, Sophia Knowles-Mofford, Neil Belton, Ronny Heiremans, Katleen Vermeir, Paul Finch, William Knowles-Mofford, Lydia Morris, Ludovic Hunter-Tilney, Roger Burrows, Mike Featherstone, Richard Webber, Elisabeth Schimpfössl, Michael Keith, Gregory Asmolov, Luna Glucksberg, Anna Tylor, Tom Hoogewerf, Gabriel Feltran, James Weitz, Norma Jones, Jan Derry, Chris Jones, Bernard Walsh, Jessica Knowles-Mofford, Gill FitzHugh, Mark Fisher, Ursula Owen, Diana Litton, Mark Dunford, Rowland Atkinson, Tim Butler, Deborah Reade, Jo Hopkins, Jane Plastow, Liz Hutchinson, Sam Liebmann, John McKiernan, Edward Hillel, Angelo Martins Junior,

ACKNOWLEDGEMENTS

Maria Garner, Melissa Sweeting Knowles-Mofford, Larry McGinity, Chloe Nast, Ash Amin, Juliette Kristensen, Alena Ledeneva, Abbas Nokhasteh, Paul Halliday, Kirsten Campbell, Sally Wyatt, Ben Collins, Alicia Rouverol, Eric Litton, Carol Rivas, Will Davies, Lynne Segal, Charlotte Fairclough, Claire Maxwell, Jane Kenway, Patrick Knowles, Charlotte Cole and Jane Collins.

Notes

PRELUDE

1 Estimates vary: 'The World Now Has More Than 20 Million Millionaires', https://www.consultancy.uk/news/28371/the-world-now-has-more-than-20-million-millionaires

2 'World Wealth Report 2021', https://worldwealthreport.com/resources/world-wealth-report-2021/

3 'Eight Billionaires Own as Much as Poorest Half of Global Population', https://philanthropynewsdigest.org/news/eight-billionaires-own-as-much-as-poorest-half-of-global-population

4 'World Wealth Report 2021'.

5 The United Kingdom now lags behind the United States, Japan, Germany, China and France. See also Cristobal Young, *The Myth of Millionaire Tax Flight: How Place Still Matters for the Rich*, Stanford University Press, 2018.

6 'Rich List 2021: How the Covid Pandemic Spawned More Billionaires than Ever', https://www.thetimes.co.uk/article/sunday-times-rich-list-2021-covid-billionaires-uk-57vjgrp7s

7 Iain Hay, 'On Plutonomy: Economy, Power and the Wealthy Few in the Second Gilded Age', in Iain Hay and Jonathan v. Beaverstock (eds.), *Handbook on Wealth and the Super-Rich*, Edward Elgar, 2016, pp. 68–93.

8 The project was called 'A Study of Everyday Life in the Alpha Territories', and ran from 2012 to 2015, funded by the Economic and Social Science Research Council. My colleagues were Roger Burrows, Rowland Atkinson, Tim Butler, Richard Webber, Mike Featherstone and Mike Savage. Luna Glucksberg was the research assistant.

9 Raja Shehadeh, *Palestinian Walks: Notes on a Vanishing Landscape*, Profile Books, 2008; Teju Cole, *Open City*, Faber & Faber, 2011; Iain Sinclair, *The Last London*, Oneworld, 2017; Walter Benjamin, *The Arcades Project*, Harvard University Press, 2002; and Virginia Woolf, *Street Haunting: A London Adventure*(1927), Symonds Press, 2013.

10 Office for National Statistics (ONS), most recent estimate.
11 In *Alpha City: How London Was Captured by the Super-Rich*, Verso, 2020, the geographer Rowland Atkinson shows the effects of extreme concentrations of wealth in the displacement and worsening life conditions of other Londoners.
12 'Homelessness', *London Review of Books* (20 December 2018).

1 THE QUANT IN THE DITCH

1 The characters on which this book is based were offered a guarantee of anonymity, and so they all have pseudonyms. The Boy alone waived his right to anonymity, making it possible for me to name his bar.
2 Mariana Mazzucato, *The Value of Everything: Making and Taking in the Global Economy*, Penguin, 2018.

2 BANKERS IN GLASS TOWERS

1 David Kynaston, *The City of London*, vols. 1–4, Chatto and Windus, 1994–2002.
2 Linda McDowell, *Capital Culture: Gender at Work in the City*, Blackwell, 1997.
3 Rowan Moore, *Slow Burn City*, Picador, 2016.
4 Ibid.
5 Chris Rhodes, 'Financial Services: Contribution to the UK Economy', House of Commons Briefing Paper 6193 (25 April 2018).
6 Brett Christophers, *Banking across Boundaries: Placing Finance in Capitalism*, Wiley-Blackwell, 2013.
7 Ibid., p. 44.
8 Susan Strange, *Casino Capitalism*, Manchester University Press, 1997.
9 Landing slots are specific points in time when aircraft are allowed to land and take off.
10 Robert Frank, *Richistan*, Piatkus, 2007.
11 'Borough Profile', accessed Tower Hamlets website, https://www.tower hamlets.gov.uk, since removed.

3 MAYFAIR MAGIC

1 'May Fair', in *Old and New London*, vol. 4, Cassell, Petter and Galpin, 1878, British History Online, https://www.british-history.ac.uk/old-new-london/vol4/pp345-359

2 Hedge funds are now in decline, with 580 closing globally in 2018. At their height, they held $2 trillion of assets under management. Reasons cited are falling fees, falling returns, a growth in the number of hedge funds chasing profits, and regulation more likely to be enforced. Robin Wrigglesworth, Laurence Fletcher and Lindsay Fortado, 'Keeping It in the Family', *FT Weekend* (26/27 January 2019).

3 'London Private Equity Firms', https://www.crunchbase.com/hub/london-private-equity-firms

4 'Private Equity Moves beyond London in Search for Deals', https://www.ft.com/content/15403ff2-150a-11e9-a581-4ff78404524e. Estimates vary and it is difficult to get a precise figure, particularly in a shifting landscape, as London is described as 'all fished out', and since 2017 has lost private equity firms elsewhere.

5 'Hedge Funds', Investopedia, checked 28 November 2019.

6 Wrigglesworth, Fletcher and Fortado, 'Keeping It in the Family'.

7 This comes from the High Court Family Division Decisions publicly available documents on the Bailii website.

4 MAYFAIR NIGHTS

1 Market report on the Wetherell website, https://wetherell.co.uk, accessed April 2016 but since removed.

2 Ibid.

3 Frank Mort, *Capital Affairs: London and the Making of the Permissive Society*, Yale University Press, 2010.

4 This is difficult to establish, but, in *Londongrad*, Fourth Estate, 2010, Mark Hollingsworth and Stewart Lansley suggest this rate for prostitutes serving top-end-hotel clients.

5 MILKING FISH

1 Criticisms of private equity tend to focus on its taste for leveraging and financial engineering, rather than its short timescales.

2 In *Rich Russians*, Oxford University Press, 2018, Elisabeth Schimpfössl explains this particularly lucidly.

3 'Larry Gagosian', https://www.interviewmagazine.com/art/larry-gagosian

4 'Larry Gagosian: The Fine Art of the Deal', https://www.independent.co.uk/news/people/profiles/larry-gagosian-the-fine-art-of-the-deal-398567.html

5 Jan Dalley, 'Art in a Spin', *FT Weekend* (22/23 February 2020).

6 Sharon Zukin, *Naked City: The Death and Life of Authentic Urban Places*, Oxford University Press, 2010.

7 Jan Dalley, 'Can the Art World Clean Up Its Act?' *Financial Times* (21 February 2020).

8 'UK Art Dealer Matthew Green Charged in a $9 Million Picasso Money-Laundering Sheme', https://news.artnet.com/art-world/matthew-green-charged-money-laundering-us-1236929

6 A GAME OF CLUBS AND MONOPOLY

1 'A Home from Home', https://www.economist.com/britain/2015/09/17/a-home-from-home

2 'Club Ties' (June 2013), accessed on the *Spectator* website, https://www.spectator.co.uk, but since removed.

3 'Tory Leadership: Farage Donor Robin Birley Puts Money Behind Boris Johnson', https://www.thetimes.co.uk/article/tory-leadership-farage-donor-robin-birley-puts-money-behind-boris-johnson-v9qt3j02n

4 'Tigers, Tarts and a Family Feud', https://www.thetimes.co.uk/article/tigers-tarts-and-a-family-feud-sqzqtzc9f7n

5 'George: The Private Club where Murdoch and Cameron Courted', https://www.theguardian.com/politics/2012/apr/27/george-private-club-cameron-murdoch

6 Rachel Sherman, *Uneasy Street: The Anxieties of Affluence*, Princeton University Press, 2017.

7 HIS GRACE'S BEES

1 'Berkeley Square, Westminster', https://hidden-london.com/gazetteer/berkeley-square/

2 'Arabs Pay £345m for Berkeley Sq', https://www.thisismoney.co.uk/money/news/article-1555932/Arabs-pay-163345m-for-Berkeley-Sq.html

3 'One in Ten Mayfair Properties Has Middle East Owners', https://www.morganpryce.co.uk/knowledge-centre/exclusive-news-articles/one-in-ten-mayfair-properties-has-middle-east-owners

8 KEEPING IT IN THE FAMILY

1 Thomas Picketty, *Capital in the Twenty-First Century*, Harvard University Press, 2017.

2 'The Rise of the Family Office: Where Do They Go Beyond 2019?', https://
www.forbes.com/sites/francoisbotha/2018/12/17/the-rise-of-the-family-
office-where-do-they-go-beyond-2019/#4aa310d25795

3 Nathan Brooker, 'Uncovering London's Hidden Wealth', *FT Weekend*
(21 March 2020).

4 Gemma Acton, 'Panama Papers Shine Light on London Real Estate' (11
April 2016), https://www.cnbc.com/2016/04/11/panama-papers-shine-
light-on-london-real-estate.html

5 'Explore the Panama Papers Key Figures', https://www.icij.org/investiga
tions/panama-papers/explore-panama-papers-key-figures/

6 Hollingsworth and Lansley, *Londongrad*, p. 18.

7 'The Power Players', https://www.icij.org/investigations/panama-papers/
the-power-players/

8 Acton, 'Panama Papers Shine Light'.

9 In 'Family Offices and the Contemporary Infrastructures of Dynastic
Wealth', *Sociologica* 2 (2016), Luna Glucksberg and Roger Burrows
cite a financial journalist who suggests family offices date to 1971.
I also benefited from Glucksberg's notes taken during the Swiss
conference.

10 Peter York, *The Blue Riband*, Penguin, 2013, pp. 52–4, quoted in Glucksberg and Burrows, 'Family Offices and the Contemporary Infrastructures
of Dynastic Wealth'.

11 Their sample is small, but significant in the absence of other data. They
interviewed 311 family office users online and twenty-five officers from
family offices.https://www.ubs.com/global/en/global-family-office/reports/
global-family-office-report-2020.html

12 York, *Blue Riband*, pp. 47–9, quoted in Glucksberg and Burrows, 'Family
Offices and the Contemporary Infrastructures of Dynaslic wealth'.

9 WORKING THE SPLIT

1 John Urry, *Offshoring*, Polity, 2014; and John Urry, 'The Super-Rich and
Offshore Worlds', in Thomas Birtchnell and Javier Caletrío (eds.), *Elite
Mobilities*, Routledge, 2014, pp. 226–40.

10 THE BURNING TOWER

1 'The Real Meaning of "Rachmanism"', https://www.nybooks.com/daily/
2019/12/23/the-real-meaning-of-rachmanism/

2 For a full account of this see, Andrew O'Hagan, 'The Tower', *London Review of Books*, vol. 40, no. 11 (7 June 2018).

3 Information accessed https://www.trustforlondon.org.uk, but since removed.

4 Grenfell Tower Inquiry, Phase One, Report, October 2019, presided over by Sir Martin Moore-Bick.

5 O'Hagan, 'The Tower'.

6 For a full account of this, see ibid.

7 'Social Housing in the Borough', https://www.rbkc.gov.uk/housing/social-housing/local-housing-information

8 P. Hubbard and L. Lees, 'The Right to Community? Legal Geographies of Resistance on London's Gentrification Frontiers', *CITY* 22(1) (2018): DOI 10.1080/13604813.2018.1432178

9 'Challenging the Gentrification of Council Estates in London', https://www.urbantransformations.ox.ac.uk/blog/2018/challenging-the-gentrification-of-council-estates-in-london/

10 'White Riot: The Week Notting Hill Exploded', https://www.independent.co.uk/news/uk/home-news/white-riot-the-week-notting-hill-exploded-912105.html

11 Information accessed Institute of Race Relations website, http://www.irr.org.uk, but since removed; 'Rights, Resistance and Racism: The Story of the Mangrove Nine', https://blog.nationalarchives.gov.uk/rights-resistance-racism-story-mangrove-nine/

12 Sus law refers to section 4 of the 1842 Vagrancy Act, which gave police powers to arrest anyone they suspected of loitering with intent to commit an offence. The Runnymede Trust describes it as a key mechanism in the racialization of the streets: http://www.irr.org.uk/news/fighting-sus-then-and-now/

13 'The "rebel" history of the Grove', https://irr.org.uk/article/the-rebel-history-of-the-grove/

14 'Grenfell Tower Cladding Failed to Meet Standard', https://www.bbc.co.uk/news/uk-43558186

15 'Grenfell Tower Inquiry: Phase 1 Report Overview', https://assets.grenfelltowerinquiry.org.uk/GTI%20-%20Phase%201%20report%20Executive%20Summary.pdf

16 Andrew O'Hagan, 'Letters', *London Review of Books*, vol. 40, no. 12 (21 June 2018).

17 O'Hagan, 'The Tower'.

11 LIVING IN TRIANGLES

1 Prospectus accessed Eton College website, https://www.etoncollege.com, but since removed.

2 Shamus Rahman Khan, 'The Ease of Mobility', in Thomas Birtchnell and Javier Caletrío (eds.), *Elite Mobilities*, Routledge, 2014, pp. 136–48; and Shamus Rahman Khan, *Privilege: The Making of an Adolescent Elite at St Paul's School*, Princeton University Press, 2011.

3 A term developed by French sociologist Pierre Bourdieu in *Distinction: A Social Critique of the Judgement of Taste* (1979), Routledge, 2006, pp. 2–3. It refers to a way of being socially that comes from the distinctions bestowed by cultivating certain kinds of taste. A 'cultured disposition' implies mastery of the art of living certain kinds of lifestyles, shaped by luxuries and entitlements.

4 Wednesday Martin, *Primates of Park Avenue*, Atria Books, 2015.

5 'Number of Billionaires around the World in 2019, by Gender', https://www.statista.com/statistics/778577/billionaires-gender-distribution/

6 'Men Account for 90% of All Global Billionaires', https://www.verdict.co.uk/90-percent-millionaires-male/

12 THE WAY DOWN

1 'What is It Like to Live on Britain's Most Expensive Street', https://www.theguardian.com/money/2014/apr/07/londons-most-expensive-street-kensington-palace-gardens

2 'Coming out' persisted into the mid-1960s and beyond. See Sophie Campbell, *The Season: A Summer Whirl through the English Social Season*, Aurum, 2013.

3 It is extraordinary that this persisted into the mid-1960s, when Lady came out. For a fuller account, see ibid.

13 PATROL

1 'The Bizarre Secret of London's Buried Diggers', https://www.newstatesman.com/business/2014/06/bizarre-secret-london-s-buried-diggers

2 Sophie Baldwin, Elizabeth Holroyd and Roger Burrows, 'Luxified Troglodytism? Mapping the Subterranean Geographies of Plutocratic London', *arq* 23(3) (2019), pp. 267–82: DOI 10.1017/S1359135519000356. This fantastic study explains the basement digging in this and other boroughs between 2008 and 2017. See also Roger Burrows, Stephen Graham and Alexander Wilson, 'Bunkering Down? The Geography of Elite Residential Basement Development in London', *urban Geography* (2021): DOI 10.1080/02723638.2021.1934628

3 Kensington Society website, http://www.kensingtonsociety.org/. See also 'Kensington High Street, South Side', in *Survey of London*, vol. 42, London, 1986, British History Online, https://www.british-history.ac.uk/survey-london/vol42/pp77-98

4 Annabel Walker, with Peter Jackson, *Kensington and Chelsea: A Social and Architectural History*, Antler Books, 1987. This study provides useful accounts of the recent history of Kensington. Lord Kensington's estate, Phillimore Estate and Holland House were some of the grand houses of the area.

5 Roger Burrows and Caroline Knowles, 'The "Haves" and the "Have Yachts": Socio-Spatial Struggles in London between the "Merely Wealthy" and the "Super-Rich"', *Cultural Politics* 15(1) (2019), pp. 72–87: DOI 10.1215/17432197-7289528

6 Simon Thurley, 'How Kensington Became Part of London' (2019), Kensington Society Annual Reports, http://www.kensingtonsociety.org/wp-content/uploads/Annual-2019%E2%80%932020.pdf

14 DIRTY WINDOW

1 In the summer of 2017, at the Old Bailey in London.

2 Schimpfössl, *Rich Russians*, p. 112.

3 Hollingsworth and Lansley, *Londongrad*, p. 197.

4 'Russian Corruption is Poisoning Britain', https://www.thedailybeast.com/russian-corruption-is-poisoning-britain

5 Karen Dawisha, *Putin's Kleptocracy: Who Owns Russia?*, Simon & Schuster, 2014. This study describes in detail the regime of Vladimir Putin.

6 'Investor Visa (Tier 1)', https://www.gov.uk/tier-1-investor

15 WAITING

1 'Pampered Prince Puts Sun King in Shade', https://www.theguardian.com/uk/2002/nov/16/monarchy.jamiewilson

2 'Domestics: UK Domestic Workers and Their Reluctant Employers', https://www.bl.uk/collection-items/domestics-uk-domestic-workers-and-their-reluctant-employers

3 'Britain's Butler Boom', https://www.cnbc.com/id/100644298

4 'The Servants Making $150,000 a Year', https://www.bbc.com/worklife/article/20160119-the-servants-making-150000-a-year

5 'More Butlers Do It as London Embraces Incomes with Eight Digits', http://www.butler-valetschool.co.uk/media-press/more-butlers-do-it-as-london-embraces-incomes-with-eight-digits

6 Accessed on Mr Henderson's website, now defunct.
7 'More Butlers Do It as London Embraces Incomes with Eight Digits', https://www.butler-valetschool.co.uk/media-press/more-butlers-do-it-as-london-embraces-incomes-with-eight-digits

16 MADE IN CHELSEA

1 In *Reality Television and Class*, Routledge, 2012, Beverley Skeggs and Helen Wood indicate that reality TV is staged and fake.
2 In 2009, Dr Brooke Magnanti revealed herself to *Guardian* journalist India Knight as the author of the Belle de Jour blogs and books, revealing her life as a £300-an-hour prostitute, when she ran out of money while writing her PhD. How many students and well-educated young women who are not poor take this route to support their studies and lifestyles?

17 STUFF

1 'Meet the Billionaires Who Live in the World's Most Expensive Apartment Building', https://www.businessinsider.com/who-lives-in-londons-one-hyde-park-2013-3?r=US&IR=T
2 *How to Spend It* (FT, 15 June 2019), p. 39.
3 Bourdieu, *Distinction*.
4 Crispin Thurlow and Adam Jaworski, 'Visible–Invisible: The Social Semiotics of Labour in Luxury Tourism', in Thomas Birtchnell and Javier Caletrío (eds.), *Elite Mobilities*, Routledge, 2014, pp. 176–93. See also Crispin Thurlow, 'Expanding our Sociolinguistic Horizons? Geographical Thinking and the Articulatory Potential of Commodity Chain Analysis', *Journal of Sociolinguistics* 24(3) (2020): DOI 10.1111/josl.12388, for a sophisticated analysis of enactments of privilege.
5 Andy Beckett, 'How to Spend It: The Shopping List for the 1%', *Guardian* (19 July 2018).
6 *How to Spend It* (FT, 13 December 2019).
7 Sociologist Emma Spence draws on her first-hand experience as crew on luxury yachts to suggest that watching television is a favourite activity. Emma Spence, 'Performing Wealth and Status: Observing Super Yachts and the Super-Rich in Monaco' (2015), in Iain Hay and Jonathan Beaverstock (eds.), *Handbook of Wealth and the Super-Rich*, Edward Elgar, 2016.

18 GOBBLED BY AN OCTOPUS

1 Deloitte Private, 'Family Office Personal Risk and Reputation Management', https://www2.deloitte.com/content/dam/Deloitte/uk/Documents/corporate-finance/deloitte-uk-family-office-personal-risk-and-reputation-management.pdf

19 RICHES AND RISK

1 Frank, *Richistan*, p. 203.
2 Schillings website, https://www.schillingspartners.com/#why-us, checked 24 June 2020.

20 DEAD STREETS

1 'Bunker Mentality: How Wentworth Golf Club Won the War', https://www.thegentlemansjournal.com/article/bunker-mentality-wentworth-golf-club-won-war/
2 'Petr Aven: The Russian Oligarch with an Eye for Art, Not Yachts', https://www.ft.com/content/f328a740-6233-11e7-8814-0ac7eb84e5f1
3 ONS data for 2018–2019 show downward trends for the Virginia Water section of the Borough of Runnymede, for all types of crime.

EPILOGUE

1 'Pandemic Makes World's Billionaires Even Richer', *FT Weekend* (24/25 October 2020).
2 'Luxury Yacht or Hermes Bag? What the Wealthy Are Buying', *Financial Times* (1/2 August 2020).
3 *New York Times* (6 June 2020).
4 ONS 2018–2019.
5 Press release, 24 May 2020.
6 'Westferry Planning Row: Jenrick Texted Property Developer, Documents Show', https://www.bbc.co.uk/news/uk-politics-53172995
7 'Pandemic Makes Wealth Tax More Likely than Ever', *Financial Times* (4 July 2020).
8 'Tax Office Turns Heat on Rich Families', *Financial Times* (22 February 2020).

9 'HMRC Targets Wealthy in Push on Tax Evasion', *Financial Times* (1 August 2020).

10 'Carbon Emissions of Richest 1% More than Double those of Poorest Half of the World', https://www.oxfam.org.uk/media/press-releases/carbon-emissions-of-richest-1-more-than-double-those-of-poorest-half-of-the-world

11 James Dale Davidson and Lord William Rees-Mogg, *The Sovereign Individual: How to Survive and Thrive during the Collapse of the Welfare State*, Simon & Schuster, 1997.

Index
(by Paula Clarke Bain)

Page numbers in *italic* denote illustrations. Page numbers in the form 285n2 indicate endnotes.